Praise for *The End of the Gay*

'What a fabulously timely, well-researched and argued book. The gay world has to be ready for the coming fight. It is hard to doubt that much of what has been achieved in a lifetime (mine for example!) is threatened by a new tsunami of authoritarian rightists. McCrea lays out a highly convincing wake-up call for the whole LGBTQI community. Queer or ally, I urge you to read it.'

Stephen Fry

'I hope this important book sparks a conversation rather than a cancellation. While many of the book's ideas are controversial, it is high time the LGBT community holds an open discussion about its core values and political strategies'

Yuval Noah Harari, author of *Sapiens*

'Ronan McCrea poses questions from the heart, urgent questions designed to help secure a safe and egalitarian future for all gay people; for though there has been welcome progress there is visible, audible push back. The stomach-churning awfulness of the opening story of his savage public humiliation at age thirteen will never leave you. Nor should it. The future has to be homophobia-free and this book will play a significant role in ensuring it is.'

Mary McAleese, former President of Ireland

'A thoughtful and timely reckoning with the triumphs and vulnerabilities of the gay rights revolution. Lucid and provocative, Ronan McCrea shows how far we've come – and how easily it could all unravel.'

Yascha Mounk, author of *The Identity Trap: A Story of Ideas and Power in Our Time*

'Did the movement for gay equality overreach by embracing freedom without responsibility? Did it induce a backlash by mortgaging itself to an alphabet soup of radical causes? Ronan McCrea's manifesto for moderation is sure to be controversial – and, for just that reason, deserves attention and debate.'

Jonathan Rauch, Senior Fellow at the Brookings Institution, author of *Gay Marriage: Why It Is Good for Gays, Good for Straights and Good for America*

'Ronan McCrea has written a brilliantly argued book that mixes pragmatism and principle seamlessly. He shows that standing up for unlimited personal freedom is perilous in practice and unwise in principle, and that such a stance does not even serve the well-being of those who argue for it. His focus is on gay rights, but the lessons he offers apply across many areas of our collective social, cultural and political lives. People engaged in the struggle for personal liberation should pay close attention.'

Barry Schwartz is Professor Emeritus at Swarthmore College and the author of *The Paradox of Choice*

'This is a fascinating and thought-provoking book. Ronan McCrea never shies away from challenging readers to reconsider their assumptions, and from setting out some difficult realities for the gay rights movement, as well as charting the extraordinary progress it has made in a few short decades. In making the case that progress is not irreversible – and indeed, is today at risk – and that this is a product not just of external conservative forces, but internal tensions within the gay community, this book has important insights and implications not just for gay rights but for all civil rights movements as they mature and confront the need to consolidate their early wins.'

Sonia Sodha, *Guardian* columnist

'This timely book asks challenging questions of the gay rights movement. Whether we agree or disagree, all members of the LGBTI+ community and our allies need to consider the author's analysis.'

Leo Varadkar, former Prime Minister of Ireland

The End of the Gay Rights Revolution

THE END OF THE GAY RIGHTS REVOLUTION

How Hubris and Over-Reach Threaten Gay Freedom

Ronan McCrea

polity

Copyright © Ronan McCrea 2026

The right of Ronan McCrea to be identified as Author of this Work has been asserted in accordance with the UK Copyright, Designs and Patents Act 1988.

First published in 2026 by Polity Press Ltd.

Polity Press Ltd.
65 Bridge Street
Cambridge CB2 1UR, UK

Polity Press Ltd.
111 River Street
Hoboken, NJ 07030, USA

All rights reserved. Except for the quotation of short passages for the purpose of criticism and review, no part of this publication may be reproduced, stored in a retrieval system or transmitted, in any form or by any means, electronic, mechanical, photocopying, recording or otherwise, without the prior permission of the publisher.

ISBN-13: 978-1-5095-6999-1 (hardback)
ISBN-13: 978-1-5095-7000-3 (paperback)

A catalogue record for this book is available from the British Library.

Library of Congress Control Number: 2025937100

Typeset in 11.5 on 14pt Adobe Garamond
by Fakenham Prepress Solutions, Fakenham, Norfolk NR21 8NL
Printed and bound in Great Britain by CPI Group (UK) Ltd, Croydon

The publisher has used its best endeavours to ensure that the URLs for external websites referred to in this book are correct and active at the time of going to press. However, the publisher has no responsibility for the websites and can make no guarantee that a site will remain live or that the content is or will remain appropriate.

Every effort has been made to trace all copyright holders, but if any have been overlooked the publisher will be pleased to include any necessary credits in any subsequent reprint or edition.

For further information on Polity, visit our website: politybooks.com

Contents

Terminology

I have generally used the term 'gay men' when referring to same-sex attracted men and 'lesbians' when referring to same-sex attracted women. I have used the term 'gay people' when I am referring to both gay men and lesbians. This term can also be taken to cover bisexual people in so far as they are same-sex attracted. To have said 'gays, lesbians and bisexuals' every time I needed to refer to same-sex attracted people would have made the text much more a chore to read. It will be clear from the context when 'gay sex' refers to sexual activity between men alone or to sexual activity between men and sexual activity between women. The terms 'gay rights', 'LGBTQ+' or 'LGBTQIA+' have all been used at various points in the text in relation to movements, campaigns and organizations. It will usually be the case that 'gay rights' refers to the rights of same-sex attracted people while 'LGBTQ+' and 'LGBTQIA+' refer to a wider category including various other categories such as trans people, intersex people or people who identify as queer.

Acknowledgments

I owe a great deal to my agent Caroline Hardman and editor George Owers for taking a chance on this book and for insightful feedback and advice at many stages of the process. Their commitment to taking on projects that others might shy away from is truly admirable. I would also like to thank those at Polity Press for their work on the book, especially Flo Winkley, Susan Beer and Rachel Moore. I would especially like to thank the anonymous reviewers whose reports significantly improved the final text. Mariana Chaves, Scott Frisby, Méabh Gallagher, Johann Hari, Barry McCrea, Paul O'Connell, Francis Sweeney and Steven Vaughan deserve particular recognition for their very detailed and helpful comments on the text as well as for input on the publication process. I would also like to thank Trudi Charles, Kieron Dunleavy, Jim Holden, Brian Kennelly, Alison MacKeen, Gillian MacKenzie, Lucinda Miller, Stephen Murphy, Vincent Nolan, Katya Segal and Scott Slattery, who all fed into the writing or other elements of the process in very helpful ways. None of them should be taken to agree with all of the arguments made in the book. The UCL Faculty of Laws has continued to provide a stimulating workplace that values the free exchange of ideas. The staffs of the library of the School of Slavonic and East European Studies, the Institute of Advanced Legal Studies, Campden Hill LTC, Café Tropea and Caffè Nero on Upper Woburn Place all provided wonderful spaces in which to write. I thank *Current Legal Problems* for their permission to use some of the material in Chapter 4.

By chance, the text of this book was finalized twenty-five years to the day since I was diagnosed with non-Hodgkin's lymphoma. I remain grateful to the many people who helped me through that time and hope that if any of those reading this book are passing through similar challenges, highlighting this coincidence will be a source of hope. I dedicate this book to the memory of Willem Arondeus, who showed by his own actions that, as he put it, 'homoseksuelen niet per definitie zwakkelingen zijn'.

1

Deliverance?

In June of 1990, a charity tennis event was held in Dublin. Some of the top male players in the world, very generously, took time out of their Wimbledon preparation to fly over and play an exhibition tournament to raise money for *GOAL*, a charity working to alleviate poverty in the developing world. I was then thirteen years old. Ireland is a small country in which tennis is very much a minority sport, so it didn't have any top-level tournaments. This was the only chance to see the stars play live. Even better, for a child of my age, the *GOAL Challenge*, as it was called, offered the chance of being a ball-boy: a one-off opportunity to touch the hem of international tennis royalty as it passed through Dublin by actually being on court with stars of the game. I tried to apply long before they were even accepting applications. When they did start the recruitment, I was one of the first in, and so had my place.

When the day rolled around, things lived up to expectations. There was a grass court surrounded by a temporary stadium in the pictur-esque campus of Trinity College in the centre of the city. It didn't quite compare to Wimbledon's Centre Court but looked pretty similar to the stadium courts of the warm-up tournaments that I had seen on television and that was easily glamorous enough for me. The same could be said of players who came. They were not the ones who were likely to contend for the Wimbledon title but were good players, top thirty in the world, or former champions now in decline. The most famous face in 1990 was former world number one Mats Wilander. The star of the show, however, was the French player, Henri Leconte, who had never won a grand slam title but who had a reputation for stealing the show with crowd-pleasing jokes and clowning around.

And he didn't disappoint. In fact, he got going as soon as the players and ball-boys had taken their positions on court. My first reaction was confusion as I was pretty sure that there was no reason for him to be staring at me; I was only there as a ball-boy and the balls hadn't even been taken out of their tins yet. But he did appear to be looking right at me. Then the laughter started to rise from the bleachers, getting louder as more and more people in the crowd started to get the joke.

He was definitely staring right at me. He had one hand theatrically resting on his hip and had the other hand out in front of him swishing from side to side as it hung limply from his wrist. By this stage there was no doubt in my mind that he was staring at me and that the crowd were laughing. I hadn't had any sexual feelings by that stage so I wasn't fully aware of what 'gay' meant but I had a dim feeling of recognition; a kind of semi-conscious knowledge that his swishy gestures were related to the vague feeling of difference from other boys that I had felt.

My main memory was a panicky 'what do I do now?' feeling. What is the recommended course of action when the star of the show is leading a stadium full of people in mocking you for something you are only half aware of but which makes you deeply ashamed? My main concern was ensuring that awareness of what happened did not leak into my wider life, where it threatened to wreak havoc. I began to worry that my father, who had given me a lift in, might not yet have left and might be seeing what was going on. Discussing what had happened would have meant talking about things that I needed to remain unsaid but, if no one from home or school had seen and I managed to keep going till it stopped, I could never speak of this again. In the end I think I did what was probably the best thing I could have in the situation. I tried to pretend I was unaware of what was happening and just stared straight ahead even though my burning cheeks must have given the game away.

Of course, Henri Leconte was soon on to the next joke, the tennis got underway and afterwards I dutifully reported to my parents that I had had a great time. No one, or almost no one, remembered the fun at the ball-boy's expense. My own memories of the event had a kind of dream-like quality, so much so that when I thought back on it decades later, I began to wonder whether it had actually happened.

However, my memories also included the seemingly surreal fact that Leconte's antics had been mentioned the next day in *The Irish Times* (Ireland's main liberal-left newspaper). While this detail seemed suffi-ciently strange to reinforce the idea that I was confusing a dream with reality, it also offered the possibility of verification. After a quick look through *The Irish Times* archive, there it was in in the edition of 20 June 1990. With the headline 'Good-Humoured Display Gives £25,000 to GOAL', one of the paper's main sports writers wrote:

> Champagne corks popped from executive boxes, people walked about noisily and all four seasons arrived in one day. All-told not unlike Wimbledon really, which will have suited Guy Forget, Henri Leconte and Darren Cahill who, along with the temporarily inactive Mats Wilander, partook in yesterday's sixth running of the annual GOAL tennis challenge on the well-coiffured lawns of Trinity College. [...] In keeping with its tradition, this was a typically good-humoured event exhibition, with all the protagonists willingly catching the prevailing mood – invariably none more so than Leconte.
>
> The showman in Leconte didn't take long to emerge ... about five seconds actually. For his first trick he imitated an effeminate ball-boy.

I remember the newspaper open on the kitchen table the next day and that, as I read the story, my main thought had been 'Oh God, he is talking about me ... The newspaper is saying this about ME.' This was followed by a flash of panic that people I knew might read it and I would be recognized as the 'effeminate ball-boy'. I didn't know exactly what the word 'effeminate' meant but had a good enough guess at the likely meaning to know that doing what I normally did with unknown words, namely ask my mother what it meant, risked awkward questions about something that absolutely had to remain concealed. I felt my cheeks burn again and then an instinct that this was too much to deal with kicked in. I closed the paper and subconsciously decided to forget that any of this had happened, an approach I maintained till my trip back to *The Irish Times* archive over three decades later.

It was all a long time ago and I certainly don't want to see Henri Leconte cancelled because of any of this (I don't believe in cancelling people for their misdeeds and, even if I did, after more than three decades whatever informal statute of limitations applies to these things has surely expired). I doubt that Leconte or almost anyone in the crowd has any memory of what he did that day. The Henri Leconte of today may be a much nicer person than he was in 1990. He may well now happily have openly gay friends. Many of those who jeered along from the stands were likely part of the thumping majority of Irish voters who voted yes to gay marriage in 2015 and who now probably think they never looked down on gay people.

I have to admit that I do still think badly of him. Most adults don't find pleasure in picking on a child in front of thousands of people. But, as *The Irish Times* report accurately noted, he was merely 'catching the prevailing mood'. Gays were not part of society and were, at best, to be laughed at. If a ball-boy looked or acted gay and was mocked by a tennis star for that, the ball-boy had it coming. It wasn't just Henri Leconte who thought so; it appeared at the time that virtually everyone did. Indeed, back then, I didn't even think he had done anything wrong myself. It seemed obvious that I was the problem, not him. I even asked him for his autograph after the match (this level of self-abnegation must even have surprised him; he did look quizzically at me as he signed the back of the KitKat wrapper on which I was collecting players' signatures (in my excitement I had left my notebook at home)).

When taboos disappear, it is very hard to imagine the power they once had. What people didn't even clock as unusual is more revealing than anything else of how enveloping the cloud of prejudice and disrespect that hung over the day-to-day lives of gay people at the time was. How a stadium full of people could have looked at a top tennis professional mocking a child for appearing gay, to the laughter and jeers of over a thousand spectators, and thought nothing scandalous had happened. How a journalist from Ireland's most liberal newspaper could see the same thing and report it as being an indication of what a 'good-humoured event' it had been. It all speaks to a social reality now alien to us.

Of course, Ireland in the early 1990s was more conservative on sexual issues than most of North America and Western Europe. The tourist guidebook *The Rough Guide to Ireland 1990* advised gay readers (its inclusion of advice for gay travellers marked it out, at the time, as an edgy modern travel series) 'Be aware that intolerance is not just a product of the legislators, bigotry is rife and public displays of affection are out of the question.'[1] But, even in more liberal places and more recent times, the predominant social attitudes towards homosexuality were jeering and hostile to an extent that we struggle to recognize today. In both the US and UK, a majority of the population continued to regard same-sex sexual activity as wrong until well into the new millennium.[2] The tennis world didn't change so quickly either. As late as 2001 in swinging liberal

London, the winner of the Wimbledon title that year, Goran Ivanišević, told the press that a linesman who gave a call that he disliked looked 'like a faggot a little bit, you know', with the liberal *Guardian* newspaper describing this as 'post-match humour'.[3]

What this all underlines is how the past truly is a foreign country and how the part of that foreign land that is most inaccessible to us is its mentality. When you see photographs of nineteenth-century life, the visible differences like horse-drawn carriages and constricting clothes are initially the most striking but it is the invisible differences that are the really big ones. At a push, I can imagine travelling around by horse and wearing a bowler hat or flat cap. What is much harder to do is to place yourself in the mental world of the inhabitants of that era: what they instinctively thought of as normal, taboo or scandalous. And, although I have been discussing the recent past, the change in attitudes to homosexuality in the past few decades has been so immense that the attitudes of the people of the time are almost as inaccessible to us now as those of the era of corsets and frock-coats.

Were a player of Henri Leconte's status to pull a similar stunt today, there would certainly be no laughing or jeering but condemnations, grovelling apologies, terminated sponsorships and promises from the main bodies in professional tennis to 'do better'. But I suspect the reaction of most people would not just be 'He really shouldn't have done that' but a genuinely shocked 'What the hell did he think he was doing?' Today, Leconte's actions would not be unpopular, they would be unthinkable. The shift in norms has been so total that what was just a laugh and a bit of fun in 1990 would be regarded as having taken leave of your senses in 2025.

That is why this story should be a happy one, and it is. But only partly. It serves as a reminder of the almost miraculous nature of the transformation in the fortunes of gay people that we have witnessed. Ours has been a triumph that has been comprehensive and decisive to an extent that the gays and lesbians of 1990, let alone 1950, could not have imagined. The triumph covered not just the removal of actively oppressive laws and policies but also the development of a whole range of measures that actively affirmed and protected gay people and their relationships. When I was a ball-boy in 1990, laws criminalizing gay sex were still on the books in Ireland, something that was only changed in

1993 following a ruling of the European Court of Human Rights. By 2015, same-sex marriage, rules against discrimination at work and in the provision of goods and services had all been introduced.

But something much more substantial than law reform had happened. The change was actually in the social water we all swim in, what the philosopher Charles Taylor calls the 'social imaginary'.[4] For Taylor, the social imaginary is 'something much broader and deeper than the intellectual schemes people may entertain when they think about social reality [...] rather [it consists of] the ways people imagine their social existence, how they fit together with others, how things go on between them and their fellows, the expectations that are normally met, and the deeper normative notions and images that underline these expectations'.

In relation to homosexuality, it is this 'social imaginary' that has changed. Until recently, homophobia felt like it made sense in a deep, almost unconscious, way to most people. It resonated with their underlying expectations and beliefs about life and the world. The daily lives of gays and lesbians were shrouded in a fog of hostility and contempt that was so widely accepted that its impact on them was invisible to most people. Then, with astonishing rapidity, this fog lifted. The effect was miraculous. Instead of going through daily life expecting that most people you interacted with, from work colleagues and shop assistants to fellow passengers on the bus, would be hostile or disgusted if they knew the truth about you, gay people could, largely, drop their guard and get on with their lives.

Of course, the triumph has not been total. There are many people who remain anti-gay and there are issues in areas, such as bullying in schools. But, overall, if you could go back in time and tell gay rights campaigners of the past in almost any country in the West what things would be like in 2025, even the most optimistic of them would be astounded. The extent of the triumph can risk bleeding into triumphalism and demands for endorsement that ought to make genuine liberals a little uncomfortable. Big corporations, law firms, investment banks have all piled, at least until recently, onto the gay rights bandwagon; many employers and public bodies fly rainbow flags, encourage staff to wear rainbow lanyards or to join 'ally' groups, with potential career damage to those who do not want to do so. Corporate ads feature gay couples, firms sponsor floats at gay pride events and sponsor diversity events at which they insist that this endorsement of gay freedom and equality is about their values.

You can be forgiven for cynicism in this regard. While many employees of these companies are sincere in their 'allyship', if the current commitment of banks, corporations and law firms is, as they often say, about their values and not a calculation of which way the wind is blowing, then why was Goldman Sachs not offering to sponsor a float in the 1980 Gay Pride event? Moreover, as wags on X/Twitter have shown, even before the recent corporate cooling on diversity issues, many of the companies that bedecked their European and American websites in pride colours when Gay Pride month rolled around did no such thing on their Middle Eastern websites, where this message was less popular. Corporations being self-interested and shamelessly jumping on bandwagons shouldn't shock anyone but the fact that self-interest pushed the corporate sector to publicly endorse gay rights only underlines the impression of a revolution that has been sweeping in its scale and seems permanent in nature.

So why the unease? Doesn't this all sound great? Like the Jews in the biblical tale of Exodus who left slavery in Egypt and reached the Promised Land, gay people have left misery behind them and completed (an equally miraculous) journey to their Promised Land of freedom and equality. But arriving in the Promised Land does not mean that the story is now over and that all will be well. As Jewish history shows, reaching a Promised Land is not a guarantee of remaining there permanently. Neither is it the case that the skills and habits that successfully got you to the Promised Land will necessarily be the best ones to make life in that land as good as it can be once you have got there.

In this book, I will suggest to you that although the modern West is the best time and place to be gay in recorded history, there are reasons that gay people, and gay men in particular, should feel uneasy. There are increasingly convincing grounds for thinking that the freedom that gay liberation has won for us will not be and, indeed, may never have been, sustainable. This unsustainability has two sources, one external and one internal, which overlap in an important way. The external source is familiar. If the general public can move from laughing along with bullying, homophobic behaviour to regarding such behaviour as utterly beyond the pale in the course of a couple of decades, what is to stop them switching back again?

Homosexuality has been thought of in different ways at different times but, over the course of Western history, open acceptance of homosexuality has been rare. Certainly, there have been times, such as during the Roman Empire, when some forms of gay sex have been tolerated. Even in less permissive times, legal restrictions often have been softened by a degree of blind-eye turning (especially for figures such as James I of England, or Frederick the Great of Prussia, whose powerful status allowed them to hide their desires in plain sight). Even in the repressive Victorian era, Oscar Wilde had been able to, as he put it, 'feast with panthers', without getting into legal trouble, until he launched an ill-judged prosecution for libel against the Marquess of Queensberry. Anita Kurimay's fascinating study of gay life in Budapest describes how, at the turn of the twentieth century, the official police journal noted that 'while the law in theory is relatively strict about male homosexuality, in real life its application is not' (although things later became more oppressive under the communist regime).[5] But, as Kurimay notes, much of this tolerance came from a desire to keep a lid on homosexual activity by maintaining the veil of silence that surrounded homosexuality intact.[6]

The degree of de facto toleration may have waxed and waned over the centuries. But the kind of open acknowledgement of the legitimacy of homosexuality and the treatment of gay relationships as the moral and legal equal of straight relationships, which we recently won in most of the West, is unprecedented. It would be foolish in the extreme to think that after centuries of persecution and concealment, a couple of decades of tolerance marks an irrevocable change and that hostility to homosexuality has been permanently extinguished.

Despite this, the main gay rights organizations appear to regard the battle on gay rights as permanently won. They seem to see their task not as hanging on to the degree of freedom we have miraculously obtained but as increasing the scope of their demands to include active validation and expanding their campaigns into an ever-widening range of issues from which they previously steered clear. This approach is highly risky. In the modern West, gay freedom gained traction only after a massive revolution had already overturned long-established norms around heterosexual sexuality. This book will argue that a number of political, social and demographic changes underway across the West give reason to think that the gay rights revolution, like the broader sexual revolution on which it depended, is likely to run into more, not less, opposition in the future and that gay rights organizations, devoted to the hubristic view that history is on their side, are ill-equipped to deal with this reality.

The internal source of unsustainability is perhaps even more challenging for gay people to engage with. Gays and lesbians are used to thinking about how to defend their freedom from threats arising from the outside but, after a long history of discrimination and ridicule, are understandably reluctant to engage in self-criticism. However, there are good reasons to think that gay freedom is rendered more vulnerable by the form that it has taken among gay men. Put bluntly, the sex-positive, no-rules-other-than-consent, approach to sex that arose out of the sexual revolution, and which has been embraced with particular enthusiasm by gay men, is proving damaging to many of us and makes gay freedom in general even less politically sustainable than it would otherwise be.

The sex-positive approach of the sexual revolution starts from the reasonable premise that individuals are the best judge of what is good for them and what will make them happy. Accordingly, choice in sexual matters should be maximized. Sex should be, to use the writer Aaron Sibarium's term, 'disenchanted';[7] that is to say, it should be freed from restrictive taboos and should be regarded as an activity of no inherent weightiness, which can be engaged in with no consequences if that is what individuals want. Free of restrictions and taboos, people should, on this logic, have naturally found the kind of sexual existence that best suits them. But the reality is more complicated.

There can be no doubt that for gay people the freedoms of the 2020s provide a vastly better environment than the 1950s. But, at the same time, a consistent message has been coming through for decades in health statistics, in surveys of gay men's lives and in gay novels, that sexual freedom, while wonderful and necessary, has its drawbacks. Too much of that freedom can hinder rather than help gay men to live the kind of lives most of them want to live in the longer term. As concerningly, health statistics still show that gay men have both significantly higher numbers of sexual partners (with resultant high levels of sexually transmitted disease) and that higher levels of loneliness, mental health issues and addiction among gay men have persisted, even as societal homophobia has decreased.[8]

If gay men's sexual culture has developed in such a way that its over-emphasis on sexual freedom is impeding our ability to live healthy and happy lives and to have the kind of lasting relationships that most of us say we want, that is obviously a reason to think about whether we might want to change that culture. But this internal challenge overlaps with the external challenge in a way that means that the potentially damaging impact of this sexual culture cannot be kept 'in house'. Writing back in 2008 about the gay dating website *Manhunt* (a pre-smart-phone predecessor of *Grindr*), Matthew Joseph Gross wrote, 'We don't tell straight people about *Manhunt*. We don't even tell them it exists. And even when we do, we usually don't tell them what it's really like.'[9] And he is right. Many gay men have a desire to avoid, as the journalist Owen Jones put it during the mpox outbreak in 2022, 'washing the dirty linen in public',[10] that is, a desire to obscure from straight view the reality of the notably higher level of casual sex among gay men.

The reality is that for gay men (and lesbians) having straight people on side isn't just something that is nice to have, it is existential. Gay people will always be a small minority. We are fated to rely for our freedom on 'the kindness of strangers'. That is, on the benevolence or tolerance of the vast straight majority, which, over the centuries, that majority has rarely been willing to give. Even if you yearn for life in a gay environment and move to a city like San Francisco, you will still be in a context where the straight population is more than 80 per cent of the total. We will be, always and everywhere, a small minority whose personal and political freedom rests in the hands of the straight majority.

While some might argue that the straight majority does not care what gay people get up to, historically that has not been the case. In the past in much of the West, when gay freedom appeared inconsistent with the overall societal approach to sex, the straight majority usually criminalized male homosexuality. This situation lasted for centuries, with decriminal-ization occurring only when the sexual revolution had loosened the overall sexual framework and other sexual (straight) freedoms had become well accepted. The reality is that gay freedom advanced only as part of a much wider current of sexual freedom that swept the Western world in the second half of the twentieth century, in which straight people gave themselves much more sexual freedom and redefined marriage. It was only then that, belatedly and often reluctantly, they agreed to apply the new more liberal paradigm to gay people and their relationships.

Gay men, with their notably libertine sexual culture, have placed themselves at the very outer boundary of the freedom won by the broader sexual revolution. If there is any turn in the broader culture against the sexual revolution more generally and if the boundaries of sexual freedom come under pressure, it is gay freedom that will be one of the first outposts to fall. As this book will show, there are more than a few indicators that such a backlash against the sexual revolution more generally is imminent and may even be underway.

This backlash draws on a host of factors. Populist political movements hostile to liberalism, to feminism and to identity politics are in the ascendant. Feminists of both left and right are disillusioned with some of the revolution's key tenets. Demographic change across the West and a rising awareness of the complicated, often antagonistic, relationship between the short-term desires and people's longer-term goals are driving new sources of opposition to an 'anything goes' sexual culture.

For our own happiness as well as the political sustainability of our liberation project, gay people must take on board how fragile our freedom is. Liberalism is in crisis across the West, particularly its post-1968 version, which was particularly favourable to gay rights. Gay men in particular must find a way to move their freedom back from the outermost limits of sexual liberation to safer territory further behind the front lines. This may be painful, and may involve difficult decisions about whom and what goals it is feasible to fight for, as well as the difficult task of looking at ourselves and our weaknesses and taking a more nuanced approach to the idea of sexual freedom and the good of following one's desires. This is a less joyful project than the utopian idea that all we needed to do was harness the energy of an ever-strengthening liberalism to push our revolution ever further and achieve happiness in an ever-more sexually free paradise: but times change and circumstances change.

A few decades ago, more freedom and more campaigns against discrimination were what gay people in the West needed. But now, in most of the West, the state no longer discriminates against gay people and there are significant legal, social and commercial pressures to dissuade others from doing so. It is a mistake to assume that the answer to your current problems is to get more of the things you needed decades ago. After all, the sexual freedom that gay people previously lacked is now present in abundant quantities. Would even more of it enhance their current lives? Failing to adapt your goals, repeating once useful but now stale slogans, and imagining that the threats to your freedom today are the same as those that came from the now shrivelled opponents you previously vanquished, is a recipe for future failure.

Abandoning the belief that your movement is bound to triumph over time is frightening. Looking honestly at the downsides of what you have achieved and adapting your goals, worldview and political strategy is uncomfortable. People are generally most angered not by hearing things that they think are false but by hearing things that they wish were false but which they worry might be true. There is, however, no other choice. This is not about judging or denigrating anyone (I have done plenty of stupid and embarrassing things in my own life), or about oppressive measures designed to roll back gay rights. On the contrary, my aim is to think about how gay men (and lesbians, who will be caught up in any backlash) can best preserve and make the best use of the freedom we have miraculously achieved.

Some of the concerns I highlight, such as over-reach by the gay rights movement, apply equally to gays and lesbians. Others, such as the downsides of anything-goes approaches to sex, apply much more to gay men. That said, even if some of my concerns do not relate to lesbians themselves, they are of relevance to the freedom that lesbians currently enjoy. The reality is that, despite the fact that their concerns do not always align, gay men and lesbians share a joint liberation project. Legal rights such as same-sex marriage and employment protections were granted to gays and lesbians as part of a single same-sex attracted category rather than to gays and lesbians separately.

The further unfortunate reality is that, not least because of the sexism that tends to foreground the concerns of men over those of women, societal thinking around gay rights has focused disproportionately on gay men. This has sometimes had incidental beneficial effects (lesbian sex has not been criminalized as regularly as sex between men) but it has also meant that issues relating to gay men have tended to affect how both gay men and lesbians are treated. The upswing in homophobia that arose out of the AIDS crisis, for example, affected both lesbians and gay men, even though lesbians were not an at-risk group for the disease. Therefore, while many of the issues I highlight are not issues that arise for lesbians, how gay men deal with these issues is likely to be of importance for the survival of lesbian rights too.

The success of the revolution that established gay freedom was not inevitable and is not guaranteed to endure. It never suffices for any revolution merely to get rid of the old order. The fact that what went before was bad is not enough to provide ongoing justification for what replaced it. As the eighteenth-century philosopher Edmund Burke learned from the French Revolution, to survive any new order must recognize that some elements of the old order had some uses. Sustaining a revolution requires former revolutionaries to apply themselves to the less romantic and less emotionally satisfying task of managing the trade-offs that inevitably exist in an imperfect world. The gay rights revolution is threatened by a hubristic approach in relation to both its core beliefs (that ever increasing choice and ever expanding freedom are always beneficial) and its political security (the assumption that history is on its side and gay rights are destined to triumph in the long run).

A dose of modesty is in order. The freedom gay people have won in recent decades is truly a miracle. But the miraculous nature of our triumph should bring home to us that that triumph is not guaranteed to last. Indeed, it is very possible that after a few decades with the wind at our backs, the gay rights movement in the West is heading into less favourable weather. Recognizing that our aim ought to be holding on to what we have won rather than assuming that the boundaries of our revolution can be pushed ever wider may end up being vital to the survival of our freedom in the long run.

2

An Incidental Revolution

In the centre of Tallinn in a square called Freedom Square stands a large monument called the War of Independence Victory Column. The victory it refers to is the victory of Estonian forces in the 1918–20 fight for Estonian independence from the USSR, though it also represents those who resisted the Soviet occupation from 1940 onwards. Estonians are proud of their fight for freedom and rightly so. Many Estonians fought very bravely over many years to allow the country to finally escape from Russian domination in 1991, and the restoration of Estonian independence radically transformed the lives of most Estonians for the better. But the reality is that, despite this heroism, the success of the Estonians' struggle was not mainly a result of Estonian efforts. There was no chance of such a tiny country breaking free of its much larger neighbour if the USSR overall had not disintegrated at the start of the 1990s. The fact that Estonian independence depended on wider events makes it inherently vulnerable.

The gay rights movement is vulnerable in a similar way. It has its heroes, brave people who faced oppression and imprisonment and who made big sacrifices to advance the cause. But, like Estonian independence, the political success of the gay movement was mainly an incidental effect of a much bigger set of changes. Without the broader sexual revolution that transformed the norms around heterosexual sex and relationships, gay rights campaigns would never have made much, if any, headway.

The emotional success of the gay rights movement in transforming how gay people thought of themselves was one that gay people brought about mainly by themselves. More radical voices played a huge role in this by arguing that 'gay is good' and challenging the sense of shame many gay people felt. But the political and legal success of the movement that made gay people free through the repeal of laws and changes in the view of wider society was mainly not due to considerations specific to homosexuality itself. Rather, gay freedom advanced because it was the logical outcome of the individualistic liberal worldview that came to dominate Western societies' approach to sex in the late twentieth century.

That is not to doubt that gay rights pioneers were brave, even heroic. They made an enormous difference by making the issue of gay rights a subject of political dispute at all. They were not pushing an open door. Far from it. Activists had to push hard to open the door to gay rights and had to deal with energetic opponents who were pushing with all their might to keep that door closed. But, without the broader transformation in norms around straight sex and relationships, those activists would have been pushing against a locked door that no amount of pushing could have prised open. The wonderful freedom gay people obtained was therefore incidental: a side effect of wider changes in heterosexual mores without which it could not have been achieved.

A Minority without Critical Mass

It is not surprising that the political fate of gay people was mainly not in their own hands. Gays and lesbians represent a very small proportion of the population. Some surveys show large numbers of young people now claim some form of identity that is not purely heterosexual. But this is not reflective of an increase in what most people have regarded as being actually gay or lesbian. In one episode of *Sex and the City*, Charlotte, usually the most conservative of the main characters, ends up falling in with a crowd of lesbians.[1] She is having a great time talking, drinking and dancing with them. After a few outings, the group suggests that she join them for a skiing holiday. Charlotte is thrilled, until one of the group takes her aside and asks if she is gay. Charlotte has to concede that she is sexually attracted to men and not to women but, hoping to still be invited on the trip, she argues that 'there's a very powerful part of me that connects to the female spirit'. 'Sweetheart', her interrogator responds, 'that's all very nice but if you're not going to eat pussy, you're not a dyke.'

Crudely put, but the point is clear. It might be fun to toy with your sexual identity or to identify with one of the amorphous categories represented by the expanding list of letters (LGBTQIA+) that are now used to refer to gay people, but actual homosexuality as it has long been understood refers to something more concrete, namely significant, sustained sexual and emotional attraction to members of your own sex. When it is defined in this way, the numbers of gays and lesbians (and bisexuals with significant and sustained same-sex attraction) become very small.

A 2021 study in the journal *JMIR Public Health and Surveillance* tracked the prevalence of the search term 'gay porn' as opposed to 'porn' in the US to come up with a figure of two to four per cent of men being primarily attracted to other men, with slightly higher figures in big urban areas, and slightly lower in rural areas.[2] A much larger proportion of young people may identify as 'queer' or 'LGBTQ+', but it would seem that for young men at least, when they have their computer open late at night and no one is looking, only a very small percentage reveal sexual desires that reflect actual homosexuality. Given different patterns of pornography use between males and females, it would be more difficult to estimate the lesbian population in this way but there is no reason to think the proportion would be significantly higher (most surveys suggest that gay men outnumber lesbians). The figure of in and around four per cent is in line with a series of polls and surveys taken in the US since the early 1990s.[3] Gay people, at least in the long-understood sense of same-sex attraction, are therefore not just a minority, they are, and will always be, a very small minority, whose political fate will depend on their ability to convince straight people to support them.

Furthermore, the key claim of the gay rights movement, namely that same-sex sexual relationships deserve equal status with heterosexual relationships, is one that involves a profound challenge to the patterns, ceremonies and institutions that most people use to make sense of their lives. It is not just that for almost all of the main religions in Western society homosexual relationships represented a violation of core norms of their sexual ethics. Even non-religious people tend to think of key moments in their lives such as birth, marriage and death in ways that require significant adaptation to accommodate homosexuality.

This always strikes me when I attend a gay wedding. Given how recently gay people were outcasts, there is often an extra poignancy to the event. Maybe it is a case of me projecting my feelings onto the crowd, but I usually notice a heightened degree of emotion among the guests. My best guess is that this comes from an awareness of the individual emotional struggle that the brides or grooms must have gone through to get to that point, as well as of the wider political struggle to get gay marriage.

There is nothing lesser about these weddings, but there is something different. At most of the straight weddings I have attended there has been a strong sense of inter-generational torch passing. When a man and woman marry there is usually a sense, which is more or less explicit, depending on the kind of ceremony they have, that they are repeating what their parents did when they got married and that, all going well, their own children will do the same in the future.

This sense of repeating cycles is one that is enormously comforting to most humans, dealing, as we have to, with the fact of our inevitable death. You will die yourself, as will everyone who is dear to you, but your life fits into bigger cycles that go on and on. At a gay wedding, it is almost always the case that, in marrying someone of their own sex, the brides or grooms are not doing what their parents did. While gay people can have children (and some straight couples can't or don't want to), reproducing is much less part of the package than in a heterosexual relationship, and any children that a gay couple may have will not have been produced from the sexual union of the spouses in the way that is normally the case for straight couples.

Riding the Wave of the Straight Sexual Revolution

The triumph of the gay-marriage movement was that, in many countries, a majority of society was persuaded that, despite these differences, same-sex couples could be accepted as part of the institution of marriage. This step required a reimagination of how marriage had been seen for centuries. But, just as the struggle to bring down communism was not carried out, with Estonia as the main consideration in people's thoughts, that reimagination of marriage was mainly not done with gay people in mind.

This is hardly surprising. It was never likely that the 96 to 98 per cent could be persuaded to engage in a reimagination of a fundamental social institution to accommodate the two to four per cent. Rather, as I will discuss below, the legalization of gay marriage was a big deal for gay people. But, viewed in the context of marriage more generally, it can be seen as a tidying up exercise that followed from a fundamental reimagining of the nature of marriage carried out by the heterosexual majority for themselves.

The truth is that the movement for same-sex marriage could not have got off the ground without this earlier change in the meaning of opposite-sex marriage. This is true of the wider revolution in the treatment of gay sexuality more generally. The gay rights revolution was an incidental revolution. In the sexual revolution that flowered in the period from the 1960s onwards (its first seeds having been sown much earlier), the straight majority liberalized rules around sex and reimagined marriage, so that both were much less restrictive and much more focused on individuals' self-realization.

It was this huge change in heterosexual mores in the post-war decades that opened the door to gay liberation. It reduced the work of gay rights activists from working to liberate homosexuality per se to the more attainable but still difficult task of getting heterosexuals to include gay people within the terms of the liberal, egalitarian and individualistic paradigm that straight people in the West had established for themselves. The gay rights revolution, in other words, was a secondary outcome of the much bigger change in attitudes to heterosexuality that has occurred in Western societies.

The wave of sexual liberalization that the modern gay rights movement managed to surf to victory was centuries in the making. Certain instincts that underlie liberal political principles were almost certainly always a part of human life. Even when we were living in caves, I am sure there were people in the tribe seen as busybodies, whose excessive interest in the doings of others caused eye-rolling and irritation. But the application of the idea of letting people do their own thing and live their own lives to the realm of politics and the state took some time and was far from inevitable. By the second half of the twentieth century an individualistic liberal paradigm that drew on a number of philosophical ideas that had been around for centuries, such as Protestant individualism, separation of religion and state and various Enlightenment ideals, achieved hegemonic status in much of the West.

The sweeping advance of liberal individualism in the post-war period, which eventually included a sexual revolution that ushered in unprecedented sexual liberalism, was helped by a number of factors. The victory of the liberal democracies in the two world wars (albeit that in both conflicts they were allied with an undemocratic Russia) gave a boost to liberal principles. The challenge to key religious claims posed by the theories of Charles Darwin and others, as well as the wider secularization of many European societies that got underway in the nineteenth century, significantly reduced the broader influence of religious bodies, which had, in general, been dedicated to a conservative approach to sexual morality.

As the feminist critic of the sexual revolution, Louise Perry, has pointed out, previous historical periods of greater sexual freedom were also 'self-limited' by the lack of good contraception[4] and, I would add, the lack of good treatments for venereal disease. But, by the 1960s, the invention of the contraceptive pill and development of treatments for sexually transmitted infections such as gonorrhoea and syphilis meant that the social and medical consequences of a more freewheeling sex life appeared, at least for a time, to have become much less severe. In addition, with affluence permitting an expansion of the welfare state in many countries, the ability of lone parents to raise children single-handedly also increased.

By the 1970s, for the first time in history, it appeared that loosening the rules around sex and permitting people to indulge in sexual relation-ships outside marriage need not necessarily result in an upsurge in destitute fatherless children, struggling single mothers or waves of disease. These developments, along with a more general cultural trend towards individualism and self-realization, all bolstered the idea that what one did in one's sex life was one's own business and brought about the complete change in both legal rules and broader social mores that we know as the sexual revolution. This revolution encompassed both legal and social changes, which fed off each other. Changes in social attitudes to sex and marriage helped to promote changes in restrictive laws, and those legal changes then improved the social status of relationships and practices that had previously been seen as illegitimate, socially taboo or shameful.

This wasn't something that happened suddenly in the 1960s. Some of the trends had been underway in the West for some time. Movements seeking the emancipation of women, for example, had been active long before the 1960s, as had trends towards less restrictive attitudes towards female sexuality. In his memoir of the last decades of the Austro-Hungarian empire, Stefan Zweig noted that by the early twentieth century, people laughed at how comically concealing the women's clothing of just a few decades earlier had been.[5] Similarly, the decline in the influence of religion over most European societies dated back to well before the twentieth century. However, in the 1960s and 1970s, these and other trends reached a tipping point. Increasingly, secular and individualistic Western societies began to regard norms that restricted sexual expression and enjoyment as unduly repressive.

At the same time, the works of feminist authors such as Simone de Beauvoir, Betty Friedan and Germaine Greer found an increasingly receptive audience for their arguments against the web of restrictive rules and expectations in which women were enmeshed, including oppressive expectations of sexual purity. These arguments also helped to facilitate the development of gay rights by undermining the idea that it was immoral for men and women to depart from gender-typical ways of behaving. After all, if women's choices in relation to work, education and clothing should not be constrained by what was expected of their sex, why should people's choice of partners be similarly constrained?

By the 1960s, these changing norms began to have an impact at a legal level. In 1959 the British Parliament passed the Obscene Publications Act, which significantly relaxed censorship of works with sexual content, particularly after the famous 1963 failed prosecution of the publishers of D.H. Lawrence's *Lady Chatterley's Lover* on charges of obscenity. In the United States a similar relaxation flowed from a series of Supreme Court rulings, beginning with the 1964 judgment in *Grove Press Inc. v. Gerstein*, in which five of the nine judges ruled that Henry Miller's novel *Tropic of Cancer* could not be censored, on the grounds that it was not 'utterly without redeeming social value'. Title VII of the Civil Rights Act of 1964 prohibited employment discrimination on grounds of sex, while a year later France enacted legislation allowing married women to work without the permission of their husband. The UK Parliament legislated for equal treatment at work in 1970 and expanded this right beyond the workplace in 1975.

By the end of the 1960s, laws in the West were taking decisive steps away from punishing those whose sexual choices fell outside traditional parameters and increasingly prioritized individual autonomy. In 1965, the US Supreme Court ruled in *Griswold v. Connecticut* that the constitution granted married couples a right of access to contraception, a right it extended to unmarried couples in 1972 in *Eisenstadt v. Baird*.

In Europe, it was parliaments rather than the courts that took the lead. 1967 saw the French National Assembly pass the Loi Neuwirth, which relaxed restrictions on the provision of contraception. In the same year, the UK Parliament legalized abortion and expanded access to contraception. Having paused to catch their breath, British politicians then proceeded to liberalize the law around divorce in 1969.

These changes rippled on through the 1970s. In the US, Title X of the Public Health Act 1970 was used to expand provision of contraception to the poor. In the course of the decade either unilateral or no-fault divorce had been introduced in Australia, Austria, Belgium, Denmark, France, Greece, Italy, Luxembourg, the Netherlands, Portugal, Sweden and West Germany. By 1980, abortion had been decriminalized in Austria, Denmark, France, Italy, Luxembourg, the Netherlands, Sweden and West Germany. The era of significant legal restriction of heterosexual sexual freedom in the West was clearly coming to an end.

Reform Breeds Revolution

Many of those who advocated liberalizing laws around sex did not intend to bring about a revolution in sexual mores. If you read the record of the debates on the various reforms that passed through the British Parliament in the late 1960s, it is clear that most supporters of reform thought that they were merely softening the hard edges of the existing rules around sex and marriage to lessen the suffering of those who found themselves unable to live up to their strict standards of chastity followed by stable heterosexual monogamy. As Louise Perry writes of the 1969 Divorce Act: 'it does not appear that supporters of the Bill knew what was coming. They believed that their reforms would be an act of kindness towards [...] those trapped in a relatively small number of particularly unhappy marriages.'[6]

But as things turned out, reform of divorce law in the UK was part of a wider transformation that saw the societal perception of divorce change from something that was rare and scandalous to an everyday part of life. Similarly, as we will see, decriminalization of homosexuality did not result in the pitying toleration of men who couldn't help themselves from yielding to their 'shameful' desires, though this is what many of those who promoted decriminalization thought they were providing.

Instead, it was one step in a wider transformation of homosexuality from a hidden source of shame to an openly acknowledged and often celebrated form of human sexuality.

Like Mikail Gorbachev, whose *perestroika* ('restructuring') and *glasnost* ('openness') were intended to reform the Soviet system but ended up unleashing forces that swept it away, 1960s sexual reformers who sought to ease some of the harsher aspects of the old sexual order fuelled forces that overturned it altogether. Legal changes that on the face of it were not that radical reflected, and ultimately reinforced, wider social changes that were much more revolutionary and which resulted in the wholesale dismantling of the old regime around sex. Under the old regime, sex had been something that was largely out of sight, rarely spoken of and default forbidden other than within heterosexual marriage. Under the new set-up, sex was regularly portrayed and discussed, and having sex became a choice (indeed almost an expectation) that all adults could make, whether married or not. Under this regime, individual choice, not cultivation of collective virtue, was paramount and any attempt on the part of the state or other people to interfere in the sex lives of others was regarded as inherently suspect.

The Reluctant Extension of Straight Freedom to Gay Sexuality

Yet, the application of this freewheeling paradigm to homosexuality took much longer. Many straight people may have embraced free love during the 1960s but were reluctant at the time to give the same latitude to gays (I don't find this surprising; in my teenage years the laddish characters most devoted to getting with as many girls as possible were very often the most vocal homophobes). The poet Philip Larkin may have written that 'Sexual intercourse began in nineteen sixty-three [...] between the end of the Chatterley ban and the Beatles' first LP'[7] but the swinging sixties were not very swinging at all for gay people.

The moment that is often seen as giving the modern gay rights movement critical mass, the Stonewall riots in New York, did not happen until the summer of 1969 and the movement itself did not start to make real progress until the middle of the next decade. While legalized contraception and no-fault divorce were standard across the West by the end of the 1970s, laws criminalizing gay sex lingered on the books of some European states until the 1990s and of some US states until the 2000s.

There was something about homosexuality that made tolerating it seem a bigger ask. Yes, most mainstream religions regarded homosexuality as a sin, but that was also true of pre-marital sex and divorce. There is something unsettling for many people about homosexuality, which goes beyond its violation of the old rules that confined legitimate sex to marriage. For most straight people, their sexual desire for the other sex is part of what defines them as a man or a woman. As has been noted by one gay author, for heterosexuals, their sex drive is bound up with a desire for the other, for intimacy with a body that is inevitably to a large degree unknowable to them. Same-sex desire on the other hand involves desire for the kind of body that one already knows intimately, which is radically different and, in its proximity to desire for oneself, somewhat unnerving. 'Gays', he concludes, 'will always present a challenge to something innate in the group that make up the majority in society.'[8]

The acceptance of the legitimacy of gay relationships, I would add, also offers a more profound challenge to the traditional order than toleration of cohabitation, divorce, sex and procreation outside marriage. Most other forms of disobedience against the traditional sexual order may abate over time. The single mother may one day wed, the divorcee may settle into a stable second marriage, the promiscuous man may 'find the right girl' and settle down. In all of these cases there is the chance that the reality of the initial rebellion becomes progressively more obscure over time and the rebel may end up living a life that, to those unaware of their history, looks indistinguishable from that of those who followed traditional norms. Gay and lesbian relationships cannot be reconciled to the traditional order in this way. These relationships, when they endure, even if they take otherwise conformist form, will still remain obviously divergent from traditional norms of sexuality, a constant visible reminder of the replacement of a once-dominant approach to matters of sex and sexuality.

In any event, whatever the reasons were, the recognition of gay rights claims as a legitimate part of the broader freedom provided by the sexual revolution took longer than heterosexual claims and left some people uneasy, even those who were otherwise liberal. Betty Friedan, 1960s feminist icon, for instance, acknowledged that the whole idea of homosexuality made her 'profoundly uneasy'.[9] She was not alone in her unease. Surveys of public opinion in the US and UK showed that hostility to homosexuality lingered long after attitudes to other forms of sexual behaviour had loosened. In the United States in 1991 fully 74 per cent of respondents told pollsters that sex between adults of the same sex was 'always wrong' while in the same survey only 26 per cent of respondents said the same about pre-marital sex. It was only in 2010 that the number of Americans saying that gay sex was always wrong dropped below fifty per cent, and it was not until 2016 that more than half of respondents agreed that same-sex sexual activity was 'not wrong at all'.[10]

Similarly, in the UK the 1987 British Social Attitudes survey reported that well under thirty per cent of respondents said they regarded pre-marital sex as wrong but in the same survey 75 per cent of respondents said they thought that sexual relations between adults of the same sex were 'always wrong' or 'mostly wrong'. Only eleven per cent of respondents said that such relations were 'not wrong at all'. It was not until 2010, some 43 years after the initial moves to decriminal-ization, that the 'not wrong at all' option had more support than 'always wrong' or 'mostly wrong' combined.[11] France was somewhat ahead of the anglosphere, with 54 per cent of people coming to believe that homosexuality was 'a way like any other to live your sexuality' by 1986. Nevertheless, despite its long tradition of toleration of affairs and private sexual freedom, as late as 1975, 64 per cent of French people were of the opinion that homosexuality was either 'a sickness that should be cured' or 'a sexual perversion that should be combatted'.[12]

This unease meant that progress was slow. The utilitarian philosopher Jeremy Bentham wrote a pamphlet in favour of decriminalization as early as 1785,[13] and some countries with French-influenced legal systems had copied the decriminalization of gay sex that occurred during the French Revolution as part of a wider copying and pasting of French legal rules. But, in most other Western countries, criminalization was the norm until well into the second half of the twentieth century.

As the sociologist Jeffrey Weeks puts it, the whole recent history of homosexuality is a 'complex process of definition and self-definition'.[14] The modern approach relies very much on the idea of gay people as a category. But this way of thinking only became prominent from the late nineteenth century onwards, after a number of researchers, particularly in Germany, began to promote the idea of homosexuals as a class of people with a particular set of desires, rather than focusing on forbidden sexual acts.[15] There has been a lively debate among academics about the degree to which it is even possible to talk sensibly about homosexuality in the past, given how differently people thought about these issues in other eras.

However, as David Halperin points out, although friendship and male love, for example, have often been discussed very differently from questions such as sodomy and effeminacy, there are definite 'genetic traces' of our modern notion of homosexuality identifiable in how people thought and acted in earlier times.[16] The sociologist Mary McIntosh, though critical of the idea of homosexuality as a condition that defines a group, noted how England in the seventeenth century saw the appearance of 'references to homosexuals as a type and to a rudimentary homosexual subculture'.[17] Although Foucault argued that it was not until the eighteenth and nineteenth centuries that societal thinking began to regard the homosexual as 'a species' rather than simply the perpetrator of forbidden acts, there are traces of the former further back. The historian Tom Holland notes how Agostino di Ercole was burned to death in Florence in 1348 for being a 'dedicated sodomite' but 'barely acknowledged his guilt', insisting that it was impossible for him to resist his nature. There was also, in that era, some recognition that this sexual identity produced characteristics that went beyond sex acts: Holland describes how, seventy years later, also in Florence, Bernardino of Siena, a Franciscan missionary and virulent preacher on the topic of the evils of sodomy, organized a bonfire of the vanities, in which he 'set fire to a massive pile of the fripperies and fashions to which sodomites were notoriously partial'.[18]

In any event, whether what we now see as anti-gay laws and attitudes were thought of as repression of a series of forbidden acts or as repression of a category of people, as the nineteenth century turned into the twentieth century and the idea of gay people as a distinct class strengthened, the first stirrings of what would become the modern gay rights movement began to emerge. In 1897, Magnus Hirschfeld founded the *Scientific Humanitarian Committee*, which pushed for decriminalization of homosexuality in Germany.[19] Although this campaign did not succeed, it was influential, particularly in countries that were influenced by German social and scientific thinking. In the Hungarian half of the Habsburg Empire, for example, 1909 saw two lectures favouring decriminalization of gay sex given to the Hungarian Association of Legal Scholars, while in 1910, *Huszadik Század*, the best-known progressive social science journal in Hungary, endorsed the idea of decriminalization.[20] While Hirschfeld's campaign ultimately failed, the existence of such a campaign shows an atmosphere that was becoming very gradually more promising. In the 1940s, before the emergence of significant gay rights campaigning, Sweden and Switzerland rescinded their criminalization of sex between men; but overall, large-scale progress had to wait until well into the post-war period.

Gay-rights campaigners faced different obstacles and had different resources available to them in different countries. Indeed, the kind of opposition that they faced influenced the dynamics of the gay rights movements that emerged and the arguments that they put forward. In Catholic countries like Spain and Ireland, the Catholic Church was a key opponent. In the US, the well-organized Christian Right played a similarly important role. In the UK, on the other hand, while conservative Christian campaigners were active (including mounting a prosecution of the paper *Gay News* in the late 1970s), the more secular nature of British society meant that religious opposition was much less of a factor. In addition, the Church of England was notably divided on gay issues, with senior figures notably sympathetic on issues such as decriminalization.[21]

The political cultures of different countries also provided campaigners with different philosophical and political resources on which they could draw. In the US, the strength of the ideas of liberty and the pursuit of happiness in American legal and political culture was a key resource, as was the revolutionary tradition of liberty and equality in France. In Spain and Ireland, gay rights movements could draw strength from broader movements that sought to step away from the illiberal Catholicism that dominated both countries until the end of the 1970s.

Despite these differences, there were also notable similarities in the gay rights movement across the West in the second half of the twentieth century. Early groups, operating in a fiercely anti-gay atmosphere, tended to have a message that would later seem quite minimalist. In the United States, despite the intense conservatism of the post-war era, which included a purging of gays and lesbians from the civil service in the 'Lavender Scare', activists were able to make use of the strong protections afforded to free speech by the US Constitution to get an embryonic gay rights movement off the ground. The early 1950s saw the foundation of 'homophile' groups, such as the largely male Mattachine Society, the largely female Daughters of Bilitis, and the mixed One Inc., all of which held talks and meetings on gay topics and argued for reform of anti-gay laws. In 1958, One Inc. scored a major victory when the Supreme Court held that its magazine, *One*, could not be held to fall foul of laws restricting the posting of obscene material.

As in the US, Britain in the 1950s saw an intensification of persecution (notably in surging numbers of arrests and prosecutions for offences such as gross indecency or importuning for an immoral purpose). But it also saw the foundation of the Homosexual Law Reform Society, whose status as the 'first and only organization publicly sympathetic to the problems of homosexuals' the historian Stephen Jeffery-Poulter noted, meant it also ended up providing support to many gay men who came to it for emotional and practical help.[22] Similarly, in France, 1954 saw the foundation of the Association Arcadie, which established a magazine and social club, as well as pushing for increased acceptance of homosexuality.

The Acceptance of Privacy, Not Pride

These groups were notable for their pursuit of limited, conservative goals, which would later be seen as too apologetic and minimalist. Their main aim was tolerance not equality. Arcadie, for example, had as its objective 'to present homosexuals as respectable, cultured, and dignified individuals deserving of greater social tolerance'.[23] This minimalism was inevitable in societies that still regarded homosexuality as scandalous. In America and Britain, decriminalization was the key early goal (France had decriminalized gay sex during the French Revolution, though it did have an unequal age of consent). On this front, as the 1950s turned into the 1960s, a gradual liberalization of norms could be detected. In 1962, although at the time all US states maintained criminalization of gay sex, the prestigious *American Law Institute* produced its Model Penal Code, under which private gay sex would cease to be a crime, a recommendation enacted by Illinois in the same year.

A similar pattern of progress was underway in the UK. An upsurge in arrests for same-sex activity and some high-profile trials in the 1950s provoked a degree of public debate. In 1957 the *Wolfenden Committee* was established, whose mandate included a review of the laws criminalizing gay sex. The resulting report was a major milestone on the road to decriminalization in England and Wales. It backed decriminalization, not because its members thought of homosexuality as good or morally neutral, but because they thought there ought to be 'a realm of private morality and immorality, which is, in brief and crude terms, not the law's business'.[24] As the 1960s turned into the 1970s, the idea that broader commitment to private autonomy meant that criminalization of gay sex was no longer appropriate began to become the normal position among Western democracies. In 1969, West Germany and Canada decriminalized male homosexuality, being followed by Austria in 1971, South Australia (the first Australian state to do so) in 1975, and Spain in 1979.

Even when some legal progress was proposed, the inclusion of homosexuality within the scope of the sexual freedoms established by the sexual revolution was grudging and minimalist. The American Model Penal Code may have proposed decriminalization of private sodomy, but it also proposed the introduction of an offence of soliciting for sodomy. In other words, if gay sex happened, it was to be tolerated, but go looking for it and you deserved punishment. What is more, even these minimal steps remained too much for many. In the United States as late as 1986, over half of the states maintained anti-sodomy laws, which a majority of the US Supreme Court upheld as constitutional in their ruling in *Bowers v. Hardwick*.

Progress in the UK was also slow and partial. The decriminalization of male homosexual behaviour, eventually passed by the British Parliament in 1967 some ten years after the recommendation of the Wolfenden Committee, was very minimal in nature.[25] Parliament did not decriminalize gay sex and then apply the usual rules in relation to ages of consent to it. Instead, legislators chose to leave the general criminalization of sex between men in place but to create a limited exception to that criminal status when both parties were over twenty-one and the act was done in private. The privacy requirement was strictly interpreted by the courts (it was held not to cover either acts done in a private home in which a third person was present, nor acts done in hotels). In addition, it did not apply to the merchant navy, the armed forces or to Scotland or Northern Ireland. Indeed, the UK authorities refused to apply the provisions of the 1967 Act to Northern Ireland until ordered to do so by the European Court of Human Rights in 1982.

The idea that 'Gay is Good', as the slogan of more radical activists went, had little or no political or legal traction. Even those politicians who worked hard to get decriminalization through legislatures were no supporters of gay pride. When the Lieutenant Governor of California exercised his casting vote to get decriminalization through a deadlocked State Senate in 1975, he justified his decision on the basis that it was totalitarian for the state to regulate private sexual conduct, not that homosexuality was morally acceptable.[26]

In the UK, Roy Jenkins, the reforming Home Secretary who worked tirelessly to get the decriminalization through the House of Commons, referred to homosexuality as 'a disability' whose sufferers 'carry a great weight of shame their whole lives'.[27] Lord Arran, who helped shepherd the Bill through the House of Lords, noted that 'no single noble Lord or noble Lady had ever said that homosexuality is right or a good thing. It has been universally condemned from start to finish by every single member of this House.'[28] His hope was that gays would 'show their thanks by comporting themselves quietly and with dignity' and was clear that 'any form of ostentatious behaviour now or in the future or any form of public flaunting would be utterly distasteful ... [and] make the sponsors of this bill regret that they had done what they had done'.[29]

The legal and political arguments that achieved success for gay people were based not on a claim that homosexuality itself had any merit or claim to toleration. Instead, the argument that won the day was the idea that a broader commitment to individual sexual autonomy required that homosexual behaviour be legal, even if most people thought of it as immoral and disgusting. When, in 1981, the European Court of Human Rights found that blanket criminalization of sex between men violated the European Convention on Human Rights, it justified its decision on the basis that:

> the present case concerns a most intimate aspect of private life. Accordingly, there must exist particularly serious reasons before interferences on the part of the public authorities can be legitimate [...] although members of the public

who regard homosexuality as immoral may be shocked, offended or disturbed by the commission by others of private homosexual acts, this cannot on its own warrant the application of penal sanctions when it is consenting adults alone who are involved.

The judges went out of their way to disassociate themselves from any claim that their ruling implied that homosexuality was to be considered as praiseworthy or even morally neutral, saying that:

'Decriminalization' does not imply approval, and a fear that some sectors of the population might draw misguided conclusions in this respect from reform of the legislation does not afford a good ground for maintaining it in force with all its unjustifiable features.[30]

Indeed, in the US, it was only when advocates for decriminalization succeeded in framing their case in terms of respect for privacy, rather than respect for homosexuality, that they achieved success. The Supreme Court ruling upholding the constitutionality of laws criminalizing gay sex in the 1986 case of *Bowers v. Hardwick* began:

The issue presented is whether the Federal Constitution confers a fundamental right upon homosexuals to engage in sodomy and hence invalidate the laws of the many States that still make such conduct illegal and have done so for a very long time.[31]

In contrast when, in 2003, a majority of the Supreme Court struck down such laws the judgment framed this issue very differently, arguing that:

In stating the claim to be whether there was a fundamental right to engage in consensual sodomy, Bowers had misapprehended the claim of liberty that had been presented to the Supreme Court.

A majority of the Court then proceeded to find criminalization unconstitutional on the basis that there was *'an emerging recognition that liberty gave substantial protection to adult persons in deciding how to conduct their private lives in matters pertaining to sex'*.[32] In other words, when the claim was based on an argument that homosexuality per se deserved protection, it lost. But when gay rights advocates successfully reframed the issue as one of respect for sexual autonomy and privacy in general, they won.

From Tolerance to Equality

That said, though slower to come and more grudgingly given, the legal tolerance of homosexuality was not an end point but a beginning. Law and social norms have a symbiotic relationship. Social norms influence the content of the law but the law also helps to form social norms. Judges and parliamentarians may have wanted merely to ease suffering of gay men (lesbian sex was less often criminalized) and to respect liberal principles of private autonomy, while leaving intact the wider social and cultural disdain for homosexuality. But the fact that the criminalization of sex for gay men had been removed contributed (along with other factors such as more and more people realizing they knew and liked someone who was gay), as many social conservatives feared, to a wider de-stigmatization of homosexuality.

The drift from 'we won't punish this' to 'I have the right to do this and there is therefore nothing wrong with it' is hard to resist. As the legal and social atmosphere became more permissive, gay rights movements in a number of Western countries had the space to expand into more radical territory. Activists no longer restricted themselves to seeking pity and tolerance. They wanted equality. This new attitude was reflected in the name change of the UK's Society for Homosexual Law Reform, which in 1970 was rebranded as the Campaign for Homosexual Equality.[33]

A further change occurred with the emergence of much more radical groups like the Gay Liberation Front in the US and UK and its French equivalent the Front homosexual d'action révolutionnnaire (all founded between 1969 and 1971). These groups saw gay rights as part of a movement that sought radical change to society's approach to sex, family and gender in its entirety. As Dennis Altman put it in his influential 1971 book *Homosexual: Oppression and Liberation*, 'the oppression of homosexuals [...] is part of the general repression of sexuality and our liberation can only come as part of a total revolution in social attitudes'.[34] This tension, characterized by Jeffrey Weeks as being between those who sought inclusion and equal citizenship and those focused on transgression and challenging the traditional order,[35] reflected, as will be discussed later, a longstanding division in the gay rights movement that persists to this day.

But, whether gay groups were seeking equality or revolution, it was undeniable that the attempt to limit gay rights to the minimum of decriminalization proved unsustainable. When gay sex was a crime, it was hard to argue, for example, that an employer should not be able to sack an employee who was regarded as a criminal by the state. But, once decriminalization had recognized gay sex as a permitted, and therefore legitimate, form of sexual activity, it became easier to draw analogies between the rights of gays and lesbians and those of other groups, such as women or ethnic minorities, whose claims for protection against discrimination had achieved significant success in the 1970s, 1980s and 1990s.

Gay-rights activists in the US drew explicit analogies between the campaigns that sought to prohibit discrimination against African Americans and those seeking to end discrimination against gays and lesbians. The historian George Chauncey compared the more radical approach of the gay liberation movement to the Black Power movement, arguing that 'in proclaiming and even cultivating their sense of difference from the national norm, gay people followed the lead of African Americans, Chicanos, Jews, Italians and others who were embracing the differences they had once downplayed'.[36] Those with a less radical agenda sought analogies in the 1960s Civil Rights movement. For example, Evan Wolfson, one of the early activists for gay marriage, analogized laws against same-sex marriage to the anti-miscegenation laws struck down by the US Supreme Court in *Loving v. Virginia* in 1967.[37]

Indeed, the conservative writer Christopher Caldwell lamented how the success of the Civil Rights campaign of the 1960s provided, both in the US and across the Western world, a template for other disempowered groups to follow. This template was particularly helpful to groups such as gays and lesbians, which started out with limited public support. Because African Americans were almost universally recognized as having been unjustly treated, if a group could successfully analogize their cause to the African American cause, it would add significant moral weight to their campaign.[38] By 1990, Steven Epstein was describing how gay politics had moved to focusing on 'a proto-ethnic gay identity'.[39]

Nonetheless, as was the case in relation to decriminalization of gay sex, the recognition of gay claims in areas such as discrimination law took much longer than for other groups. Laws preventing discrimination on grounds of sexual orientation at work did not come into force in the European Union until 2003. Federal level protections in Canada, Mexico, Australia and the US had to wait until 1995, 2003, 2013 and 2020 respectively.[40] But, ultimately, the case for granting gays and lesbians analogous freedoms and protections to those granted to other groups proved irresistible.

The ultimate recognition of the success of the gay rights movement in transforming the societal treatment of homosexuality from a disorder and a crime to a form of human sexuality on a par with heterosexuality was the recognition of gay marriage. This is still a work in progress, even in the West. Around half of EU member states, for example, continue to prohibit it. Nevertheless, in many countries, support for gay weddings has moved from a position that was so fringe that not a single mainstream party supported it in the 1990s, to being something that it would be considered a public scandal to oppose. A number of countries now even require prospective immigrants to indicate awareness of, and tolerance for, same-sex marriage as a condition of naturalization or immigration.[41]

But, again, this seemingly miraculous success was incidental. The victory of the campaign for same-sex marriage would not have happened without the work of gay rights activists. But it was only secondarily about gay people. It was a downstream, almost incidental effect of the broader revolution in the societal perception of the nature and function of heterosexual marriage. The idea of same-sex marriage made no sense in the context of the traditional view, which regarded marriage as an institution whose main function was to encourage the formation of stable families in which to raise children.

Under this view, marriage, sex and procreation were intimately bound up with each other. If the overall goal was to provide children with a stable two-parent home this meant that pre-marital sex (with its risks of single motherhood) should be avoided. Viewing marriage in this child-centred way also meant that if a couple failed to resist the temptation to have sex and an unmarried woman became pregnant, it was expected that the father of the child would marry her. Marriage was expected to mean 'till death do us part'. If, after a few years, the spouses were no longer 'feeling it', divorce was not considered an acceptable option. As the writer and gay-marriage activist Jonathan Rauch noted, the personal fulfilment of the spouses was not the primary concern and the very heavy expectations that we now place on marriage in terms of providing love, excitement and meaning were also less prominent. As he puts it:

> the couple did not necessarily expect deep personal fulfilment in marriage, a certain amount of adultery was taken for granted, and more of what would today be considered abusive or dysfunctional marriages were thought to be tolerable.[42]

The decline of this child-and-stability-focused vision of marriage was one of the major developments of the era of the sexual revolution. With the development of reliable contraception, it became possible to reduce the risk of unwanted pregnancy. In addition, from the 1960s on, cultural approaches that emphasized individual autonomy and fulfilment became increasingly dominant. This inevitably began to affect people's view of the function of marriage, causing the rise of what the psychologist Eli Finkel termed 'the self-expressive marriage'. Couples increasingly saw their marriages as being a way to meet their own romantic, sexual and emotional needs and as part of the realization of their individual life goals.[43] The shift in divorce law that got underway across the West in the 1970s, which provided increasing recognition of the right of one spouse to end a marriage unilaterally, reflected this shift.

Under this post-sexual revolution version, sex before marriage is fine and marriage, which may or may not involve children, is postponed until the couple have established stable adult lives. The function of marriage on this view is to confirm and strengthen the spouses' pre-existing commitment to each other.

The steady eclipse of the child-focused model of marriage by a self-expression-focused model explains why much of the Western world became open to same-sex marriage. If marriage is primarily about self-fulfilment and about mature adults committing to each other, then why exclude same-sex couples? For Jonathan Rauch, this explains both the impulse to extend marriage to same-sex couples and the residual resistance among conservatives. He writes:

> Same-sex marriage, [...] is in some sense the ultimate symbolic assault on what is left of the unity of sex, marriage, and procreation. 'Ultimate', I might add, in both senses of the word: 'extreme', but also 'last', the blow that completes the most destructive demolition work of the sexual revolution. After gay marriage, [...] how can sex, marriage, and procreation ever be put back together again?[44]

There is something in this. Even countries that had swallowed divorce, cohabitation and pre-marital sex without huge controversy saw furious resistance to legalizing same-sex marriage. By the turn of the millennium America had long been reconciled to freedom for straight people to marry and divorce as they saw fit, but same-sex marriage was one of the key issues in the 2004 presidential election. George W. Bush's electoral guru Karl Rove identified it as something that would drive conservative voters to turn out to vote and devoted huge resources to highlighting it as an issue. In the period up to 2012 some thirty-two states passed constitutional amendments prohibiting recognition of gay marriage.

Gay marriage also proved particularly controversial in France. French society is famous for its tolerance of affairs and is notably unjudgemental of private life. Gay sex was decriminalized in 1791, while François Hollande, the President between 2012 and 2017, had four children out of wedlock and while in office, left his partner and had affairs with a prominent journalist and then a prominent actress, all without much public reaction. But, in 2013, France was convulsed by huge demonstrations that saw hundreds of thousands protest against same-sex marriage for weeks on end.

Despite this opposition, the wider triumph of the individualistic and autonomy-based logic of the sexual revolution meant the case for same-sex marriage was too strong to resist; it seemed too unfair for straight people to apply to themselves a model that said marriage was all about adults committing to each other but then, when it came to gay couples, to turn around and insist that marriage was all about stability for children.

A judge of the Court of Appeal in the UK put the issue memorably in a (pre-gay marriage) ruling which established that same-sex couples could be recognized in the same way unmarried straight couples were for the purposes of inheriting a partner's tenancy. 'Parliament having swallowed the camel of including unmarried partners within the protection given to married couples', he declared 'it is not for this court to strain at the gnat of including such partners who are of the same sex as each other.'[45] In other words, the big development had been the abandonment of the old, traditional, marriage-focused paradigm for a more relaxed, individual-focused approach. The inclusion of the treatment of same-sex couples within this more relaxed paradigm was just a tidying-up exercise.

The key point is that the main development permitting both decriminalization of homosexuality and the legalization of gay marriage was the revolution in *straight* norms around sex and marriage. A liberal, self-fulfilment-focused paradigm was applied to straight sex and straight marriage and was then, gradually and often grudgingly, extended to gay sex and gay relationships. This extension needed the courageous effort of gay activists to bring it about, but it could never have succeeded on the basis of the efforts of gays and lesbians alone.

Without the shift to a liberal, self-fulfilment focused paradigm for straight sexuality, the movement to lift restrictions on gay sexuality could not have got off the ground. Indeed, as was the case with decriminalization, the full application of the logic of that reimagining of marriage to same-sex couples took some time; it was not until heterosexual marriage had been fundamentally changed for quite a while that the idea of same-sex marriage even began to be discussed. Unilateral or no-fault divorce was the norm in most of the West by 1980; the very first country to legalize same-sex marriage did not do so until 2001.

It is a strange realization that the legalization of gay marriage was not primarily about gays and lesbians. But one of the insights of getting older is the realization that, even in your own life, many things are not really about you – and your ability to determine your fate is often very limited. Hollywood may rejoice in telling people that they can do or be whatever they want but, in reality, most of our fate is determined by forces much larger than we are. A female serf in the Middle Ages could have all the dreams, ambitions in the world but would be unlikely to achieve them no matter how hard she worked or how much get-up-and-go she had.

Gay-rights activists in the same era (assuming they could have thought in these terms) could have been the most skilful political operators in history but would have had no chance of success. Though we all like to take credit for our successes, our victories in life usually rely as much on the hand we were dealt as our own endeavours. Broader historical forces gave gay rights activists from the mid twentieth century on openings that previous generations did not have. Those activists put in great efforts and pushed to advance their agenda with bravery and skill but without the changes wrought by those bigger forces they would have been pushing against a locked door.

The fact that the gay rights revolution would have been impossible without the broader change in straight sexual mores underlines its vulnerability. Gays and lesbians were not capable of bringing about their legal, political and social liberation themselves and they are unlikely to be able to defend their gains on their own. We are a tiny minority who will never be able to fully determine our political fate ourselves.

Just as free Estonia sits on the edge of the democratic world, uncomfortably close to Russia and dependent on the backing of larger and more powerful allies to remain free of Russia's grip, gay freedom is also on the frontlines. Gay rights are at the very edge of the territory conquered by the sexual revolution. They are the outcome that was furthest from and most radically opposed to the old order that had governed sexual life in the West for a very long time. Moreover, like democratic Estonia, the survival of these rights depends mainly on their continued ability to win the backing of larger allies, in our case the large straight majority. Gay freedom will be particularly vulnerable to any broader cultural changes that move society in a more conservative direction. Contrary to what most people appear to think, such a change is increasingly likely.

3

Sexual Freedom and the End of History: The Post-Liberal Moment

My grandparents were good people. Devoted parents, doting grand-mother and grandfather, caring neighbours. They had a hands-on kindness towards people in difficulty that would put to shame those who think that solidarity with our fellow humans extends only to holding and advertising the correct opinions. Some of this came from their upbringing. Although in their old age they lived in Dublin, they had both grown up on small farms in rural Ireland in the 1920s and 1930s, where money was scarce and the Catholic Church's influence was extremely powerful. The negative impact of the Church's approach to issues of gender, sex and sexuality on the Ireland of that time have been extensively ventilated but I think that my grandparents' strongly religious upbringing shaped them in positive ways too. It gave them a strong sense of compassion in other ways, especially their belief that they had a duty to help those around them who were vulnerable, be it through poverty, illness or mental-health troubles.

They were, however, as I said, people of their time. I remember sitting in their always stiflingly over-heated sitting room in the early 1990s watching a news report on Irish TV about the campaign to get the government to stop dragging its feet and to abide by the 1988 ruling of the European Court of Human Rights that had ordered Ireland to decriminalize gay sex. 'They should be burnt' was my grandfather's immediate reaction. My grandmother, who was more liberal (and liked to disagree with him in any event), chimed in with the softer-edged: 'I feel sorry for them. They have a disease.' They never knew I was gay. When I did come out to others, I didn't think it was right to upset them and thought they would never really get their heads around it. After all, their conservatism on sexual matters was not limited to homosexuality; it was part of a broader set of beliefs on sex, family and marriage that they had inherited from the cultural and religious atmosphere in which they grew up.

Maybe I was underestimating their flexibility, though I still think I did the right thing. But, looking back, my reasoning is instructive. I didn't tell my grandparents because they were old and, given the circumstances of their upbringing, I thought they wouldn't be able to cope with the idea of a gay grandson. By the late 1990s I could assume that, though my grandparents would have struggled, my aunts and uncles (who grew up in the 1950s and 1960s) would be better able to cope with the information and that my cousins (who grew up in the 1980s and 1990s) would have few, if any, issues with it. This chain of reasoning was correct (in this case, each successive generation did have less of an issue with homosexuality). More importantly, it reflected deep-seated ideas about the direction societies take over time.

My view was that each generation could be expected to be more and more at ease with gay people because being anti-gay was 'old-fashioned'; something that resulted from growing up in circumstances that no longer applied in the modern world. The 'modern' approach was to be progressively more tolerant. Young people who grew up in a social atmosphere in which the sexual revolution had made its influence felt would be ever more permissive in relation to the full range of issues around sex and gender (pre-marital sex, homosexuality, abortion, trans issues). My grandparents were not enamoured of sexual liberalism, I thought, only because they had not been sufficiently exposed to it in their formative years.

My view reflected the wider liberal confidence that we have left the illiberal past behind. In the long run, liberal approaches to sex would prove, it was assumed, universally appealing. We were convinced that, as the intellectual historian Matthew Rose put it, 'the frontier is closed, there is no going back'. But I increasingly worry that this approach, though correct in relation to Ireland in the 1990s, is too complacent and that it mistakes a recent and largely Western trend for a universal irreversible process.

Gay people in most of the West won their freedom by successfully placing their small boat in the current of sexual liberation that swept the Western world from the 1960s on. That current carried them to a place of unimagined freedom and equality. But being swept along by powerful currents is only good if the current is flowing in the right direction; if there is a more conservative turn in society and the current starts to flow in a less welcome direction, the gay and lesbian boat could easily be swept to a more repressive and unhappy place. There are a number of reasons to believe that the blithe confidence that embracing the sexual revolution is modern and that the cultural current is bound to keep flowing in a liberalizing direction is badly mistaken.

Worse, because gay and lesbian liberation represents the outer extreme of the sexual revolution it is particularly vulnerable to any conservative shift. It is, after all, the step that took longest to achieve, and the step that sparked the most intense resistance from those of a conservative outlook. It is also the step that is more radically at odds with the old unity of sex, procreation and marriage than any other element of the sexual revolution. This makes it all the more likely that gay rights will be among the first to go if there is any kind of cultural shift against the sexual revolution more generally.

Am I falling into paranoia here? Does the fact that I grew up in a still-homophobic society mean that I am hyper-vigilant, nervily scanning the horizon for threats and convincing myself that every passing cloud represents a coming storm? Isn't acceptance of gay rights not now deeply embedded in the politics of Western democracies? Have corporates and politicians not been crowding on to the gay rights bandwagon? Have workplace EDI departments in many places not become ever more restrictive of the rights of employees to dissent from the gay rights orthodoxy? And are older generations that were the most hostile to homosexuality not gradually dying off?

I have to concede that the answer to these questions is, mainly (but not entirely), yes. Most people in Western Europe, Australia, North America and most of South America regard the key issues of the gay rights revolution (decriminalization, same-sex marriage, etc.) as closed. Such debates as there are focus largely on trans issues (in relation to which gays and lesbians are themselves noticeably divided). But I am still convinced that it is unduly optimistic to see the recent triumphs of gay rights as representing the irreversible end of a process rather than as a particular stage in a story that may develop in a number of different ways. Regarding the victory of gay rights as the culmination of a process can be thought of as an example of what I would call 'The End' thinking. That is the idea that, like in a film, when certain events have unfolded, the story is over, 'The End' comes up on the screen and the credits roll.

In relation to the sexual revolution this kind of 'The End' thinking is very prevalent. On this view, the story of the gay rights revolution in the West can be summarized (admittedly simplistically) as follows: 'Gays and lesbians were oppressed for centuries. Then there was decriminalization in some, then all, countries. This was followed by anti-discrimination laws and, finally, same-sex marriage. Virtually everyone realized that this was for the best. The End.' A similar view is often prevalent in relation to the emancipation of women, under which the story runs: 'Women were oppressed for centuries, then we had female suffrage, then reforms to laws on marriage, sex and work. The End.'

The problem is, there is no way of knowing whether the thirty years of tolerance of homosexuality, after centuries of oppression, marks the end of such oppression or merely a blip, or, indeed, whether fifty years of commitment to sex equality has brought a definitive end to wholesale and longstanding oppression of women. What seems permanent often passes away. The history of Europe is littered with countries and empires that existed for centuries but which have disappeared from the map.

Are sexual freedom and the greater toleration of homosexuality that such freedom brought ultimately of near-universal appeal? It is almost certainly too early to know. As I have already noted, opinion poll data on both sides of the Atlantic show that it is only in the last ten to fifteen years that the number of people who thought that same-sex relationships were not morally wrong exceeded the number of people who thought that such relationships were always or mostly wrong. That is the blink of an eye in historical terms.

I remember seeing a politician from Ireland's largest party canvassing for votes at my local train station in 1997. I had been reading inspiring histories of the gay rights movement, so overcame my embarrassment and asked her what her view was on legalizing same-sex marriage. She looked at me with a mix of confusion and disdain, as if I had asked what her policy was on the establishment of brothels on Mars. After a moment of mutually embarrassed silence she said 'Does anyone have a policy on that?' In 2025 it may seem unthinkable that gay marriage would ever be repealed in Britain, France, the US or almost anywhere else it has been legalized, but we forget how in most places in the 1990s (let alone the 1960s) legalizing it was unthinkable.

Surprising losses are no less likely than surprising gains. The only way that anyone could be confident that questions such as gay marriage are definitively settled is if they believe in a version of 'the end of history'. This term goes back a long way but its most recent prominence comes from a famous book written in the early 1990s by the political scientist Francis Fukuyama. Written in the optimistic afterglow of the fall of the Berlin Wall, Fukuyama argued that with the collapse of communism, we had come to 'the end of history' in the sense that liberal democratic capitalism had seen off its rivals and was 'the only game in town'. To be fair to Fukuyama, his thesis was more subtle than many of his later detractors alleged and he did hedge his bets by alluding to the possibility that religion or nationalism could provide the basis for conflict in the future. But, overall, he argued that liberal democratic market capitalism could be seen as the end point of an evolutionary process of human government and that, over time, it would become progressively more prevalent.[1]

For a time, this kind of thinking appeared to be correct. All the indicators did seem to show that liberal democracy was the way of the future. The post-1989 period saw a wave of democratization sweep much of the world. Moreover, the achievement of liberal democracy appeared to be irreversible. The traffic seemed to be all one-way; numerous communist and other forms of dictatorships were becoming democracies, no democracies were becoming autocracies. Where democracy had not yet taken hold, as in China, it was assumed that, over time, economic development would go hand-in-hand with liberalization and democratization. This complacent attitude was understandable. After all, hadn't it been necessary to pen those living under autocratic communism in Central and Eastern Europe behind concrete walls, minefields and barbed wire to stop them fleeing to the democratic West?

But, as we now know, history didn't end. China did not become more liberal nor more democratic as it became more economically developed. Neither, for that matter, did the increasingly wealthy oil monarchies of the Persian Gulf. Even more disturbingly, countries such as Poland and Hungary, which had enthusiastically embraced liberal democracy, began to move away from liberal democratic practices in important respects, particularly in relation to respect for judicial independence. Even in the United States, the peaceful transfer of power following presidential elections is no longer guaranteed. The world is unpredictable and our ability to know how things will go and what issues will be controversial, even fifteen or twenty years hence, is minimal. I imagine that if you had asked one hundred thousand Danes in 1985 what the biggest issue in Danish politics would be in twenty years' time, I doubt a single one of them would have said 'blasphemous cartoons'; yet in 2005 the controversy over cartoons of the Prophet Mohammed in the newspaper *Jyllandsposten* overshadowed all other issues in Danish political life.

The complacency caused by regarding the achievement of liberal democracy as an irreversible end point isn't just a matter of failed predictions; it causes serious problems. For example, the European Union required all states that sought to become members to demonstrate that they had embraced liberal democracy. But because no one imagined that liberal democracy, once achieved, could be reversed, the Union failed to develop effective procedures that could be deployed when states such as Poland and Hungary began to move away from liberal democratic values after joining. This has left the Union like a nightclub with tough bouncers on the door but no internal security, which then finds itself unable to deal with patrons who start fighting on the dancefloor once they are inside.

'Outdated' Homophobia?

The parallels to gay liberation are striking. For many people, the liberalization of norms and rules around homosexuality is seen not just a social and political change, but as a form of modernization that, once achieved, is irreversible. I have often heard someone's anti-gay views described as 'out of date' or 'old-fashioned', as if gay rights were a form of technology that made homophobia redundant in the same way that the personal computer did away with the need for typewriters. But, when you look at old photos, you can see that what we think of as modern at any particular moment may appear anything but a decade or two later.

A woman photographed in the 1980s with big hair and big shoulder pads would have thought she was giving off the message that she was modern and successful, but looking from 2025 at a photo of that era, the only message we can see is '1980s'. Embracing gay rights might look modern now but might just look '2010s' to someone in forty years' time.

Yet, for many, perhaps most people, the story of the criminal status of gay sex or the legalization of gay marriage is viewed as a one-way historical process, a story with a predetermined outcome in which early supporters of gay rights were 'on the right side of history', and which comes to an end when the pro-gay position achieves primacy.

This is far too determinist an approach. Just as the European Union was wrong to assume that once a member state achieved liberal democracy it would never regress, those who support gay rights would be wrong to assume that, once achieved, such rights are irreversible. Gay equality is no less reversible than liberal democracy. Both are choices that societies can make, or not make, or make and then reverse. Legal gay marriage is no more inherently modern than criminalized gay sex. Both exist in our current world and neither is guaranteed to remain in force.

Although pro-gay activists often like to identify other causes (poverty, manipulative leaders, lack of knowledge) to explain why people hold anti-gay views, the persistence of such views does not need any explanation. Hostility to homosexuality has been the norm, not the exception for most of recorded history in the Western world. The fact that in the West, after centuries of oppression, the tide has been flowing in a pro-gay direction for a few decades does not mean that that pattern will become universal or that it is not subject to reversal. There is a degree of post-colonial Western arrogance in imagining that the very recent turn in Western sexual mores represents an irreversible trend or a position that is inherently more modern than other approaches. A cursory look around at the world today should be sufficient to discredit the notion that sexual liberalism is either inherently modern or steadily advancing over time.

Sexual Conservatism Can Be Modern Too

Much of the world has steadfastly refused to embrace gay liberation and, in many areas, sexual mores overall are becoming more, not less conservative. The internet is littered with sites showing photos of women in mini-skirts in Iran in the 1960s and 1970s. Iran is not exceptional. While many in the West are certain that sexual freedom, and its incidental by-product of gay rights, could never be reversed, many countries in Africa, Asia and the Middle East are becoming increasingly conservative.

In the Arab world, the collapse of pan-Arab nationalism and socialism, along with the spread of well-funded highly conservative versions of Islam, brought about a notable conservative trend in matters of sex and gender. Beyond the Arabic-speaking world, Muslim-majority countries such as Pakistan and Indonesia have seen significant upswing in the influence of conservative and highly illiberal forms of Islam. In Africa, there has been an intensification of hostility to homosexuality and of resistance to gay rights in countries such as Nigeria and Uganda. In many parts of the world, international gay rights activism is not seen as a form of modernization and improvement but as one more instance in the long history of former colonial powers hectoring and looking down on their former colonies.

Even closer to home, in Russia, the climate for gay people has become notably more hostile with rejection of homosexuality now identified as a key marker that distinguishes Russia from the West. Poland and Hungary have also, albeit to a lesser extent than Russia, seen a worsening climate for gays and lesbians. As the Hungarian historian Anita Kurimay puts it 'gone are the days when would-be members of the European Union held up the more humane treatment of homosexuals as proof of the "cultural maturity" of East-Central European countries on their way to becoming mature Western democracies'.[2] Populist parties in a number of countries in the region have taken strong stances against gay rights and trans rights. In 2019 the ruling PiS party made opposition to LGBT rights the central feature of its successful re-election campaign, to the extent that 'LGBT' was chosen as the Polish 'word of the year' in that year's annual vote organized by the Institute of the Polish Language at the University of Warsaw.[3] Viktor Orbán's anti-gay Fidesz party is the most electorally successful since the fall of communism and has been in power since 2010.

Although things improved in Poland following the victory of a centrist coalition in 2023, the same year saw the anti-gay Smer party win elections in Slovakia, while late in 2022 Georgia Meloni's highly socially conservative Fratelli d'Italia took power in Italy. Both Meloni and Orbán have acted to restrict the recognition of gay couples as parents,[4] while Orbán has enacted a law restricting access to content depicting homosexuality for under eighteens and upped the ante further in early 2025 by banning gay-pride parades (providing that facial recognition will be used to punish those attending such events). A law seeking to allow people to report same-sex couples raising children to the state authorities was passed but then vetoed by Hungary's President.[5] Neither Orbán nor Meloni have tried to repeal their countries' civil partnership laws (they might face clashes with their constitutional courts and the European Court of Human Rights if they did so) but if the wider atmosphere moves in an anti-gay direction, this cannot be ruled out.

Although those pushing for gay rights or trans rights often say that their opponents are 'on the wrong side of history',[6] they are being myopic both historically and geographically. The very most that could be said is that opponents of gay rights are 'on the wrong side of a very short period of recent history in some parts of the world' but that isn't quite as catchy. These 'right side of history' determinists fall into the same mistake identified by the philosopher Bernard Williams, who mocked those who believe that their views are 'being cheered on by the universe'.[7] The reality is that neither the universe nor history is to be found with rainbow face-paint on their cheeks, applauding the marchers and waving rainbow flags at gay pride marches. History does not have a side.

Contingent Cycles Not Inevitable Progress

The advance of liberal approaches to sex and to homosexuality in the West in recent decades is the product of a series of cultural and historical circumstances, which were not inevitable. If Gavrilo Prinzip's bullets had missed Arch-Duke Franz Ferdinand and the First World War had not broken out in 1914, would the conservative monarchies of Germany, Russia and Austria-Hungary have fallen? If they had not, would the loosening of morals that occurred in the post-war period have occurred? Who knows? The West finds itself where it is in terms of sex and sexuality not because this is the outcome of some allegedly inevitable historical process. Rather we are where we are because of a myriad of interacting circumstances, influences and contingent events, from Protestant Christian individualism and the moral weight of the Civil Rights movement to the discrediting of anything that can be made to look even vaguely analogous to the discrimination perpetrated by the fascist regimes.

46

The idea that anyone could be confident that a decade or so of gay marriage in a minority of states represents a permanent end to the issue of the status of gay relationships, following centuries upon centuries of persecution, borders on the absurd. The fall of the Berlin Wall did not represent the beginning of the end of disputes over liberalism and democracy, any more than the Stonewall riots represented the beginning of the end of disputes over the social and legal status of homosexuality. Indeed, as others have noted, attitudes to sex over the centuries have been characterized by cyclical patterns rather than linear progress. There have been a number of periods of history in the West in which sexual mores have become less and then more restrictive. The Roman Empire was somewhat more permissive than the Christian regimes that followed it. Georgian Britain was more relaxed than the Victorian era and the Roaring Twenties in the US were followed by a more repressive atmosphere in the 1940s and 1950s.[8]

Some backlash against the sexual revolution shouldn't surprise anyone. No revolution is perfect or suits everyone, even if it is largely successful. After an initial burst of revolutionary freedom has been enjoyed, what follows is often a rise in dissatisfaction with the downsides of the new regime and, if not a desire to restore the old regime, at least a hankering after some of its previously under-appreciated virtues. In Hungary, Poland and the former East Germany, the joyous overthrow of the oppressive communist regimes of the early 1990s was followed after a few years by a revival in the electoral fortunes of the successors to the old communist parties. This success was part of what Germans called *Ostalgie*, that is, the nostalgia for the communist era depicted in the 2003 film *Goodbye Lenin!* But, because counter-revolution usually produces something new rather than a restoration of the old order, the ex-communist parties were then swept aside and right-wing parties such as the PiS, Fidesz and Alternativ für Deutschland, which displayed authoritarian tendencies and open scepticism towards liberal democracy, surged in popularity.

In the same way, as sexual freedom ceases to be a new exciting development, awareness of its costs is starting to rise. The writer Philip Hensher described how enchanting he found the description of 1970s San Francisco in Armistead Maupin's much-loved *Tales of the City* series of books. The city was, he said 'a haven of liberality and sexual freedom to which his worldwide readers dreamt of escaping'. But, a few decades later, he felt that 'The sad truth is that everywhere now is a little bit like San Francisco, with internet dating, amateur strip nights in bars and, if you want it, casual sex in sex clubs. And now the San Francisco culture is here in our own cities, it turns out to be not quite as adorable as it seemed in Maupin's books.' [9]

In both the US and Europe, there is some evidence that a turn against the sexual revolution in general and in gay rights in particular is becoming more likely. In the US there are a number of cultural straws in the wind coupled with a more marked dynamic on the right that suggest that some of the forces that have driven the success of the gay rights revolution in the past few decades are weakening.

Even before the shattering defeat suffered by liberals in the 2024 presidential election, some detected a new traditionalism among the elite. In 2022 an essay in *The New York Times* declared 'New York's hottest club is the Catholic Church.' [10] The essay argued that among elite fashionable young people in New York 'Catholicism is the new hip thing, partly as a rejection of progressive morality, partly as an aesthetic posture among the fashionable New Right.' *Slate* magazine decried the treatment of this phenomenon as a 'fun, sexy trend story' but did not disagree that there was indeed a trend underway in which 'young, cool intellectuals – bored by the corny politics of their liberal peers – have found transgressive delight in embracing the rituals of traditional Catholicism, along with at least some of its moral stances on sex and gender'. [11] *Vanity Fair* noted in the same year how this new religiously tinged socially conservative position 'has become quietly edgy and cool in new tech outposts like Miami and Austin and in downtown Manhattan, where New-Right-ish politics are in'. [12]

Beyond elite circles, something is stirring too. The internet-driven growth of phenomena such as 'tradwives' (women committed to extreme traditional gender roles in marriage) and 'incels' (straight men whose single status leads them to denigrate women) shows that there is growing resentment in non-elite circles towards feminism's transformation of the role of women and the loosening of gender roles it brought about (a loosening which was one of the factors facilitating the advance of gay rights). Figures like Andrew Tate have become extraordinarily popular among young men, with a consistently demeaning message about women and gay people.

Louise Perry thinks (and hopes) that the UK is on the point of a move towards a more conservative sexual atmosphere. She approvingly quotes the writer Katherine Dee, who argues that 'the pendulum with sexuality is going to swing, big time [...]. We're diving headlong into something that's been simmering in the background since 2013–14.'[13] This view received at least partial support in a 2024 survey of British adults aged eighteen to twenty-seven, the results of which showed a striking shift in the sexual mores of young adults. The percentage who said that they or their friends 'commonly have sex on one-night stands' had collapsed from 78 per cent in 2004 to 23 per cent in 2024. Younger people had also become notably more favourable to marriage. In 2004, 39 per cent of the sample had said marriage was irrelevant. Only 21 per cent of the 2024 sample had the same opinion.

Given that in recent times there has been significant cultural pressure on elites to appear to be pro-gay, it is likely that a degree of 'preference falsification' has been at work, which is causing people in elite social groups to conceal any anti-gay views they may have. But, as Timur Kuran, the political economist who coined this term has noted, change can occur very rapidly when a number of people are seen to buck the prevailing view. Once this happens, those who have been consciously or unconsciously falsifying their own preferences become willing to cease doing so. Voters can move surprisingly quickly to embrace positions that were previously seen as unthinkable. This dynamic can be seen in the work of Portuguese scholar Vicente Valentim, who recently showed how the increase in support for the populist right in Western democracies has occurred too quickly to be accounted for by changes in people's beliefs. He suggests that the better explanation is that voters already held reactionary views, which they had not acted on because they perceived them to be socially unacceptable.[14]

Centuries of hostility do not evaporate in a decade or so. Given how recently homosexuality was widely negatively regarded, there must be a large pool of anti-gay feeling ready to be reactivated if the social and political atmosphere moves in a conservative direction. If this occurs, it is not hard to see how political positions such as repealing gay marriage or even recriminalization, which are now seen as beyond the pale, could become mainstream. The unthinkable can become thinkable very quickly. Who, after all, would have predicted ten years ago that open refusal to accept the result of a presidential election would not have been political death for a US politician?

Whether or not the trends among trendy New Yorkers or in angry corners of the internet represent the tip of a more socially conservative iceberg, something is definitely underway on the right of American politics that threatens to undermine what had seemed to be an emergent consensus in which both left and the right appeared to regard gay rights as a done deal. This is part of a broader realignment. In his 2021 book *A World after Liberalism*, the intellectual historian Matthew Rose sketches the changing intellectual currents among the American right. As he summarizes, 'liberalism is losing its hold on Western minds [...] a new conservatism, unlike any in recent memory, is coming into view. Ideas once thought taboo are being reconsidered, [...] debates once closed are reopening.'[15]

Of course, even before this realignment, the passive acquiescence of the American right to gay rights was fleeting and limited. Ronald Reagan's takeover of the Republican Party in the late 1970s was in part driven by the emergence of a strong conservative Christian political movement that was motivated to a large degree by opposition liberalization of norms around abortion and gay rights. This movement provided him with significant support in his fight with the more moderate wing of the party represented by figures like Gerald Ford. But, as an increasing number of right-wing figures are now arguing, despite its apparent social conservatism, the Reagan revolution was ultimately one that boosted rather than hindered the changes, such as gay rights, unleashed by the sexual revolution.

For the conservative writer Christopher Caldwell, Reagan 'learned to sound certain conservative notes about sex in the 1970s, and even gave a barn-burning speech against abortion in 1983' [...] 'but [his] stress on "family values" [...] disguised his acquiescence to modern ways'.[16] According to the conservative political theorist Patrick Deneen, conservatives in the Reagan mould, 'have at best offered lip service to the defence of traditional values'.[17]

This was not just a matter of individual policies (Reagan signed off on the liberalization of California's laws on both divorce and abortion as governor). Reagan's opposition to gay rights and abortion may have been sincere (and that of many of his supporters certainly was) but the core of his message was always small government and individual freedom. As the intellectual historian Mark Lilla points out, Reagan's constant invocation of freedom and his ambition to reduce the scope of the state meant that the cultural revolution of the 1960s and the Reagan revolution 'have proved to be complementary, not contradictory events'.[18] Christopher Caldwell suggests that the hippy principle 'do your own thing' ends up being not so different from the Reaganesque conservative principle of 'every man for himself'. 'The 1980s', he concludes, 'are what the 1960s turned into.'[19]

In some ways, therefore, the right of American politics has, for the past few decades, been an unwitting assistant to the advance of gay rights. Republican presidents may have allowed their homophobia to drive them to neglect the AIDS crisis to a scandalous degree (Reagan) or used issues like gay marriage to fire up the socially conservative element of their base (George W. Bush), but social conservatives in the 2020s are increasingly realizing that the 'small-state conservatism' they espoused did not serve opponents of the sexual revolution. If a party's central message is individual freedom and shrinking the state, in the long run it will never be an effective advocate for the maintenance of conservative approaches to sex that necessarily seek to limit individual choice and freedom in sexual matters.

Small-state conservatives who argued against gay rights were always vulnerable to the charge that they wanted to make government 'just small enough to fit into your bedroom'. This meant that for the past few decades, with both the broader culture and the main conservative party preaching freedom, the advance of gay rights was hard to stop. By the end of the 2010s a significant number of Republicans seemed willing to accept changes such as gay marriage as a *fait accompli*. Indeed, in Congress a small but non-negligible minority of Republicans even proved willing to go along with the passing of legislation that codified the recognition of gay marriage at federal level.

However, there are now strong indicators that the left–right consensus on the desirability of individual freedom that helped the gay rights movement in the US to advance is under threat from a growing wing of the conservative movement. After almost four decades the predominance of Reaganesque, freedom-emphasizing-small-state-conservative views in the Republican Party is coming to an end. Although he did deliver tax cuts to the rich in his first term, the populist movement that twice propelled Donald Trump to the US Presidency and to near total control of the Republican Party was one that broke with key elements of the Reagan approach. In common with populist movements in much of Europe, shrinking the state is no longer a priority. Indeed, a more interventionist state and opposition to free trade are key elements of the agenda and anti-woke, anti-abortion, anti-immigration themes have played an increasing role.

While Trump himself is not particularly anti-gay, the movement he has unleashed has anti-gay figures in key positions. He has also consistently expressed support for anti-gay parties such as Fidesz in Hungary and Vox in Spain.[20] The success of Trump reflects a much wider shift in the American right. Polling data now show that US Republicans' values are much closer to those of authoritarian regimes such as Russia and Turkey than to those of conservative voters in other Western liberal democracies.[21] In any event, at seventy-eight he is unlikely to be at the helm for much longer. What the Trump movement will turn into will be influenced by the fact that within conservative circles an increasingly influential group of academics, lawyers and authors are articulating a vision of the future of the conservative movement that breaks definitively with the individual-freedom-emphasizing version of conservatism espoused by Reagan and his successors.

Advocates of this 'post-liberal' conservatism have found a ready audience in the conservative Christian constituency within the Republican Party, which felt understandably short changed from the failure of two Reagan and three Bush presidencies to stop the cultural and legal advance of the gay rights movement. Patrick Deneen, perhaps the leading intellectual figure in this movement, puts it this way: 'What has passed for "conservatism" in the United States for the past half century is today exposed as a movement that was never capable of, nor fundamentally committed to, conservation in any fundamental sense. All along it was a species of "liberalism" that rejected the core tenets of an original conservatism.'[22]

Deneen and others advocate a new, increasingly influential, approach that argues in favour of what they call 'common good conservatism'. This movement openly advocates a non-liberal or post-liberal regime, which rejects the primacy of individual liberty and which envisages the state promoting conservative and religious values.[23] Deneen unabashedly acknowledges that this new conservatism 'opposes liberalism's main commitment as liberty understood above all as individual choice'.[24] Freedom for Deneen is not the ability of individuals to choose how to live their lives but the 'learned capacity to govern oneself'.[25] Doing what one wants, in contrast is, for him, a form of slavery 'in which we are driven by our basest appetites to act against our better nature'.[26]

In an approach that overlaps to a remarkable degree with that of Islamists such as Sayyid Qutb, who inspired the foundation of the ultra-conservative Muslim Brotherhood, Deneen argues that liberalism is an 'insidious ideology' which 'ingratiates by invitation to the easy liberties, diversions and attractions of freedom, pleasure and wealth'.[27] He suggests that the conservative movement in America is increasingly rejecting its previous endorsement of the classical liberal promotion of individual autonomy in favour of an approach that rejects pluralism and the previous conservative emphasis on limiting government. As *Politico* magazine summarizes, the movement argues, 'that a strong central government should endorse a socially conservative vision of morality and enforce that vision in law'. 'We are', Deneen declares, 'entering the time *after liberalism*.'[28]

It is hard to think of an agenda more likely to set alarm bells ringing for gays and lesbians than a plan to have the state 'endorse a socially conservative vision of morality and enforce that vision in law'. These are the very principles used to justify criminalization of gay sex in the past. It is hard to see how either same-sex marriage or laws protecting gay people from discrimination would thrive in a state dedicated to these post-liberal principles. Lest anyone have any doubts about what a loss for liberalism might mean for gays and lesbians, Deneen is clear that post-liberal conservatism is 'socially conservative, anti-gay marriage'[29] and advocates 'forms of legislation that promote public morality and forbid its intentional corruption'.[30] Indeed, Susan McWilliams Barndt, a political scientist and the daughter of Deneen's intellectual mentor Wilson McWilliams, has criticized Deneen in particular for 'his hostility to the gay community', noting that this hostility was not something of which her father would have approved.[31]

What is more, the growth of post-liberalism deprives the gay rights movement of the shared vocabulary and values that they could previously use to reach out to those on the right. In the past, while most on the right did disagree with gay rights advocates about what respecting freedom required in the context of homosexuality, they shared common recognition of the value of freedom. Sharing that set of values allowed for discussions in which the conservative side could share some of the instincts underpinning the position of those arguing for greater sexual freedom. This meant that persuasion was much more possible than in a debate with those whose top commitment is the imposition of a conservative legal and social order.

The 2024 election has already shown that in the US the consensus that bound both parties to a series of shared norms is a thing of the past. If post-liberal conservatism becomes dominant on the right, a joint commitment to liberal values on the right and left will also cease to be a feature of the American system. As Deneen admits, the movement's aim is that liberalism will no longer represent the system within which different strands of opinion fight for primacy. Rather, liberalism will represent one party in a system in which it has to compete with more authoritarian opponents.[32]

Post-liberalism is not yet the dominant ideology of conservative America but it has dramatically increased its influence on the American right in recent years. Deneen's 2018 book *Why Liberalism Failed* was an unexpected hit, even making it onto Barack Obama's summer reading list. It has been complemented by the work of a host of other writers, academics and lawyers, all making the same core claim that there must be a break with individual autonomy and that the state should take a hand in promoting conservative morality (with gay rights high on the target list of the immoralities to be curtailed). The moderate conservative David Brooks described the influence of this movement as the 'terrifying future' of American conservatism.

Poll data show Republicans reversing their previous warming to gay rights. A Gallup poll in 2024 showed that the long increase in Republican support for gay marriage had ended with only 49 per cent of Republicans expressing support, down from 56 per cent in the previous poll.[33] The 2025 poll showed a further decline to 41 per cent. Politics is, as Matthew Rose notes, 'a lagging indicator of cultural change'. The figures driving this movement may not, he argues, be well known by veteran Republican politicians or senior editors of conservative magazines, but they are what is animating young aides and junior staff.[34]

A number of young senators, such as Josh Hawley and Marco Rubio (later Secretary of State), have been supportive,[35] and its increasing influence was underlined when J.D. Vance, a convert to traditionalist Catholicism and an avowed fan of Deneen, secured the nomination as Donald Trump's Vice-President. Matt Gaetz, President Trump's first choice for Attorney General in his second term, identified which way the wind was blowing in the party. In 2015, as a member of the Florida state legislature he was pushing for the state to repeal its ban on gay people adopting children and was lobbying his father (a state senator) to support this move. By 2022 as a member of the US House of Representatives, he was opposed both to laws banning discrimination on grounds of sexual orientation and to legislation codifying the recognition of same-sex marriage in federal law. By 2024 he was referring to 'degenerate LGBT propaganda'.[36]

Though the risk is real, it is important not to overstate it. Despite attempts by some legal scholars to argue that common good conservative approaches are part of the American legal tradition,[37] liberal values and the recognition of freedom as the right of individuals to be free to choose for themselves how they want to think, speak and live are deeply woven into American political and legal culture. Any attempt to institute an authoritarian conservative regime would face serious pushback from judges and voters.

The example of abortion is frightening but also reassuring. It is frightening in that the overturning of *Roe v. Wade* shows that individuals can suddenly find the state interfering in intimate areas that they were long accustomed to regarding as matters for themselves alone. But the abortion example is also encouraging, in the sense that it showed limits to popular desire for more restrictive policies in areas of sex and reproduction. Since the Supreme Court ruling overturning *Roe*, the abortion issue has proved to be a vote loser for Republicans. Large numbers of voters have been turned off by the draconian restrictions proposed by legislatures in some conservative states and the Republican Party has backed away from proposals to legislate for restrictions at a federal level.[38] There are, it seems, for the moment, significant limits to the popular appetite for state interference in matters of personal morality.

That said, the fact remains that in many states severe restriction of a right that many women had regarded as a key milestone on their journey to equal status is now a reality. The wing of the conservative movement that was implacably opposed to abortion and which is as implacably opposed to gay rights is gaining in influence within the Republican Party. This movement's hostility to gay rights can draw further strength from the gay rights movement's old enemies such as the Christian Coalition, as well as newer cultural trends such as the growth of Andrew Tate-style homophobia.

The idea that opposition to gay rights will progressively fade away in the United States is unrealistic in the extreme. A Christian-inspired, post-liberal threat to gay rights is very much an American rather than a European trend. But what is not purely American is the reality that a sexual 'end of history' that permits gay rights advocates to relax and assume that their cause is destined to triumph in the long run is no more feasible in Europe than America. In some ways, the risk to gay rights in Europe may be even greater than in the United States.

4

The Illusion of the Universal Appeal of the Sexual Revolution

At first glance, the situation in Europe does appear to be much more promising than in the US. Conservative Christian political movements are largely absent from the European political scene. Certainly, as in the US, the populist right is growing. But the approach of populist parties to gay rights in Europe is more mixed. Some parties, like Fidesz, are hostile to gay rights (and even more so to LGBTQ+ rights). But others, such as the Partij voor de Vrijheid in the Netherlands, have cited defence of gay rights as part of the reasons people should favour their campaigns to limit immigration. Indeed, one of the co-leaders of one of the largest and most radical populist parties, Alternativ für Deutschland, is a lesbian. However, as in the US, a host of different factors are combining to make the future of gay rights in Europe at least as uncertain as it is in the US.

Once you set aside the notion that the advance of gay rights, like the advance other liberal causes, is historically inevitable, it becomes apparent that the situation in Europe is particularly difficult to predict with any certainty. Western Europe has, in the past half century, gone through three enormous changes, each of which, on its own, would have been sufficient to produce endless unanticipated consequences. After more than a millennium in which Christianity had overwhelming social and cultural influence, in recent decades levels of belief and practice suddenly collapsed. For centuries, most Europeans went about their day-to-day lives believing they were being observed and judged at all times by the Christian God. Most no longer do. That change alone is likely to have a huge number of consequences that we can't possibly predict.

To add further uncertainty, after centuries in which non-Christian religious communities were a very small minority, Western Europe has, since 1960, suddenly become much more religiously diverse. If these two huge changes weren't enough, you then have to add in the effect of the revolution in terms of gender, sexuality and child-bearing, where roles, institutions and norms that governed people's life course for centuries have suddenly been overturned. Any one of these changes would produce enormously uncertain and unpredictable effects. Taken together, it means that all of the chips have been thrown into the air and no one should feel that they can predict where they will land with any degree of certainty.[1]

Demographic changes are one source of uncertainty. Western Europe includes many of the countries that have gone furthest in terms of gay rights, such as France, the UK, the Netherlands, Sweden and Spain. These are all countries that have also had very significant migration from outside Europe in recent decades. Very large increases in ethnic and religious diversity cannot but bring about a very large amount of change. Everyone knows that people coming in from other cultures bring with them different languages, different ways of dressing and different cuisines. But truly accepting diversity goes beyond accepting that people eat different things or dress differently. It also involves accepting deeper differences: the reality that in some cultures, predominant beliefs about social and moral issues can differ from the beliefs that have come to predominate in Western Europe. Such differences are particularly likely to be significant when newcomers come from a different religious background from that of the native population.

Because, as the demographer David Coleman notes, demographic change in Europe is at a scale unprecedented in peacetime,[2] the changes it will bring are likely to be significant. Some of these will be positive and some will not (and what kinds of change you regard as positive may well depend on your political preferences). A very high proportion of immigration to Europe is from places where the predominant approach to homosexuality is strikingly conservative. This has to have some impact on societal attitudes. If, for some reason, a large number of people from Alabama moved to Luxembourg, that would most likely make Luxembourg a somewhat more conservative place. Similarly, given that, overall, levels of acceptance of homosexuality in Africa, the Asian sub-continent and the Middle East are much lower than in Europe,[3] the fact that large numbers of people from these areas are moving to Europe will have some impact on future attitudes to gay rights in European states.

Much of this is down to religiosity. A strong religious identity is one of the factors that is correlated with conservative attitudes to sexual morality.[4] Europe stands out in world terms as a particularly secular continent. Levels of atheism and agnosticism are high and, even among those who describe themselves as Christian, levels of practice and belief in core Christian teachings are low by world standards. Non-practising Christians in Europe have similar views to the religiously unaffiliated in terms of their support for same-sex marriage, abortion and the separation of religion and politics.[5] In contrast sub-Saharan Africa, the Asian sub-continent and the Middle East all have much higher rates of belief. Those beliefs are also more intensely held and practised, with a much higher percentage of people telling pollsters that religion is very important in their lives.[6]

These changes have scrambled the usual left–right divides. Sixty years ago, debates around the role of religion in society in most European countries were usually a contest between Christian influences on the one hand and anti-clerical or secular influences on the other. In this contest the left usually found itself on the side of the anti-clericals, while the right tended to be more sympathetic to the Christian side. Things are much more complicated these days. Migration has brought significant numbers of Hindus, Sikhs, Buddhists and Muslims to Europe, who have made their presence felt in discussions on the role of religion.

The mixing of issues of religion, migration and minority rights has unsettled previous approaches. The left, traditionally anti-clerical but pro-immigration, has struggled to come up with a united response to claims that restrictions on religious influence should be relaxed in order to accommodate the religiosity of some migrant-origin communities. The right, traditionally favourable to religion but more sceptical of migration, has been divided between those who welcome the challenge to secular predominance this religiosity involves and those who see the accommodation of minority identities as a threat to national identity.

Although the increase in religious diversity has encompassed a number of religions, by far the most significant change that has occurred has been the emergence of a significant Muslim population in Europe. Muslims easily outnumber other non-Christian religions in Europe. Muslims made up a majority of immigrants to Europe in the first half of the 2010s and over a third since then.[7] Western European countries, which sixty years ago had small numbers of Muslims, now have a significant and growing Muslim population.

Christian-majority countries such as Russia, Ukraine and the Democratic Republic of Congo, which produce large numbers of migrants to Europe, are also highly conservative in relation to homosexuality. But the fact that such migrants share the religion of the majority means that they marry into the majority population at higher rates. This undermines their ability to maintain distinctive beliefs into later generations. Although there is variation in intermarriage rates between European Muslims depending on their ethnic background and the country in which they live, overall, inter-marriage rates between European Muslims and those of other faiths are low.[8] The key factor determining openness to interfaith marriage is religiosity.[9] Levels of openness to the principle of interfaith marriage are quite high and rise in second and subsequent generations. But, as the sociologist Sarah Carol puts it, 'if we look at actual marriages, we observe the persistence of marriage patterns across generations, with the majority of marriages conducted within the family's own ethnic and religious group. Marriage decisions are related to parental preferences, family values and levels of religiosity.'[10]

In 2017 the non-partisan Pew Forum estimated that by 2050 in the countries surveyed (France, the UK, Germany, the Netherlands, Sweden and Belgium) if migration came to a halt, Muslims would make up between nine and thirteen per cent of the population, depending on the country. If migration continued at a high rate that range would be from fifteen to 31 per cent.[11] With the exception of the period of Covid lockdowns, rates of immigration in the period since 2017 have so far been very high. Islam is therefore, by some distance, Europe's largest minority religion and is Europe's fastest growing faith. European Muslims have low levels of intermarriage and see religion as more central to their identity than non-Muslims do. This means that in the near future, the attitude of Europe's Muslims towards sex and sexuality will inevitably be a significant and growing element of the overall European approach.

This is relevant to gay rights because sociological data show a very strong correlation between being Muslim and holding conservative views on sexual matters, particularly homosexuality.[12] As the political scientists Pippa Norris and Ralph Inglehart pithily put it, the 'true clash of civilizations' between Muslims and non-Muslims (at least in the West) relates to 'eros not demos', that is, to sexual freedom, not democracy. Their World Values Survey showed that approval of democratic values in Muslim societies at 87 per cent was actually one per cent higher than in Western societies. While the level of approval of gender equality was higher in the West (82%) there was still a robust 55 per cent approval in Muslim societies. On homosexuality, however, there was a chasm with only twelve per cent approval in Muslim societies (versus 53% in the West). This 41 per cent gap was much higher than for other issues of sexual and romantic freedom such as abortion (where the gap was 23%) and divorce (a 25% gap).[13]

While European Muslims are somewhat more liberal than those in Muslim-majority societies, they remain, overall, highly conservative in relation to homosexuality. In his moving book on his experiences of growing up as a Muslim of Pakistani origin in the UK, Sarfraz Manzoor identifies homosexuality as something that is particularly difficult for British Muslims to accept. He tries to be hopeful and cites his own journey towards fully embracing his gay brother-in-law and to feeling that 'gay rights are just a subset of human rights'. For Manzoor it seems 'bewildering and insane' that anyone would treat his brother-in-law differently 'simply because of who he chooses to love'. But he is too thoughtful and honest a writer to rely too heavily on this and other individual positive cases he cites. Given overall patterns, he accepts with sadness that this would be 'too neat and contrived'. His overall conclusion is much starker and worrying: 'the gap between mainstream British societal attitudes and mainstream British Muslim attitudes to homosexuality is dispiritingly wide and, frankly, I do not see many reasons to feel hopeful that it will be bridged anytime soon'.[14]

In relation to the UK, Manzoor's pessimism was backed by a 2016 poll that showed that 52 per cent of British Muslims thought that homosexuality should be illegal (a view held by only eleven per cent of the British public overall). Fewer than one in five (18%) thought it should be legal. Forty-seven per cent also told pollsters that it was unacceptable for a gay person to be a teacher (a view held by fourteen per cent of the wider population).[15] A 2009 Gallup poll also showed only a vanishingly small minority of Muslims in the UK agreed with the proposition that homosexuality is morally acceptable.[16]

The extent of these differences in relation to homosexuality varies from poll to poll and it is true that British Muslims are notably conservative compared to Muslims in other European countries. Despite the disdain most anglophone commentators show towards France's approach to religion and state, French Muslims are in fact much more liberal than their British counterparts on this issue, with 35 per cent of them agreeing that homosexuality is morally acceptable (German Muslims were in a middle position at nineteen per cent). But, even accounting for the fact that the particularly intense conservatism of the UK's Muslim population may have driven some of Sarfaz Manzoor's pessimism, the relatively liberal French Muslims were still strikingly more conservative than the rest of the population (the percentage of the non-Muslim French population saying that homosexuality was morally acceptable was fully 43% higher at 78%).

This cannot be dismissed as a passing phenomenon that will fade as migrants adjust to life in their new homes. Some polls have found that younger generations are no less conservative than their parents and may even be more so.[17] As the Shadi Hamid noted of surveys of attitudes among British Muslims:

> the 16-to-24 category consistently emerges as the most enamoured by strict interpretations of Islamic law. Apparently, youth and tolerant, liberal attitudes do not go hand-in-hand. The implication is that people who spent their formative years in Britain are more religiously conservative than their elders, despite being immersed in the British educational system rather than, say, Pakistani or Egyptian ones.

Similar patterns have been seen in France with younger generations being at least as devout and conservative as older generations, often more so.[18]

Wonderful people can hold conservative and illiberal views. I spent my childhood surrounded by good, kind, loving people like my grandparents, who were nevertheless not gay-friendly. We are all the product of our backgrounds to a great degree. I very much doubt that if I had been brought up in a different time or different place that I would have the same views I have today. But there is no avoiding the reality that migration from conservative and devout areas of the world is likely to have an impact on the future of gay rights in Europe.

Social conservatives are found among all religious groups in Europe, and among atheists and agnostics. It is uncomfortable to highlight one group, particularly because Muslims in Europe are generally, like most of us, just trying to live their lives and because they often do suffer from discrimination. But, as the largest and fastest growing religious minority, Islam is particularly important and, at a population level, Muslims stand out for their particularly conservative approach in relation to homosexuality. If, as Sarfraz Manzoor expects in relation to the UK, this remains the case across Europe and the continent's Muslims retain elements of the social conservatism that mark their ancestral homelands, then in the near future, the overall atmosphere in a number of countries is likely to be significantly less liberal in terms of sex and sexuality, in particular in relation to homosexuality.

Of course, the large-scale Muslim presence in most of Western Europe is still a recent phenomenon, so it is difficult to make confident predictions. Muslims are not a monolithic block and will come to different conclusions about the approach they and their faith ought to take to homosexuality. There are Muslim organizations such as the Los Angeles-based Muslims for Progressive Values who are pro-gay and may increase their influence in the future. Over time, there will be growing numbers of openly gay Muslims in Europe, which may affect attitudes. The presence of openly gay colleagues and neighbours may also act to change attitudes in ways that would not occur in ancestral homelands, where gays and lesbians will often have to keep a low profile.

I used not to be worried about this. After all, I was right when I wagered that my aunts and uncles would have significantly less conservative views on gay issues than my grandparents and that what I thought of as 'old-fashioned' conservative views on homosexuality would fade over generations. But the factors that drove that change may not apply to the same degree to many European Muslims. On average, religion is much more central to the identity of Muslims than non-Muslims in Europe.[19] Islamic communities in Europe retain strong institutional links to conservative movements in those ancestral homelands such as the Deobandi movement in South Asia or the Turkish state's Diyanet organization, which may limit the scope for European Islam to chart a significantly more liberal course.

Indicators from the US are more hopeful, though still have concerning elements. A 2017 poll by the Pew Forum found that 52 per cent of

American Muslims agreed that homosexuality should be accepted. Though this level is lower than that in the non-Muslim population, it had risen substantially from only 27 per cent in the previous poll.[20] The last few years have seen some more worrying signs. As an *LA Times* report noted, Muslim groups have taken a leading role in campaigns against gay-inclusive curriculums that include books portraying gay and lesbian families. This has also been the case in the UK in cities like Birmingham and in Belgium, where some schools were even set on fire or vandalized as part of a campaign against gay-inclusive sex education.[21]

In the state of Maryland, the Council on American–Islamic relations put out a call for rallies against a gay-inclusive curriculum. Zainab Chaudry, the Council's Director for the state of Maryland, argued that 'The school system believes it is being inclusive towards LGBTQ parents and students [...] But in doing that, it is not being inclusive toward another set of parents and students.' The *LA Times* noted that for Chaudry this was 'just the tip of a movement "growing among Muslims in many parts of America"'.[22]

In Hamtramck, America's first Muslim-majority town, once the city council had a Muslim majority it voted to remove all gay pride flags from municipal property. In the ensuing controversy many liberals who had supported campaigns against anti-Muslim discrimination denounced this act as a betrayal. The liberal American Muslim Shadi Hamid, on the other hand, criticized the Democratic Party for its failure to accept the social conservatism of American Muslims, arguing that this amounted to an illiberal failure to accept Muslims as they are and a refusal to respect cultural diversity, an argument that implies that he thinks the predominance of anti-gay views among American Muslims is unlikely to change anytime soon.[23]

Will the more optimistic message coming from the Pew poll in the US or the less optimistic scenario seen in surveys in Europe (and particularly in the UK) where the Muslim population is proportionately larger prove to be the indicator of the future? It is impossible to know. It is certain that some European Muslims will conclude that they are perfectly happy to support toleration of homosexuality and others will reach the opposite conclusion. It is always necessary to treat people as individuals and not to assume you know anyone's views simply from their religious identity.

I remember when I was nineteen and worked in a fast-food restaurant on the Champs Élysées, just down from a huge gay club called Queen. One evening I served a visibly gay man on his way to the club. As soon as he left, the (white) manager Paul said to me 'Tu l'as vu, ce type, en anglais on dit "poof" non?' ['Did you see that guy. In English you say "poof" no?']. I hadn't come out and didn't want to cause a scene but didn't want to go along with the homophobia, so I disingenuously replied 'Oh, ça se dit pas en anglais. C'est un peu péjoratif.' ['Oh, you don't say that in English, it is a bit pejorative.']. Paul exclaimed 'Péjoratif?! C'est pour ça que je l'ai dit!' ['Pejorative?! That's why I said it!']. It was Mo, the deputy manager, who grew up in Algeria and was married with children, who said quietly to my colleague 'Ronan a raison, il faut respecter les gens' ['Ronan is right, you should respect people'].

But differences at population level cannot be wished away. Some European Muslims will eat pork and others will hold to the traditional religious prohibition on doing so but at a population level, a society that goes from being five per cent Muslim in 2000 to thirty per cent Muslim in 2050 is likely to be a society that has, overall, a lower per capita pork consumption in 2050 than at the turn of the millennium. Similarly, the fact that individual Muslims will take different approaches to the question of homosexuality does not change the fact that there is a significant likelihood that the overall effect of a growing Muslim population will be to move society in a more conservative direction, particularly given that, as a group becomes a larger percentage of society, its ability to sustain distinctive norms and withstand assimilationist pressures will generally increase.

The pressure to adopt more liberal approaches to sexuality will also be diminishing as the broader society is likely to include rising numbers of post-liberal conservatives and those disillusioned with the sexual revolution (be they incels, conservative feminists or tradwives). High levels of migration will also mean that conservative Christians, Hindus, Sikhs will also be increasing in number. Indeed, it is notable how the issue of homosexuality has caused more conflict within the Anglican Communion than any other issue, with intractable divisions opening up between more liberal branches such as the US Episcopalian Church and the Church of England and branches in places like Nigeria, which are much more conservative. There will also likely be, it should be noted, beneficial elements to these changes: a society with a higher Muslim population will, for instance, probably have less alcoholism, stronger family bonds and less atomization.

There is already some evidence that these trends are already starting to shift attitudes to homosexuality. In the UK, a poll by the Theos thinktank showed that traditionally liberal London, the gay capital of the UK (and maybe even of Europe), but also a city whose high migrant-origin population means it has particularly large numbers of Muslims as well as above average numbers of conservative Christians, Hindus, Jews and Sikhs, was significantly more hostile to homosexuality than the rest of the country (29% of Londoners agreed that homosexuality was at least sometimes wrong compared to 23% of the rest of the country).[24]

In France, where a majority accepted homosexuality well before that was the case in the US and UK, a 2019 survey showed for the first time an increase in those saying that homosexuality was an illness or a perversion.[25] Social changes cannot be isolated from politics. In the long run, a more socially conservative electorate will produce more socially conservative politicians. After all, the reason that most politicians in Western Europe are in favour of gay rights now when a majority were opposed forty years ago is not because today's politicians are braver and more principled than their predecessors. It is because politicians follow the lead of the electorate. Indeed, in the 2024 general election in the UK, it was notable how some of the candidates of far-left parties, which drew a lot of support from Muslim voters due to foreign policy issues, were notably cooler on gay rights issues than they had been in the past and, in some cases, became actively hostile.[26]

Anyone who doubts that demographic change can change the political system need only look to Israel, where the arrival of large numbers of immigrants from the former Soviet Union and the high birth rate of religious conservatives have radically changed the nature of Israeli politics. Because both groups tend to have hard-line views on relations with the Palestinians, political positions that most Israelis considered extreme in the 1990s are now part of the political mainstream.

I realize that these are deeply uncomfortable points to make. In fact, if someone didn't feel uncomfortable about making them, it would make me wonder about their motives. I should also emphasize that I am not advocating for policy propositions here in response to the trends that I have discussed. Policies in relation to migration, religious freedom and discrimination have to take into account a range of humanitarian, economic, cultural and other factors beyond the issue of gay rights. My point is that the gay rights movement, used to operating in a steadily liberalizing atmosphere, needs to prepare itself to operate in a more conservative environment.

Before understandable discomfort with some of my points pushes you to dismiss these worries as prejudiced fearmongering, ask yourself how you can be confident that there is not something in them? Is it because you deny that, overall, newcomers to Europe tend on average to have more conservative views on homosexuality? Or is it because you don't deny that correlation but believe that a more socially conservative population will somehow not affect the political or social atmosphere? Maybe it is because you believe that history has a pre-determined direction and, even if there is such a correlation now, all faiths tend, over time, towards liberalism and separation of law and religion?

These are, I am afraid, comforting fantasies of inevitable liberal triumph whose main use is as an emotional crutch to avoid the messy reality that life is not neatly divided into privileged evil oppressors and saintly victims of oppression. The reality is that history does not have a predetermined direction and the world is not divided into emotionally satisfying categories. It would be very comfortable if all the opponents of gay rights were rich white businessmen with inherited wealth, spouting homophobic insults while they planned to keep workers, racial minorities and women down between puffs on their cigars. But life is not like that. Often different groups that have suffered discrimination have clashing interests and people who are discriminated against in one way can themselves discriminate in others.

Although praising diversity is part of the credo of many gay rights advocates, I am not sure they really value deep diversity in relation to attitudes to sex, sexuality and gender. Assuming that everyone will come to love sexual freedom involves a profoundly homogenizing world view that amounts to a rejection of diversity. Europe cannot expect to have a rapidly diversifying population and to expect to be able to neatly channel the resulting changes so that any social patterns that liberals like remain unaffected.

In a situation of rapid and profound change, it is impossible to be certain that the very particular trajectory followed by Christianity in most of the West, namely a story of rapid decline in levels of practice and belief and increasing embrace of secular politics and sexual liberalism, will inevitably be copied by other religious groups (including other forms of Christianity). In the past, scholars were certain that the decline of religious influence over society was an inevitable by-product of modernization. However, the emergence of rich and developed but still conservative and devout societies in the Gulf, the increase in the influence of political Islam in the 1980s and 1990s and the rise of Hindu nationalism in India all put paid to this notion.

Indeed, European Christianity looks like the exception not the rule. In places such as Africa, levels of belief, practice and sexual conservatism among Christians remain very high. Intellectual historians such as Mark Lilla and Charles Taylor have shown that the advance of ideas such as the separation of religion and politics was not inevitable: it was instead the product of the very specific mix of factors at work in European history, such as the destructive nature of the wars of religion of the sixteenth and seventeenth centuries, and features of Christian theology, such as Jesus' recognition of the separate nature of secular and religious authority (Jesus is famously said to have stated that his followers should render 'unto Caesar the things which are Caesar's, and unto God the things that are God's'). This recognition of separate spheres, Charlies Taylor argued, provided 'cracks in Christian theology' in which secularism grew 'like weeds'.[27] Indeed, even when secularism has been established in other areas of the world, it often takes a very different form. In India for example, the establishment of a secular state did not involve the removal of religious authority over areas such as marriage.

As Shadi Hamid has noted, Islam has its own very rich intellectual traditions that are different from those of Christianity.[28] In particular, mainstream Islamic theology does not have the same tradition of recognizing politics and religion as distinct arenas. Unlike Jesus, Mohammed was a political ruler as well as founder of the religion. While Christianity does have Canon Law that regulates internal religious matters, this is much less extensive in its scope than the Muslim tradition of Sharia. There is, as Hamid argues, little reason to assume that Christianity and Islam will end up adopting similar approaches to the relationship between law, politics and religion, unless one operates under the arrogant and colonialist assumption that the path followed by European Christianity is, for some reason, the universal path that all other religions will follow in due course.

European liberals and secularists alike have been guilty of arrogance and complacency in their assumption that their ways were inherently modern. When, in the post-war period, large-scale migration to Europe got underway from areas of the world that were notably devout and conservative, the arrogant colonialist assumption that the path followed by European Christianity was one that all faiths would eventually follow was strongly entrenched in Europe. Many assumed that the migrants would be temporary 'guest workers' who would return home. If they stayed, the assumption was that Europe's more secular and more liberal approach to gender and sexuality (even before the sexual revolution really got going) was a reflection of Europe's greater modernity and that migrants would be only too keen to embrace it. After all, at the time, sociologists had been certain for over a century that the decline of religious belief and practice were part and parcel of modernity.

But it turned out that Europe's particular ways were neither inherently more modern nor of universal appeal. Over time, indicators have accumulated that among some religious minorities along with some feminists and others, many remained unconvinced of the virtues of ever-wider sexual freedom. From the late 1980s to the mid 2000s a series of controversies, from disputes about the wearing of headscarves in French schools to the fatwa against Salman Rushdie and the murder of the staff of *Charlie Hebdo*, showed that a significant proportion of Muslim migrants and their descendants had not unequivocally embraced the secularized, post-Christian approach that predominated in most of Western Europe.

Olivier Roy, the French scholar of European Islam, highlighted why this caused significant unease. As he noted, no one was unduly concerned when a grandmother from the Rif Mountains wore a hijab after moving to live in France.[29] But many people were profoundly disturbed when her granddaughter, who had lived her whole life and been educated in France, did the same because this raised doubts in their mind about what was modern and to whom the future would belong. A symbol of a fading religious past seemed fine, a symbol of an increasingly religious future was frightening.

This trend has been reinforced by the collapse in fertility. Not only has the birth rate fallen precipitously across the West, it is secular social liberals (the core constituency of gay rights) who have the lowest birth rates of all. In the 1970s the anti-gay campaigner Anita Bryant was fond of saying 'Homosexuals can't reproduce so they must recruit.' This nasty vision of the predatory homosexual was untrue. Homosexuals may not be able to reproduce (at least through their sexual relationships) but they don't need to do so to create the next generation of gays and lesbians: homosexuality occurs spontaneously. But what Anita Bryant wrongly said of gays and lesbians is true of secular liberals. Liberals have a significantly lower fertility rate than conservatives and atheists and agnostics have the lowest fertility of any religious group.[30] Although there is some degree of convergence in birth rates between groups over time, with the fertility of religious groups remaining higher than average (and conservative religious groups higher still), the continued political predominance of secular liberals rests on their ability to continually win converts to their cause.

Secular Liberals Lose Confidence

Counterintuitively, it is the the attempts to reinforce the secular and liberal nature of the state that we have seen across Europe in recent years that best show the degree to which secular liberals are beginning to panic about their ability to keep winning these converts. The past two decades have seen a number of countries moving from arrogantly assuming that 'history' or 'modernity' would deliver the predominance of secular and liberal values (including gay rights) to starting to use the law to actively promote these values particularly among immigrants.

This attempt by a predominant but declining group to use the power of the state and the law to lock in its current dominance funnily enough calls to mind the failed 2004 attempt to insert a prohibition on same-sex marriage into the US Constitution. Anti-gay-marriage activists tried to enshrine bans in the hard-to-amend Constitution because they knew that the majority they then had would inevitably erode as older more conservative voters died off and pro-gay younger people reached the voting age.

Secular liberals in Western countries, particularly in Europe, are beginning to show the same paranoia of the declining hegemon. Between

2003 and 2007, thirteen EU member states made the granting of long-term residence to migrants subject to a compulsory integration test. Many of these tests promote knowledge of, or even make the grant of residency or citizenship contingent on being in agreement with secular and liberal principles. Tests in Germany, the Netherlands, France and the United Kingdom all highlight issues of religious freedom, equality of men and women and tolerance of homosexuality.

These worries have extended to the education system, where the schools have increasingly been placed under obligations to actively promote secular and liberal norms. In France, schools have historically been seen as having a role in promoting republican values of liberty, equality and fraternity. This was reinforced with the 2004 ban on ostentatious religious symbols, which has been justified by the political scientist Patrick Weil (who sat on the commission responsible for the recommendation to proceed with the law), on the basis of the need to disrupt the transmission of potentially oppressive identities to Muslim girls.[31]

In Denmark, even more radical measures have been taken. In areas that have high unemployment, high crime, low educational attainment and high numbers of migrants, children must attend publicly funded nurseries for twenty-five hours a week and must take classes in Danish values.[32] Even in the United Kingdom, which has long seen itself as more pragmatic and less ideological than France, things have been moving in a French direction. Following on the controversy in relation to what was being taught in some Muslim-majority schools in Birmingham, the government required all schools to teach what they called 'Fundamental British Values', which include democracy, individual liberty, tolerance of those of different beliefs and mutual respect.[33]

What these laws represent above all is a loss of confidence. It would never have occurred to secularists of the 1960s or 1970s to pass a law to encourage the secularization of migrants to Europe and their descendants. Like broader European society of the time, secularists in that era were full of post-colonial arrogance that presumed that because secularism had been achieved in Europe, it was the way of the future that 'less developed' societies would follow in due course. The same is true of liberalized norms on gender and sexuality. Until recently the 'end of history' view of sexual freedom was so predominant that no one thought it necessary to take steps to push migrants to adopt these values; everyone assumed, as I used to, that a society that tolerated sexual freedom and homosexuality was so obviously preferable that those exposed to such a society would abandon their support for more conservative and less liberal approaches.

But, as the writer Ivan Krastev has said, European liberals have been 'betrayed by their own excessive optimism'. As that optimism fades, they are becoming 'haunted by the spectre of things falling apart'.[34] There is certainly something that appears panicky about the flood of tests and programmes seeking to push secular and liberal values. And, if secular and liberal states are right to worry, then gays and lesbians are even more right to be concerned. After all, gay rights are the element of the sexual revolution that many people have found particularly difficult to embrace and the level of support for these rights in most of the countries that are the origin of the large majority of migrants to Europe is low.

Either way, it is also only fair to note that the sexual revolution which has swept through Western Europe since the 1960s has made it much more demanding for migrants to meet the demand that they sign up to the basic values of their new homes. A migrant from Algeria, Nigeria or Pakistan arriving at Paris or London in 1950 would have found things more relaxed than at home but encountered a familiar basic set up. Sex before marriage was taboo, homosexuality regarded with near universal disgust and both law and society promoted the subordination of wives to husbands.

In 2025, a migrant making the same journey will leave a still-conservative atmosphere and arrive in a place where not having sex until you are married is regarded as weird, where equality between spouses is the law and where homophobia not homosexuality is, at least for now, regarded as a (secular) sin. In relation to sex, a values gap has become a values chasm. We should recognize what a big ask this is. If I moved to Pakistan, I would find prevailing local attitudes to sex and sexuality a big challenge. I would also be very keen that any children I had would grow up with my attitudes on those questions rather than those that predominated in my new home. It is only understandable that many who come from Pakistan, or other conservative countries, to Europe feel the same. The demand that migrants accept the basic values of their new home is reasonable but we should recognize that it has become much more demanding than before and that it is Western societies that have moved the goalposts by including historically unprecedented sexual freedom and gender equality as part of society's basic values.

The Instrumentalization of Gay Rights

Gay rights have been one of the central features of the values tests imposed on immigrants. But I think gay people would be wrong to think this means that a commitment to gay rights has now become a deeply embedded principle that countries will stick by through thick and thin. The focus on gay rights in areas such as integration tests is often driven by concerns other than a genuine commitment to gay freedom.

Some of those who have highlighted opposition to gay rights as an issue in relation to migration are clearly motivated at least as much by anti-migrant sentiment as by attachment to gay rights. The Rassemblement National in France, for example, has historically been highly socially conservative but discovered an interest in the well-being of gays and lesbians when it found that gay rights were a useful means of highlighting differences between French Muslims and the rest of the population.

Tests that require migrants to indicate acceptance of homosexuality are, in important respects, not primarily about gay rights. Acceptance of gay rights is placed at the centre of integration tests because gay rights are a good litmus test of a wider willingness to compromise on one's religious identity and the cultural norms of an ancestral homeland. Questions about whether a migrant supports gay marriage in the twenty-first century can be seen as analogous to inquiries by the Spanish Inquisition back in the sixteenth century as to whether the *conversos* and *moriscos* (Jews and Muslims who were forcibly converted to Catholicism to avoid expulsion from Spain) were avoiding consuming pork. The Inquisition was driven not by a love of ham but from the knowledge that consuming pork was one of the things that those who had not sincerely abandoned their old faith would find most difficult to do. Similarly, given the recent and selective conversion to the gay rights cause of many of those keenest on demanding integration requirements, tests probing acceptance of gay rights should be seen as being at least partly driven by the awareness that acceptance of homosexuality is one of the features of Western societies that is most difficult for migrants from devout and conservative countries to accept.

Wider Doubts about the Sexual Revolution

Migration is unlikely to be the only source of a conservative turn in sexual matters. There are other indicators that ever-increasing sexual freedom is not of universal appeal. In his history of post-war Western Europe, Tony Judt sought to explain why, during the 1970s and 1980s, the baby-boom generation in the US and Europe turned against social democratic politics in favour of the tax-cutting ideology of Ronald Reagan and Margaret Thatcher. He noted that, before the welfare state was introduced, people's lives were regularly upended if they lost their job or fell sick. The welfare state had so successfully eliminated this pervasive, life-ruining uncertainty that those who had grown up knowing nothing but the security welfare systems provided took that security for granted. Without experience of uncertainty they could no longer imagine why it had been so necessary to establish a welfare state in the first place and resented the high taxes and regulatory burdens it imposed.[35]

Similarly, most of those born in the West after 1990 will have had little if any experience of what it was like to live in a sexually unfree society. They may well take this freedom for granted and will be less aware of the need to protect it. We are always more aware of what we don't have than what we have. Living in a sexually free society may heighten our awareness of its drawbacks, while blinding us to the disadvantages of less liberal approaches. Young straight people lost in a myriad of internet apps and hook-ups can, like trendy Manhattan Catholic converts, easily start to idealize the more structured world of the pre-sexual revolution era. The conservatism of young Muslims in Europe may simply mean that they are the pioneers of a wider trend in which the assumed link between youth and liberal approaches to sex and religion comes increasingly into question.

There should probably be more acknowledgement that, like all big change, the outcome of the sexual revolution will not have pleased everyone. Christopher Caldwell suggests that the alliance between feminism and increased sexual freedom was not a foregone conclusion, given that combatting men's sexual objectification of women was a key concern in the early years of the women's liberation movement. As he somewhat tartly notes, instead, as things panned out, the concerns and demands of the feminist movement such as 'the oppressiveness of marriage, […] availability of birth control, […] desirability of mixing the sexes' overlapped with the concerns of the average (male) reader of *Playboy* in the mid 1960s.[36]

Although Caldwell is right that feminist activism did, to a large degree, end up taking a supportive position towards the sexual revolution, this was not a unanimous position. In the early 1970s, a number of left-wing feminists were openly doubtful as to whether the sexual revolution would end up benefiting women. In the early 1970s Robin Morgan was already urging women to say 'Goodbye to Hip Culture and the so-called sexual revolution', arguing that it had 'functioned towards women's freedom as did the Reconstruction toward former slaves-reinstituted oppression by another name'.[37] Campaigns against pornography in the 1980s and 1990s led by figures such as Andrea Dworkin and Catherine MacKinnon were also in tension with the sex positivity of much of the sexual revolution.[38]

The 2010s saw a strengthening of theses currents within feminism. The success of the 'Me Too' movement fuelled the concern that the 'anything goes' atmosphere of the post sexual revolution era enabled a large degree of male sexual misbehaviour. Concerns about the impact of pornography on young men's attitudes to sex and to women also grew. This was followed by the emergence in the 2020s of a new strain of right-wing pro-marriage feminism seen in the writing of figures like Louise Perry and Mary Harrington who are motivated by worries that a culture of casual sex tends to serve the interests of men more than those of women.[39]

Although many left-wing feminists have disagreed with Perry's conservative solutions and criticize her for what they see as biological essentialism, there has been a lot of support for her diagnosis of the problem. Left-wing feminist Judith Green, for example, rejects what she terms Perry's 'dismal prescription' but praises Perry for having skewered 'the man-pleasing sexual culture championed and defended by liberal feminism and caddish male supremacism alike'.[40] Certainly, there remain plenty of sex positive feminists, but the alliance between feminism and advocates of sexual freedom would appear to be, at the very least, somewhat shakier than before.

There is also a wider sense of unease across the developed world that current arrangements are not proving conducive to the fulfilment of people's plans in terms of family and children. Across much of the West, women and men are telling pollsters that they are having significantly fewer children than they want to have, often because of an inability to find a suitable partner, something that would seem to indicate a failure of the post-sexual-revolution dating eco-system to provide people with the kind of relationships they want in the longer term (though a host of other factors no doubt also play a role). The proliferation of new terms such as 'breadcrumbing' (being strung along by a romantic partner who provides small indications of interest without ever engaging fully in a relationship), or 'ghosting' (terminating a romantic relationship by suddenly ignoring messages or unmatching on an app), shows that the internet is only making things worse.

As the conservative writer Ross Douthat put it: 'people reacted to the social revolutions of the 1960s first by marrying less and divorcing more and having fewer children, more of whom were born out of wedlock and then eventually by marrying much less, having many fewer children, and even – in trends from the last two decades – have less sex period'. This might be fine if not marrying and having few if any children represented what people wanted. But it is not. Most people still hope to marry and in the developed West people tell pollsters that they would like to have, on average, 2.5 children – much higher than the actual average (in 2022, 1.46 in the EU and 1.66 in the US, with both falling rapidly). Overall, there is what Ross Douthat calls a 'widening gap between what most people still say they want – relationships, marriage, children – and their growing inability to find those partners'.[41]

As John Burn-Murdoch of the *Financial Times* described in 2025, since the turn of the millennium the fall in birth rates is mainly driven by 'rising rates of singledom'. Birth rates among couples have barely dropped at all in the US. It is the rise in the number of people who are single that is causing the steep drop. While people may be happy single, Burn-Murdoch notes that 'wider data on loneliness and dating frustration suggest all is not well'. It should be noted that birth rates are also falling in some quite conservative societies too so something wider is going on, but at the very least we can say that maximizing choice has a mixed record of helping people achieve their longer-term goals.[42]

The changes of the past few decades also involve more abstract losses. We have endless books and films recounting how oppressive and restrictive many people found the conformist and conservative culture of the 1950s. But there must have been a large number of people (though probably not many gay people) who appreciated the sense of structure and order that such a society had. It must have given some people a sense of meaning and belonging to adhere to established gender roles and to feel that your marriage and reproduction fitted into a scheme that was shared by society as a whole. Taking part in long-established patterns and institutions, such as heterosexual marriage, also linked your life to the life that your parents and grandparents had lived in a way that must have been comforting, particularly when, as inevitably happens, one generation dies and another is born.

For those people, a world where gender roles, sexual partners and having children all become matters which are purely a matter of individual decision, where there are no expectations of what is the norm and in which a myriad of different kinds of family and relationships is the rule, may well have been a world that felt discombobulating, disconnected and less meaningful. There is no point in simply telling such people that they should love these changes. Like advocates of liberal progressivism more generally, partisans of gay rights should accept the reality that some people just prefer order and conformity to freedom and experimentation.

My hunch is that these feelings of loss are somewhat underreported because our accounts of those more conservative times come from the people who wrote books and made films. The people who tend to write books and make films are from the segment of society that tends to be less conformist, the very group most likely to have found the conservative set-up stifling and to have found their quality of life enhanced by its overthrow. I am one of the people for whom (like most gay people) the sexual revolution was a deliverance and a joy but that was not the case for everyone and, as memories of the reality of sexual oppression fade, nostalgia for the sense of meaning and order that the old order had may grow.

The gay writer and broadcaster Dan Savage and his husband ran a highly successful campaign in the 2010s called *It Gets Better* which sought to help young people who were being bullied for being gay. The message of this chapter is, I am afraid, something along the lines of 'It Might Well Get Worse'. Even beyond the anti-immigrant right, it is notable how shallow support for gay rights is and how quickly an attitude that gays and lesbians should shut up and be grateful for the tolerance bestowed upon them often surfaces. Claims that individuals should be exempt from anti-discrimination laws that protect gays and lesbians from being denied goods and services get much wider support than claims in relation to any other grounds. If this was part of a consistent libertarianism that would be one thing, but it almost never is.

This was brought home to me when I was providing advice to an NGO in relation to a case before the European Court of Human Rights. In this case, a Christian civil registrar in London was seeking to be exempted from having to register gay partnerships, provided that a colleague would step in and do it for her. It was really striking how both before the litigation and afterwards at academic conferences on the ruling in the case, no one would admit that they would support the right of a civil registrar to refuse to register inter-racial marriages on the same grounds. On the other hand, the claim that anti-gay discrimination should be accommodated received widespread support beyond socially conservative circles.[43]

If, like me, you value much of the legacy of the sexual revolution, you should at least consider the possibility that this legacy does not appeal to everyone and is not guaranteed to endure. There is no sexual 'end of history' and a few decades of freedom after centuries of oppression should not be regarded as the end of the story. The sexual revolution is neither of universal appeal nor of universal benefit. Whether you think greater sexual freedom and tolerance of homosexuality are good things depends on whether over all you place a higher value on things like choice, freedom and individualism than you do on things like order, conformity and continuity. As liberals are slowly and painfully discovering, their preferences for freedom, individualism and choice are not universal. As societies change and as people adapt their assessments of the relative merits of freedom and order, some societal swing in a conservative direction, at some stage, is likely. Given that gay rights are right at the edge of the territory conquered by the sexual revolution this could be a very serious development for gays and lesbians.

As in the United States, in Europe there is no one factor that on its own is likely to result in the roll back of gay rights. But there is a series of broader factors at work, all of which are diminishing the cultural pressures pushing European societies in a pro-gay direction. The gay rights revolution in the West was, for most of the last sixty years, driven by the energy of the gay rights movement in the US. In Europe, the message of that movement was amplified by American cultural prestige and close transatlantic political and cultural links. With the election of Donald Trump and the rise of post-liberalism that source of energy is gone. Indeed, it is possible that the US may begin to exert influence in the opposite direction. Trump has given explicit support to parties such as Vox in Spain that are explicitly anti-gay.[44] As foreign policy expert Gideon Rachman noted in the *Financial Times* in February 2025, the US now sees itself as more aligned with Putin's worldview, based on 'fighting for his country and for conservative values' than with European liberal democracies.[45] At the same time, demographic changes, cooling feminist attitudes to the sexual revolution and the rise of a socially conservative populist right in much of Europe all point to the likelihood that the gay rights movement is in an era when it will be facing headwinds rather than having the cultural wind at its back.

Those headwinds may already be making their presence felt. There are signs that those who have grown up knowing nothing but the post-sexual revolution settlement are becoming less supportive of some of its tenets. In the US, Gallup surveys since 2022 have shown declining levels of support for gay marriage and a fall in the numbers describing gay relationships as morally acceptable. The trend is small but comes off the back of steady rises for many years.[46] The flood of European countries adopting same-sex marriage we saw in the 2010s has ceased, with bans remaining in place in more than half of the continent's countries. Italy and Hungary have elected governments openly hostile to gay rights (and particularly to wider 'LGBT' rights). Right-wing parties in Poland, Italy and Spain have had significant success pushing a platform hostile to LGBT rights. In the US these issues are back centre stage having seemed to be a closed question just a few years ago with much of the right openly flirting with an authoritarian social conservatism which sees gay rights as a key target.

For the moment, the pro-gay elite consensus is still in control and most people are either supportive, not thinking about the issue, or are willing to keep most of their doubts to themselves. But the dynamics of preference falsification are such that it only takes a few examples of successfully bucking the consensus to unleash what Timur Kuran calls a 'preference cascade' in which people suddenly become willing to voice opinions they had been keeping to themselves. As Louise Perry notes 'things can change very quickly when people realize that there are others who secretly feel the same way as they do'.[47] This is a scenario that the gay rights movement seems singularly ill-equipped to manage.

5

Hubris: The Gay Movement Over-Reaches

In 2002, leaders in the democratic West may still have been shaken by the events of September 11th but they were supremely confident in the liberal democratic system. After all, democracy appeared not only to be the best system in moral terms. Over the previous couple of decades it had marched triumphantly through Central and Eastern Europe as well as most of Latin America, consigning communist and military dictatorships to the past.

Some Western leaders saw no reason why it should stop there. They thought that their task was not to hold on to the advances liberal democracy had made but to bring its blessings to every corner of the world. This meant that when the Bush administration was deciding how to react to 9/11, along with oil interests, fears (genuine or not) of weapons of mass destruction and a notably casual attitude to the infliction of the miseries of war on non-Westerners, they also believed that by invading Iraq they could help democracy take another step towards its destiny as the world's universal form of government.

Today's gay rights movement in Western countries finds itself in a similar position. Just as few people in 1985 foresaw the imminent collapse of communist dictatorships, the scale and speed of the gay rights victory is one that could not have been foreseen even by its most optimistic architects. This means that, in recent years, the gay rights movement has been facing its own version of the question that faced liberal democracies in the early 2000s: what to do in the aftermath of an unimaginable victory?

The invasion of a country, inflicting untold misery and causing thousands upon thousands of deaths is obviously a very different phenomenon from the waging of gay rights campaigns. But there are parallels in the underlying thought processes and assumptions of the relevant leaders. For the leaders of a number of key Western countries the triumph of liberal democracy in the 1990s did not produce a desire to luxuriate in their improbable victory or a focus on how best to ensure that new democracies remained democratic. Instead, certain that the triumph of democracy was inevitable in the long run, George W. Bush and others sought to push things further and launched a catastrophic invasion that ended up weakening support for the liberal democratic values they said they were championing.

Many gay rights organizations of the 2020s have fallen prey to similar hubris. As early as the 1990s, veteran gay-marriage campaigner Andrew Sullivan had been pondering what should happen if the main goals of the movement were achieved. Addressing leading American gay rights groups in the early 1990s Sullivan said: 'The goal of any civil rights movement should be to shut itself down one day. And, once we get marriage equality and military service, those of us in the gay rights movement should throw a party, end the movement, and get on with our lives.'[1]

I don't fully agree that once the main items on the gay rights had been achieved the movement should have shut down altogether. After all, there was still some important work to be done in terms of combatting residual discriminatory attitudes as well as work to help gay people in the very large part of the world in which the gay rights revolution had made little progress. But Sullivan was entirely right that victory should have brought about a change in approach.

The improbable, even miraculous, extent of the gay rights victory should have prompted a recognition that, viewed in the context of centuries and centuries of oppression, holding on to the newly achieved status quo of legal equality in the medium term would be a good result. But, just as a number of Western leaders thought that the triumph of democracy in Europe should be followed by an attempt to spread it in the Middle East, today's gay rights leaders, in a similarly hubristic fashion, see their role not as holding on to what we have gained but in seeking out new territories to conquer. They seem to have decided that past success shows further success is guaranteed and have expanded their demands, creating new enemies and making the continued thriving of gay freedom more generally increasingly dependent on the success of their new and increasingly ambitious campaigns.

The Demand for Active Validation

The expansion of the claims made in the name of the gay rights movement has happened in two main ways. One has been to ratchet up what states, organizations and individuals must do in order to be regarded as fulfilling their obligations to gay people. While the gay rights movement grew out of the classical liberal claim of a right to be left alone, there has been an increasing tendency to require active validation of homosexuality seen in demands that businesses or state bodies fly gay flags, make statements or take other actions to show that they support gay pride and same-sex marriage.

Gloria Gaynor's famous 1983 cover of the song *I Am What I Am* deservedly became a gay anthem with its defiant message that we have 'one life with no return and no deposit, one life so it is time to open up your closet'. But the approach that the song recommends when it says 'I am what I am. I don't want praise I don't want pity' is one that is rejected by many gay rights organizations today, who appear committed to demanding ever more extensive degrees of praise, pity and sundry other forms of active validation.

For example, the largest gay rights organization in the UK, Stonewall, developed an extremely elaborate 'Workplace Equality Index'. Its 2021 version had questions that ran to some 4,000 words. Under this scheme it was not sufficient for companies to avoid discriminating on grounds of sexual orientation. Instead, the development of a large suite of policies and taking of a range of active steps were required. Things such as allyship programmes, verifying that suppliers are 'committed to LGBT inclusion, community engagement work and ensuring that LGBTQ+ inclusion is embedded across every stage of an employee's journey through an organization' were necessary to do well on the submission.[2] In case anyone had doubts about the scope of this duty, Stonewall was clear that the duty to focus on an employee's specific needs as an LGBTQ+ person 'covers everything from recruitment and induction, to training and internal communications, all the way through to exit processes'.[3]

In the US, the Human Rights Campaign had a similar programme called the 'Corporate Equality Index'. Doing well on this index also required going way beyond avoiding discriminating against gay employees or even the formation of allyship groups and the like. It required 'at least five efforts of public commitment to the LGBTQ+ community'. This included the equivalent of a kind of gay tithe seen in the duty to provide 'philanthropic support via cash or in-kind donation to at least one LGBTQ+ specific organization'. In a slightly chilling echo of George W. Bush's 'you're either with us or against us' thinking from the era of the 'War on Terror', the Index also called for business to adopt guidelines that 'prohibit philanthropic support of non-religious organizations with an explicit policy of discrimination towards LGBTQ+ people'.[4]

The damaging message that setting out such an extensive set of demands sends is that accommodating gay people needs extensive work and reconsideration of all established arrangements. This is a message that comes dangerously close to validating the claim of the self-described homophobic writer John Derbyshire, who believed that mainstream organizations should not accept gay people because any organization that admits gay people on equal terms eventually loses its purpose and becomes an organization dedicated to promoting homosexuality.[5]

The extensive demands made by groups such as Stonewall and the Human Rights Campaign have the effect of rendering untrue the arguments that underpinned the successful campaigns of the late 1990s to mid 2010s, namely the moderate argument that all gay people wanted was for society to lay off discriminating against them and that doing so did not require fundamental changes nor the forcing of anyone to endorse beliefs they don't hold. Indeed, worryingly for a movement born in claims of individual freedom and the right of the individual to dissent from majority norms, there have been repeated instances where, in the name of protecting gay rights, attempts have even been made to remove individuals from courses of study or fire people from their jobs not because of at-work conduct, but because they have expressed disapproval of homosexuality on social media. The University of Sheffield, for example, removed a student from its Master's degree in Social Work for expressing the view on Facebook that homosexuality was sinful,[6] while a housing charity sought to demote an employee for saying that gay marriage was 'an equality too far' on the same site.[7]

This has, rightly, been controversial in that it appears to run counter to some of the liberal principles that gay rights advocates relied on to get their movement off the ground. Indeed, requiring active validation of gay identities is in tension with the central plank of modern liberal thinking. As the philosopher John Rawls famously argued, a liberal state should be neutral as to ideas of what constitutes a good life and should leave it up to individuals to decide these matters for themselves. For true liberals, the state has no more business saying 'gay is good' than 'gay is bad' and certainly has no business punishing people for expressing in their own time their view that homosexuality is not ideal.[8]

New Aims, New Enemies

The second way in which gay rights groups have expanded their claims has been by finding new categories of people whose demands can be analogized to and therefore included within those of the gay rights movement. The most high-profile change in this regard has been the embrace of the cause of trans rights as a central plank of what had previously been the gay rights movement. During the course of the 2010s and usually in the lull following the legalization of same-sex marriage, major gay rights organizations such as Stonewall in the UK and the Human Rights Campaign in the US dropped their previous policy of regarding gay and trans questions as separate and redirected a large proportion of their campaigning towards trans issues.

The change did not stop there. The movement advocating for lesbian, gay and bisexual people was gradually transformed by the addition of various other groups. The groups became so numerous that using full words became impractical and each group had to be given its own letter. The list of additional categories is not fixed but to the original LGB (lesbian, gay and bisexual) categories not only was a 'T' added to cover transgender rights; the list was further augmented by a 'Q' ('queer' rights), to which 'I' (the rights of intersex people) and 'A' (asexual people) are sometimes added. The rights of 'non-binary' people, that is those who do not fully identify with being either male or female, are often also included and a '+' sometimes appears at the end of the list of letters. This '+', according to the 'The Center', a community centre for what it calls the 'LGBTQ+ community' in New York City, 'is used to signify all of the gender identities and sexual orientations that letters and words cannot yet fully describe'.[9]

The expansion of the LGB rights movement into an LGBTQIA+ movement has created controversy and new enemies. One of the central demands made by LGBTQ+ organizations in the name of trans rights has been a right of access to single-sex spaces on the basis of self-identification for transwomen. This has caused heated clashes with feminists concerned that this right compromises the rights of women particularly in areas such as women's sports, single-sex prisons and shelters for survivors of sexual or domestic violence.

In a similar vein, a number of gays and lesbians and others have objected to the demand for a 'gender affirming' approach to children who identify as transgender. Their worry is that this approach brings the risk that young people who would otherwise develop into gay and lesbian adults with no lasting trans identity will be encouraged to transition to the opposite gender with all of the life-long medical complications that hormone treatment and genital surgery bring. In addition, some intersex people have questioned whether the issues they face due to having chromosomal medical conditions fit within a movement focused on sexuality and gender identity. Others have queried whether a movement whose founding aim was to prevent people from being punished or discriminated against because of who they had, or wanted to have, sex with is the right vehicle through which to represent the interests of asexuals.

Finally, some gay critics regard some of the categories such as 'queer' (defined by the Gay and Lesbian Alliance against Defamation as those 'whose sexual orientation is not exclusively heterosexual') as trivial and insulting. The gay writer James Kirchick worries that:

> Such an expansive definition, however, means that anyone – including heterosexuals – can now identify as queer. Not long ago a male journalist [Terrell Jermaine Starr] 'came out' as queer on Twitter while making sure to note that 'I'm attracted to a wide range of women, but not men at all.' [...] What regular gay people strived long and hard to transform into one identity attribute among many, to make as relevant to a person's character as their eye color or shoe size, queers seek to italicize and imbue with transgression. 'Queerness' is an attempt to revive homosexuality's lost radical splendor, which is the inevitable consequence of the attainment of rights and the spread of decency. [...] a heterosexual who 'comes out' as queer disrespects a long and harsh struggle and reeks of identity slumming, like the episode of *Seinfeld* in which Jerry's dentist converts to Judaism 'just for the jokes'.[10]

I can see his point. A white person who enjoys sitting on the seats at the back of the bus should hesitate before asserting that this means he has something in common with Rosa Parks and a straight person who feels like an outsider should hesitate before telling gay people that this means he is in some way in the same category as they are. It is tone deaf to the long history of involuntary exclusion of gay people to say something that amounts to 'I feel like a rebel and an outsider and therefore I associate myself with you' without pausing to consider whether the people you are associating yourself with actually want to be thought of as rebels or whether the status of outsider is one that has been painful for them.

The desire to include more people in your movement and to help them live the best lives they can could be, in principle, no bad thing but the transformation of the LGB movement into the LGBTQIA+ movement does raise some challenging issues. Some of the categories do seem to appear to be trivial (+), to be an awkward fit (I, A) or, as in the case of some of the claims made in the name of trans rights, to have some potential to clash with the interests of biological women or the interests of gays and lesbians. However, these concerns have been exhaustively aired elsewhere and are not the focus of this book. What is important for my purposes is to think about the assumptions underpinning this expansion in the goals and scope of the gay rights movement and the dangerous complacency they reveal.

Complacency and Hubris

What was it that drove key figures in the gay rights movement to change their minds and to include trans and other issues within the scope of their campaigns, even to the extent of insisting that there is 'no LGB without the T' that is, insisting that the fate of gay rights issues must be tied to the success of this wider agenda? A cynic would suggest that gay rights organizations, having built up large budgets and staff, needed new issues to justify their existence and avoid the dole queue. Of course, decisions of this nature that are multi-faceted and taken by large groups of people often have a number of motivations. Inevitably, some of these motivations will have been subconscious. Some people may have been unconsciously predisposed to being favourable towards arguments that suggested that the organization they worked for and their individual job were still important; as the novelist and social reformer Sinclair Upton famously said 'it is difficult to get a man to understand something when his salary depends on his not understanding it'.

It would certainly have been very psychologically difficult for organizations that had built up knowledge, expertise and status to decide to significantly curtail their activities or to call it a day. The fact that gay rights had advanced to the point where corporates were highly willing to come on board and were willing to donate significant sums to gay organizations would have made it even more difficult to walk away. But to suggest that the expansion in the gay rights agenda was consciously cynical goes too far. After all, there has always been *some* overlap between gay and trans issues. Both involved individuals with a deep-seated desire to behave in ways that deviate from the behaviour traditionally expected from those of their birth sex. Gay-rights activists and trans rights activists also share many of the same opponents.

That said, there are also differences. A 2025 Pew survey in the US showed that only 28 per cent of gays and lesbians said that they had a lot, or a fair amount, in common with transpeople (notably lower than the 51 per cent saying they had a lot or a fair amount in common with straight people). There is also a significant history of trans rights organizations existing separately from gay-rights organizations. The organization Press for Change was founded in the UK in 1992 to advocate specifically for trans rights. The Transgender Defense and Education Fund, National Center for Transgender Equality (NCTE) and Transgender Law Center (TLC) were all set up in the US in the early 2000s. It is important to note, however, that the leadership of gay rights groups in the 1990s and 2000s were not hostile to trans rights in principle even if they regarded them as distinct from the gay rights movement. Indeed, in the US, the National Gay and Lesbian Task Force and the National Center for Lesbian Rights provided financial and other assistance to the NCTE and TLC.[11]

Nevertheless, although arguments about potential clashes between some trans rights claims and both women's sex-based rights and the interests of young gays and lesbians were not a feature of debate at the time, there were occasions on which both LGB rights campaigners and trans rights campaigners explicitly distinguished their campaigns. For example, the right of a transwoman to marry a man was recognized by the European Court of Human Rights in the case of *Goodwin v. United Kingdom* back in 2002 at a time when only one country (the Netherlands) recognized same-sex marriages. Christine Goodwin's success before the Court relied on disassociating her claims from the claim that same-sex marriage ought to be legal.[12]

Gay-rights groups also had a significant sense that the two struggles were separate. Some of the reason for this was caution. There was a strong feeling that whatever view one took of the relationship between gay rights and trans rights, embracing the trans rights campaign as an integral part of the campaign for gay rights risked damaging the chances of success for the gay rights cause. In the US, there was a decades-long campaign, beginning in 1974, to get Congress to pass legislation prohibiting discrimination in employment on grounds of sexual orientation. Between 1994 and 2007 this legislation was proposed in every session of Congress but one.

The proposed legislation in the 1970s, 1990s and early 2000s had covered discrimination on grounds of sexual orientation only. The absence of focus on trans issues was not initially something that attracted widespread attention.[13] But, by the mid 2000s a campaign was underway to include discrimination on gender identity within the scope of the bill. The response of leading gay rights figures was to stress caution. The openly gay congressman Barney Frank and the Human Rights Campaign's political director Winnie Stachelberg both stressed that including transgender discrimination would reduce the chances of the bill passing.[14]

By 2007, things were changing and the proposal introduced in to the US Congress in April of that year included discrimination on grounds of gender identity. However, it became clear that a trans-inclusive bill could not attract majority support and a version focusing on sexual orientation alone was reintroduced. Even at this stage, with trans concerns taking up an increasing amount of attention, the Human Rights Campaign backed the trans-non-inclusive bill. No version of the legislation ever passed Congress, though its central aim was achieved when the US Supreme Court ruled in 2020 in the *Bostock* case that the Civil Rights Act of 1964 ought to be interpreted so as to cover both discrimination on grounds of sexual orientation and discrimination on grounds of gender identity.

By 2014, the attitude of the Human Rights Campaign had fundamentally changed. It adopted the campaign for trans rights as a central part of its mission. Its leader Chad Griffin delivered a formal apology to trans people saying: 'I am sorry for the times when we stood apart when we should have been standing together. Even more than that, I am sorry for the times you have been underrepresented or unrepresented by this organization. What happens to trans people is absolutely central to the LGBT struggle.'[15]

A similar story can be seen in relation to Stonewall in the UK. Until the mid 2010s Stonewall was clear that its focus was the struggle for gay rights and distanced itself from debates on trans questions. As a trans critic of Stonewall wrote in 2010 'Stonewall has the right of freedom of association, and it clearly does not wish to associate with us.'[16] By 2015, with same-sex marriage, employment non-discrimination and the repeal of the ban on gays and lesbians in the military all secured, there was a change of approach. In 2015 the organization apologized to trans people for the 'mistakes' and 'harm' in its previous approach and announced that it planned to campaign for trans equality.[17] In 2017 it produced a plan for trans equality and since then trans issues have been central to its work.[18]

So, in the space of a decade or so, the main gay rights organizations in the US and UK both switched from distancing themselves from trans issues to adopting them as central features of their work. These decisions are never about only one thing. Some of the reason gay rights groups expanded their remit to cover trans issues may have been based on conscious or, more likely, unconscious desires to keep LGB organizations relevant and well-funded in an era when most of the LGB battles had been won. The moral pressure placed by trans activists that drew on the overlaps between the gay rights and trans-rights causes also likely played some role.

But any moral reasons were equally present in the 1990s and 2000s when both organizations resolutely stuck to their decision to steer clear of these matters. An important part of what had changed, therefore, was the political calculus. Gay-rights organizations up to the 2010s were still operating in a difficult political atmosphere. A large proportion of the population still thought that homosexuality was morally wrong and majorities opposed same-sex marriage. In this atmosphere, gay rights organizations felt that they had to be cautious. A big part of their thinking was that, as Barney Frank and Winnie Stachelberg argued, gay campaigners could not afford to complicate their task of winning majority support for their gay rights work if they embraced trans rights.

Such a step would have alienated moderate straight support and gained the gay rights movement additional enemies who would be added to the still substantial ranks of gay rights opponents. In 2001 the Human Rights Campaign had actually agreed to add the phrase 'gender expression and identity' to its mission statement but was not active on trans issues, with a spokesperson for the organization Transgender Menace complaining in 2004 that 'for over a decade HRC has continued to view the transgendered as too costly for them to deal with'.[19] But by the late 2010s, with the tide running strongly in favour of gay rights, organizations like Stonewall and the Human Rights Campaign suddenly lost their fear of swelling the now depleted ranks of their enemies and enthusiastically embraced the trans rights cause.

It is here that we can see the parallel to those who reacted to the spread of liberal democracy in the 1990s by convincing themselves that they could spread democracy throughout the Middle East. Like some leaders of liberal democracies in the early 2000s, gay rights organizations of the late 2010s and early 2020s allowed a run of successes to cause them to lose their fear and to embrace hubris. They did not focus on the protection of the miraculous gains of their improbable victories but increasingly saw their task as being to push the gay rights revolution further to cover new categories and more ambitious goals. The transformation of the LGB movement to the LGBTQ+ movement has become Operation Iraqi Freedom of the gay rights struggle – a hubristic project driven by illusions of invincibility that threatens to fuel a backlash against the very freedom it aimed to promote.

The repression of homosexuality lasted for centuries and is still the rule in vast areas of the world. Active criminalization in most of the West stopped only in the post-war period, societal discrimination was rife and almost unchallenged until three or four decades ago. Same-sex marriage was not legal in a single country at the turn of the millennium and is now permitted in a small minority of countries worldwide. Looking at this situation with any kind of longer-term perspective it should be clear that the current approach to homosexuality in most of the liberal West is historically vanishingly rare, extremely recent and not guaranteed to last. We cannot know if ten or twenty years of toleration after a millennium of oppression represent the end of the story. A gay rights movement with any sense of historical perspective would realize that just holding on to the unprecedented degree of freedom we currently have would actually be a very good medium-term outcome.

Yet gay rights organizations seem confident that what has been recently won is so secure that their focus ought to be to push things further rather than to hold on to what they have. Such confidence is only possible for those who subscribe to the motto Barack Obama had sown into the carpet in the Oval Office: 'The arc of the moral universe history is long but it bends towards justice.' The sad reality is that history does not have an arc, a side or an end. It is the height of arrogance to assume that the ways of doing things that we have developed over a few decades represent an end point.

With each expansion in the movement's agenda, new enemies are made. This has included many feminists, traditionally staunch advocates of gay rights, who have been alienated by the embrace of self-ID. By falling prey to the fantasy that the triumph of their cause is historically inevitable, gay rights organizations are risking making the task of holding on to what gay people have achieved much harder. They are also making it much more difficult for gay rights campaigns in areas of the world where homophobic laws and norms still predominate to get off the ground. It is hard for African gay rights activists to argue that they just want decriminalization of same-sex activity and to be left alone when Western gay rights organizations are insisting that fundamental changes to the idea of what is a man and woman are an intrinsic element of the gay rights agenda (now shackled to an ever-lengthening list of other causes in the LGBTQIA+ acronym) and that businesses have the duty to take a dizzying range of active steps to celebrate their gay employees.

Alienating Identities

The gay rights movement's ever-lengthening list of letters and symbols is an example of the broader trap identified by the intellectual historian Mark Lilla. He was appalled by the election of Donald Trump in 2016 and sought to explain why it was that liberal America had managed to find itself losing a presidential election to such a manifestly flawed character. Lilla placed much of the blame on the degree to which liberals became enthralled with identity politics and what he identified as its 'resentful, disuniting rhetoric of difference'.[20]

An overwhelming focus on your own identity can cause you to lose connection with the wider community and can undermine your capacity to reach out to others and make common cause with them. As Lilla puts it 'every catechism tends over time to become rigid and formulaic, until it eventually becomes detached from social reality'.[21] The gay movement has been particularly susceptible to this tendency. Being able to chart your own course and to create a life you can live with honesty and integrity is important, but an excessive focus on yourself and your own identity is neither psychologically healthy nor conducive to winning over or cooperating with others.

The continual addition of extra letters to the LGB acronym in order to try to capture ever finer nuances of identity speaks eloquently to this tendency. As the political scientist Yascha Mounk, who shares many of Lilla's concerns, has pointed out, there is no combination of external labels that will ever amount to 'a satisfactory depiction of [our] innermost selves'.[22] After all, linguistic categories are approximate. I am Irish but have lived almost half my life outside Ireland. This does mean that my Irishness is different from those who have lived their whole life there but to object if someone refers to me as 'Irish' because that term does not precisely follow the contours of my personal experience, and require a new term to be invented, would be to fall into what Freud called the narcissism of small differences.

What is more, think what the likely impact would be of me asking someone I was speaking with to correct their description of my nationality and to say 'Irish/International' or 'Irish+'. All that would do would be to lessen the bond I shared with any Irish person listening as well as alienating the person who was probably only trying to make conversation when they referred to me as plain old 'Irish'. The same is true when what used to be gay rights organizations insist on the use of an ever-lengthening list of letters and symbols that, as the lesbian writer Julie Bindel put it, increasingly looks like an unbreakable wifi code.[23] All this does is to divide people from each other and demonstrate an unappealing narcissism that alienates the wider public on whose continued support maintaining the gains of the gay rights revolution depends.

I am happy to concede the theoretical case for why a very particular identity sub-group should get recognition in terms of its own letter in whatever acronym now stands in for what was the gay movement. You can also make a further theoretical argument about how individuals' right to self-define should be unlimited and why such struggles should be seen as part of gay rights campaigns. But the point comes when we see that, as Mark Lilla said (albeit in in a different context) 'the contradiction between the dogmas and social reality is becoming all too apparent'.[24]

With 55 per cent of American respondents telling pollsters that they are 'confused by all of the different letters and terms to describe the individuals who comprise the LGBTQ community',[25] gay rights organizations should bear in mind the warning of the French philosopher Raymond Aron.[26] He warned that it was important to think politically rather than ideologically. Within the confines of queer theory, one may be able to make a case that 'gender identities and sexual orientations that letters and words cannot yet fully describe' ought to be recognized with their own symbol ('+'). To insist that gay rights organizations make this part of their portrayal of their case to the wider world is disastrous.

Leveraging the Success of Gay Rights

Counterintuitively, the damaging complacency of LGBTQIA+ groups is seen most clearly in their apocalyptic rhetoric, which insists that any resistance to the expanded agenda of the gay rights movement constitutes an attack on everything that movement has achieved. In 2023 the Human Rights Campaign went so far as to officially declare a 'state of emergency for LGBTQ+ people' for the first time in its history. Its justification for doing so focused almost exclusively on pushback on access to women's sports and women's bathrooms for transwomen and restrictions on 'gender affirming care for minors'.[27] Gay-marriage pioneer Andrew Sullivan notes how this portrayal of resistance to the wider issues recently embraced by gay rights campaigners as attacks on all of the achievements of the movement to date lacks credibility:

> I get fundraising emails all the time reminding me how we live in a uniquely perilous moment for LGBTQ Americans and that this era, in the words of Human Rights Campaign [...], is one 'that has seen unprecedented attacks on LGBTQ people'. Unprecedented? Might I suggest some actual precedents:

when all gay sex was criminal, when many were left by their government to die of AIDS, when no gay relationships were recognized in the law, when gay service members were hounded out of their mission, when the federal government pursued a purge of anyone suspected of being gay. All but the last one occurred in my adult lifetime. But today we're under 'unprecedented' assault?[28]

The message behind this apocalyptic rhetoric is the same as the message that appeared on a poster in my local corner shop in London 'No Pride without Trans Pride'. The intention underpinning this slogan is two-fold. First it presents the newly embraced trans issues as equally pressing and central to the gay rights movement as the old ones of criminalization, discrimination in employment and marriage. Second, by doing this, it aims to leverage the success of the old gay rights issues to help to advance the movement's newly expanded LGBTQ+ goals. By suggesting that, for example, support for self-ID for trans people is part of an all or nothing package that includes support for other more popular issues such as gay marriage, the hope is that the majority who are favourable to gay marriage will be encouraged to set aside any doubts about self-ID. However, this is a highly risky approach.

LGBTQ+ activists may insist that their current opponents are simply the same crowd who fought decriminalization and gay marriage and that conflict on trans issues is simply a re-run of the old gay rights disputes. There is, to be sure, overlap between gay-marriage and trans-rights opponents, but there are also important differences. The tendency to see past conflicts as simply earlier versions of current conflicts and current conflicts as re-runs of previous clashes is very strong in contemporary culture but often misleads. It can be seen in the attribution of views to historical figures who, to say the least, are highly unlikely to have thought in such a twenty-first century way. The 2018 film *Mary Queen of Scots*, which portrayed the sixteenth-century Scottish Queen in a highly favourable light, had a scene in which Mary expresses highly supportive sentiments about the homosexuality of David Rizzio, one of her courtiers. Forget that Mary was a devout sixteenth-century Catholic who saw her execution as a martyrdom for her faith; as a goodie in a twenty-first-century film she had to have the right views for the twenty-first century so that the audience could know for whom to cheer. I was only surprised that when they showed her writing letters to Queen Elizabeth I, they didn't have her include an announcement of her 'she/her' pronouns with her signature.

Regarding current clashes as re-runs of past ones is very pleasing for activists. You might have missed out on the campaigns for civil rights for African Americans in the 1960s or the gay-marriage fights of the 1990s and 2000s, but you can feel like the heroes of those campaigns if you regard your current campaigns as 'our gay marriage' or your goal as 'our Civil Rights Act'. This also allows you to have the comforting implicit assurance that if you had been there in the 1960s or the 1990s, you would have been on the side of the good guys. But the reality is that, as Mark Lilla notes, 'there is no again' in politics. Times change, the issues change and the balance between pros and cons does not remain constant, either over time or between different issues.

LGBTQ+ organizations should not think that they can act as though their current campaigns amount to a 2020s re-run of the LGB campaigns of the 1990s and 2000s, when the surrounding society and, indeed, the issues, are different. Not only will they lose credibility with the public when (in the case of the debate on self-ID) the public notice that it is not just Christian conservatives but also feminists, lesbians and gays who are on the opposing side. You also risk provoking a wider backlash. If you insist that only a homophobe and social conservative would resist the presence of biological males in women's sport, then you risk a significant section of the public backtracking on their acceptance of gay rights more generally and responding 'ok fine, I am a homophobe'.

The gay rights movement has always needed straight support and needed to ride the coat-tails of the changes in straight sexual mores to succeed. Reassuring the straight majority that liberation and inclusion of gay people did not require massive adaptations to existing ways of doing things has been crucial to the political advance of the gay rights movement. The insistence that gay rights are inseparable from a much wider set of demands, including fundamental changes to categories as basic as male and female, comes dangerously close to withdrawing that reassurance and asserting that accommodating gay people necessarily involves radical change to basic social structures. This is an approach that is as likely to undermine support for the old more limited gay rights agenda as it is to increase support for the new one.

There is already some evidence that the new much wider approach is having a detrimental impact on support for gay rights measures that previously had seen steadily increasing support. A series of polls was carried out in the US in 2016 and 2019 on behalf of the Gay and Lesbian Alliance Against Defamation (GLAAD). Although the organization's own name would indicate that trans issues were not seen as part of its remit when it was founded back in 1985, GLAAD has fully signed up to the expansion in the scope of what had been the gay rights campaign. GLAAD's poll asked respondents whether they would be comfortable in certain scenarios with what the question termed 'LGBTQ' people. This terminology itself is quite divorced from real life. After all, if someone told you that they are 'LGBTQ', you wouldn't even know to whom they are attracted or what their gender identity is without asking follow up questions. In any event, the situations covered by the poll included 'learning a family member is LGBTQ', having an 'LGBTQ doctor' and 'learning my child has had an LGBTQ history lesson at school'. The poll then tabulated the proportion of people who could be considered as 'allies' of the 'LGBTQ community' (allies being those who reported being 'very' or 'somewhat' comfortable in all situations).

Overall, the results showed either a plateauing or slight decrease in comfort in most situations. Given the rapid advance in attitudes towards homosexuality and gay marriage in the US over the past few decades, this plateauing would be concerning enough. But what was even more worrying was the slump in support among 18-to-34-year-olds. This is the group most likely to have been at school or university in recent years and who, given the prominence of these issues and increased proportion of young people claiming LGBTQ+ identities, were most intensively exposed to the full expansion of the gay rights movement into the LGBTQ+ movement. The percentage of 18-to-34-year-olds who were found to be 'allies of the LGBTQ community' dropped from 63 per cent in 2016 to 45 per cent in 2018. The percentage of males aged 18 to 34 who were considered allies collapsed from 62 to 35 per cent.[29]

In France the four-decade-long steep decline in the number of people saying that homosexuality was either a sickness or perversion has now gone into reverse, rising from 13 to 15 per cent between 2012 and 2019. The number of people saying homosexuality was 'a way like any other to live your sexuality' has also ended its steady rise and has fallen from

87 to 85 per cent.[30] In America, a series of Gallup polls paint a similar picture. While support for same-sex marriage in the US grew rapidly from 37 per cent in 2005 to 71 per cent in 2023, its rise slowed notably since 2020 and in 2024 declined to 69 per cent, with support from Republicans dropping by seven to below fifty per cent.[31] This followed on the heels of the 2023 Gallup survey, which showed a steep drop in the percentage of people agreeing that 'gay and lesbian relations' were morally acceptable – with only 64 per cent agreeing compared to 71 per cent the previous year. The proportion stating that such relations were not morally acceptable rose from 25 to 33 per cent in the same period.[32]

Interestingly, in relation to trans issues, the rise in activism on the part of what had been gay rights organizations appears not to be having the desired effect. In relation to traditional gay rights issues the percentage of people agreeing with the political claims of the gay movement increased in lockstep with the rise in the proportion of people reporting that they knew someone who was gay or lesbian. This does not appear to be occurring in relation to the claims of the trans-rights movements. For example, in 2021, 31 per cent of Americans reported that they knew someone who was transgender and 34 per cent supported the right of transwomen to compete in women's sports. Two years later, the number of people reporting they knew a transperson was up to 39 per cent but the level of support for including transwomen in women's sports was down to 26 per cent.[33]

Polls in the UK tell a similar tale of the counterproductive impact of the kind of campaigning carried out by organizations committed to the 'LGBTQIA+' approach. A series of polls by YouGov showed support for the assertion that 'transwomen are women' dropping from 43 per cent agreement in 2018 to 38 per cent in 2022, with those opposed rising from 32 to forty per cent. Support for existing legal rights has been dropping rapidly. By 2024, support for the right to change legal gender (34%) had fallen well below opposition to that right (48%). Support for transwomen participating in women's sports was never that high (27% in favour, 48% against in 2018) but had fallen to very low levels by 2024 (12% in favour, 74% against in 2024). Opposition to making it easier to change gender legally had also become overwhelming (19% in favour, 63% against).[34] This confirmed the picture painted in the British Social Attitudes survey of 2023, which showed the percentage of respondents supporting the right of a trans person to change the sex marked on their birth certificate slumping from 53 per cent in 2019 to thirty per cent in 2023. The percentage who said they were 'not at all prejudiced' against transgender people also took a dive in the same period, falling from 82 to 64 per cent.[35]

It should be noted that the expansion of the gay rights agenda to cover LGBTQ+ issues is a recent phenomenon, dating from the mid 2010s, so long-term trends are not yet clear. In addition, the world has been roiled by so many dramatic events in the past ten years that one cannot be certain as to what has caused any of the changes in relation to public opinion that we are starting to observe. That said, what is undeniable is that in some of the countries in which it had its greatest success, the gay rights movement has changed over the past decade. A demand for legal equality and social acceptance for gays and lesbians has been expanded so as to cover a range of new groups (queer, asexual, '+'), and a range of new demands (more active validation of gay identities, greater restriction of anti-gay speech and prioritization of gender identity over biological sex). Some of the expanded categories such as 'queer' and '+' are sometimes trivial and risk undermining both the seriousness of the oppression previously suffered by gays and lesbians in the West (which they still suffer in many other places), as well as the credibility of gay campaigning. Others are highly controversial and have won the LGBTQIA+ movement new enemies that the old gay rights movement did not have.

Perhaps this was inevitable. The gay rights movement was always an uneasy mix of reformists focused on issues like gay marriage and radicals who, in the words of Andrew Sullivan, 'itched to transform society far more comprehensively'.[36] In recent years, with the most pressing issues for most gays and lesbians a done deal, those of a less radical bent were likely to disengage to some degree from gay rights movements, leaving us in a situation where, as Sullivan puts it, 'radicals now control everything in the hollowed-out gay rights apparatus'.[37] This control now extends to Stonewall and the Human Rights Campaign, two organizations founded to give a moderate face to the gay rights movement.

The current orthodoxy among gay rights groups in the West (now rebranded as LGBTQIA+ groups) shows little awareness of just what a miracle the liberation of gay people has been and how lucky we would be, when you take a longer historical view, to hold on to our improbable recent gains. It is unhealthy to have no doubt about whether you will fail or whether you will succeed. Feeling that defeat is certain causes hopelessness and will make it hard for your campaign to avoid lethargy. But being certain that you will win (that you are 'on the right side of history') brings hubris and complacency and makes it hard to avoid overplaying your hand or taking too many risks.

There are many causes that, like trans rights, overlap with at least some of the concerns of the gay rights movement. Campaigns like that to separate church and state or in favour of abortion rights or free-speech rights all draw on some of the same principles that animated the gay rights struggle. But overlap does not mean that these causes are one and the same and that there should be 'no gay rights without abortion rights' or 'no gay rights without separation of religion and state'.

I would hope that almost all gay people support the vast majority of the claims made in the name of trans rights, such as the right to live your life with dignity and not to be discriminated against at work (though there is probably greater disagreement in relation to self-ID, women-only spaces and treatment of children with gender dysphoria). One movement can wish other movements well and be largely supportive of most of their goals. But a prudent movement will not think that that supportive attitude means that it must also stake its future on the success of those other causes.

After all, the causes of feminism and gay rights overlap to a great degree and often share enemies but would it be a good idea for Afghan feminists or Russian feminists to adopt the slogan 'no women's rights without gay rights'? Indeed, in Iran, some limited trans-rights are recognized by the state but homosexuality is subject to the death penalty. Would portraying the two causes as inseparable be a wise path for Iranian trans activists to take? If they insisted that there can be 'no trans rights without gay rights' would it be more likely that the Ayatollahs will start conducting gay weddings or that the Islamic Republic will start to question its commitment to trans rights?

6

The King Is Dead! Now What? Radical and Moderate Versions of Gay Freedom

The distorting influence of the idea that we are on the right side of history goes beyond its role in the failure of the gay rights movement to correctly perceive the external threats that it now faces. Seeing the emergence of gay freedom as a form of inevitable modernization rather than a contingent event can fuel a tendency to see the wider sexual revolution as an unvarnished positive that should always be pushed further and further. This not only potentially alienates moderates and encourages conservatives to see opposing gay rights as a top priority. It also allows gay people to avoid recognizing how elements of the revolution may not even be in our own interests.

Looking at the downsides of your victory is no fun. I am slightly jealous of the pioneers of the sexual revolution. It is not that they had an easy time of it: quite the opposite. What they did have was clarity of purpose. The old system was rotten and the need to get rid of it made their task clear. The idea was that if society could just lay off the cruelty and prejudice that blighted the lives of single mothers, gays and lesbians, and others who fell outside restrictive sexual norms, those people would be fine. The absence of oppression would make a good life. It certainly made a better life. The lot of single mothers and of gays and lesbians in most of the West is immeasurably better than in the 1950s.

But, once the palace has been stormed and the king has been decapitated, opposition to the monarchy is no longer a sufficient agenda. The much more complicated task of designing rules for post-revolutionary life has to begin. The dissidents behind the Iron Curtain had a much clearer and more emotionally satisfying job than those who had to carry out the complex work of dismantling communist economies and managing the transition to a market economy once the Wall had fallen. Similarly, while fighting to overturn the oppressively anti-gay norms of the pre-sexual-revolution order was a clear and emotionally satisfying task, administering the post-revolutionary regime was always going to be a muddier affair which would inevitably involve difficult compromises and the recognition that all choices involve some degree of trade-off between competing goods.

The Inevitability of Unanticipated Consequences

Making a revolution sustainable often involves acknowledging that some revolutionary propositions made sense in theory but have turned out to cause unexpected problems in practice. In the early days of the USSR, the communist authorities were initially committed to abolishing private property but found in 1921 that they had to bring back limited forms of private property to stabilize the situation and stop the revolution from being overwhelmed. This was emotionally difficult and controversial but it turned out that sticking to the revolutionary principles that had made perfect sense in theory would have sunk the revolution in practice.

The Soviet experience would not have surprised Edmund Burke, who was profoundly influenced by the attempt in revolutionary France to wipe away almost every aspect of pre-revolutionary society and to start again at 'year zero'. For Burke, when you are dealing with longstanding rules or institutions, the fact that you have never known a world without them can blind you to the functions that they perform. This means that unanticipated consequences are inevitable and it is only when revolutionary change has occurred that you realize that a few of the old rules and institutions you hated had actually been doing some valuable work that you hadn't noticed till they were gone. Sustainable revolutions need to be flexible enough to make use of the positive elements of the regime they replaced.

This tendency to be blind to the work that established rules and institutions are doing for us is the inspiration for G.K. Chesterton's famous metaphor of the gate across a road. Chesterton wrote that if someone says that the gate appears to be useless and should be removed the appropriate answer should be 'If you don't see the use of it, I certainly won't let you clear it away. Go away and think. Then, when you can come back and tell me that you do see the use of it, I may allow you to destroy it.'[1] These insights are also applicable to the sexual revolution. Sexual mores in the West have been changed utterly and bear no resemblance to those that predominated sixty years ago. But, although there is currently little demand to restore the sexual *ancien régime*, there is evidence that the success of the revolution in overturning oppressive laws and norms is producing effects that were not fully anticipated and which are raising qualms, even among those, such as women and gay people, who are seen as being the revolution's greatest beneficiaries.

Recognizing that there have been some downsides to the sexual revolution is a hard message to accept when half the world is still fully committed to the kind of persecution of gay people that characterized the pre-sexual revolution era in the West. It is also an emotionally difficult exercise for those who carried out the struggle against the oppressive regime, as it involves swapping the moral clarity that arises out of that kind of campaign for the reality of grey areas, trade-offs and compromises.

For some people, it will always prove easier to postpone or avoid the emotional costs that such an exercise involves. This group seeks to keep the revolutionary struggle and its thrilling emotional clarity going by hunting for evidence of the persistence of the power of the old regime and finding new fronts on which to wage the old campaigns. By doing this they can avoid the troubling reality that the success of the revolution will rarely have brought about utopia and that their opponents' arguments, though wrong in the round, might have had some kernels of wisdom in them.

Ross Douthat identifies something of this phenomenon in the behaviour of the baby-boom generation. He suggests that their youthful rebellion in the 1960s provoked an outburst of creativity because it was attacking a conservative order that 'still felt confident, rooted, possibly enduring'.[2] But the boomer generation struggled to accept their victory. By the 2010s, the 1960s rebels and their ideology had become dominant but nevertheless we found ourselves in what Douthat called an era where 'everyone fancies himself a rebel and corporate titans posture as counter-cultural revolutionaries'. For him, this produces a strange scenario where 'traditional forms and structures that once gave rebellion purpose and clarity persist only as inertial holdovers that no one publicly defends – or else as shadows of themselves in the unfashionable hinterland, their remaining strength a purely negative force that exists mostly to persuade the cultural elite that they haven't won yet; that they're still the same rebels they were in 1968'. What this leads to is a form of stagnation whereby, lacking a strong enemy, the original critique of the now vanquished order is simply repeated 'just more loudly or crudely or tediously'.[3]

Douthat was writing about Western culture more generally, but much of what he writes of the dilemma of the victorious rebel applies to the modern gay rights movement. That movement faced powerful opponents right up to the mid 2000s at which point the forces in its favour reached a tipping point. A political, corporate and institutional stampede to the pro-gay side ensued. This left the former rebels in the awkward position of having come to represent the dominant ideology. Certainly, long-term vulnerabilities remained, but with the edifice of sexual traditionalism and socially and legally validated homophobia having crumbled, the gay rights movement should logically have become a movement of insiders using their institutional power to defend their gains. And this is, in fact, what has largely happened. The gay rights agenda can now be, and often is, defended not by the tools of the outsider and the rebel but by corporate HR departments or successful invocation of pro-gay laws against those who would discriminate on grounds of sexual orientation.

But what didn't change was the self-perception of many gay rights organizations and activists who still saw themselves as plucky outsiders, even when they had the backing of everyone from Goldman Sachs management to the trades union movement. You could see this as a harmless fantasy: allowing those who earned their stripes as genuine rebels on the front lines in decades past to keep that identity even in victory (or allowing their younger counterparts the pleasure of cosplaying that role). But there was a genuine downside. By failing to move on and accept that the times, the issues and their enemies have changed, the gay rights movement risked falling into the trap identified by Douthat. By remaining focused on critiquing a now defeated enemy, the movement ended up repeating its old, now only semi-relevant demands 'more loudly or crudely or tediously' and using the focus on the now long collapsed 'traditional forms and structures that once gave rebellion purpose' to avoid thinking about the problems their victory had produced or about ways to tweak the new settlement to make it viable in the long term.

There is a definite sense in which the continued pursuit of the old goals of the movement, most notably sexual freedom, did start to appear somewhat tedious when the law and employers had lined up to protect and cheer on whatever choices people make in their sexual lives. But, more concerningly, the focus on old, now vanquished, enemies meant that the gay movement has been deaf to concerns that the sexual revolution, which permitted gay rights to advance, was producing negative side effects that its advocates had not anticipated.

Although women are commonly regarded as some of the main beneficiaries of the sexual revolution, one can see why some question whether this is the case and think that unanticipated consequences of sexual freedom are damaging women. For the conservative feminist Louise Perry, there are 'asymmetries inherent in heterosexuality', namely that men are more interested in casual sex and casual sex is much riskier for women, due to the risks of both pregnancy and violence. This means that the current approach, which she sees as one that aims 'to encourage *all* women [...] to meet the male demand for casual sex' is one she regards as harmful to women.[4] Indeed, both Perry and Jonathan Rauch (a gay American writer prominent in the campaign to legalize same-sex marriage) have noted that, while the development of the Pill and expanded access to abortion did give women greater control over their fertility, it also had an unanticipated impact on men by allowing them, as Rauch puts it, 'to shift the responsibility for unwed pregnancies to women, giving more fathers the moral leeway to do what they were always inclined to do, which is to walk away'.[5]

The Limits of Sexual Deregulation

The conclusion Perry draws is that the sexual liberation project was always inherently flawed. Sexual liberals, she argues, have had 'the hubristic assumption that our society could be uniquely free from the oppression of sexual norms and could function just fine'. This was a false assumption and the solution is 'to re-erect some of the social guard rails that have been torn down'.[6] Although many, perhaps most, feminists strongly disagree with Perry, there are signs that her unease with the deregulatory nature of the sexual revolution is gaining traction.

Indeed, this builds on a longstanding stream of feminist thought. As far back as the eighteenth century, one of modern feminism's foundational figures, Mary Wollstonecraft, was convinced that 'the little respect paid to chastity in the male world is the source of many of the physical and moral evils that torment mankind as well as of the vices and follies that degrade and destroy women'.[7] As previously discussed, when the sexual revolution got underway two centuries later, plenty of left-wing feminists like Robin Morgan, Andrea Dworkin and Catherine MacKinnon made it clear that they felt elements of the sexual revolution, such as the increased availability of pornography, were not to the advantage of women. These critiques, from the left and the right, have gained new strength in recent years with renewed critical focus on hook-up culture, porn and sexual relationships in the workplace.

The result has been increasing pressure on the 'anything goes' and 'consent is enough' liberationist model. For example, there has been a strong trend towards a more restrictive approach to workplace sexual and romantic entanglements than was the case in the late 1990s. In 1998, Bill Clinton's relationship with Monica Lewinsky was regarded as scandalous because he was married and lied about the liaison; the fact that he was three decades older and in a position of authority in her workplace barely figured in discussions at the time (in which, disgracefully, she, who was not married and not cheating on anyone, was nevertheless portrayed as the greater sinner in sexual terms). This would, for better or worse, hardly have been the case if in 2024 Joe Biden had been found to be having a relationship with a 22-year-old intern.

Campus dating rules are also becoming increasingly restrictive. The campaigners highlighting the issue of what they termed 'campus rape culture' have generally come from the feminist left. But they have been joined by conservative figures such as leading post-liberal Patrick Deneen, who has suggested that there is a strange circularity in relation to the history of campus dating rules.[8] In the past, he notes, colleges had rules preventing female students from being present in male dorms and vice versa and social norms heavily discouraged women from being drunk or alone in the presence of men. In the 1960s, 1970s and 1980s these approaches were largely swept away by the sexual revolution. But, instead of inaugurating a utopia where men and women were free to have the relationships they chose, what followed was a flood of complaints that women were the object of significant sexual harassment and assault. Universities then had to react by developing increasingly elaborate codes of conduct around sex and dating on campus, producing a more rigid and legalistic approach than the largely social norms-based rules that predominated in the pre-sexual revolution era.

Now it should be noted that the past to which Deneen refers is actually a rather brief period of transition as, until well into the twentieth century, many universities would not admit female students. But, while his solution of a reinstatement of a socially conservative sexual culture is one that would appal most feminists, it is notable that they many of them would agree with his premise that a deregulated sexual environment has also proved unsatisfactory for many women in a way that advocates of the sexual revolution failed to anticipate.

Radical Gay Liberation as a 'Protected Opinion'

So voices on the left and the right are driving a new questioning of the sexual revolution in particular by questioning whether it has served women's interests. Do these critiques have anything of relevance to gay people? Whether or not you agree with it, there is at least a case to be made that the sexual revolution has been net negative for heterosexual women. That case cannot be made in respect of gays and lesbians. The pre-sexual revolution dispensation assigned heterosexual women a role, albeit one that many of them found unduly restrictive. Gays and lesbians, in contrast, had no legitimate role at all under the old order, making any claim that the sexual revolution has been an overall negative for gay people utterly unsustainable.

Does the fact, however, that the pre-sexual revolution era provided no space for gay people mean that their interests are best served by a sexual revolution that was as wide ranging as possible? Right from the early days, there have been disputes about the extent to which the gay rights movement should be seen as part of a wider challenge to all established norms and institutions. While the 1950s and early 1960s were dominated by very moderate, somewhat apologetic gay organizations, the late 1960s and early 1970s saw the foundation of a number of groups dedicated to seeing the gay rights struggle as part of a wider struggle. The Gay Liberation Front Manifesto of 1971 called for 'revolutionary change in our whole society'. In language remarkably similar to that often used by religious conservatives, the Manifesto declared that monogamous gay couples were 'inevitably a parody, since they haven't even the justification of straight couples – the need to provide a stable environment for their children', though it was quick to note its ambition to overturn the family more generally by adding 'in any case we believe that the suffocating small family unit is by no means the best atmosphere for bringing up children'.[9]

For some radicals, the tendency to consider absolutely all restrictions on sexual freedom as suspect went as far as querying the desirability of age of consent laws. The result was a spectacularly ill-judged ambivalence towards paedophile activism, which saw groups like the North American Man/Boy Love Association (NAMBLA) being permitted to take up membership of the International Lesbian and Gay Association (ILGA) in the late 1970s. Links between ILGA and NAMBLA were severed in the early 1990s but not before they had caused immense damage. In 1994 the United Nations' Economic and Social Council withdrew the consultative status it had granted ILGA in 1993, after a campaign highlighting its links to NAMBLA.[10] ILGA did not succeed in winning back this consultative status until 2011.

Like most utopian projects, the radical gay liberation agenda was, to a large degree, what I would call a 'protected opinion', that is, an opinion that can only be held because you know others will prevent it from being put into operation. These 'protected opinions' are fairly common across the political spectrum from open borders and defunding the police on the left to massive deregulation and abolishing income tax on the right. Those who espouse them are often not cynical. It is more a case of being easy on themselves; saying something that sounds good and which makes them appear radical and ideologically pure but allowing themselves to rely on broad generalities and abstractions rather than detailed specifics when pushed to explain how their goals would actually work. The panic that ensued among partisans of Brexit, as they desperately tried to come up with concrete, detailed objectives for the Brexit project, following their unexpected success in the 2016 referendum was a good example of what happens when a protected opinion loses its protection and has to be implemented in specific form.

Unlike Brexiteers, those who advocated overturning virtually all of society's established structures in relation to sex and the family never faced that loss of protection for their opinions. Specifying how a free-love utopia would have worked would certainly have been a challenge. It is one thing for a small and largely childless group like gay men to embrace free love. It would be quite another for the whole society to do so. The mechanics of a society in which all structures around family and sex had been overthrown and replaced were never fully specified because they could not be. They are completely incompatible with the need for stable units in which to raise children, as well as basic human instincts such as instinctive attachments to family members, jealousy and children's need to bond intensely with their parents. Certainly, the radical gay liberation movement's criticisms of traditional approaches had some strong points. But that is what the movement was, an oppositional movement with an often-valid critique of the problems and unfairness of established rules and institutions, rather than a movement with a viable plan for what to replace them with.

Despite the radicalism of many activist groups, right from the start others thought it would be best to see gay relationships as analogous to straight relationships and sought access to, rather than the overturning of, the institutions that applied to straight life. In May 1970, less than a year after the Stonewall riots, a gay couple, Richard Baker and James McConnell, (unsuccessfully) sued the state of Minnesota for refusing to allow them to marry.[11] For more radical queer activists, aping heterosexual institutions was the very last thing that gays and lesbians should do. Indeed, when the campaign for same-sex marriage got going in a serious way in the late 1980s and early 1990s, its pioneers faced significant hostility from a large number of gay activists. The writer Andrew Sullivan, whose 1989 article for the *New Republic* magazine[12] and 1993 book *Virtually Normal*[13] did an enormous amount to place the issue of gay marriage on the public agenda, remembered in 2012: 'Marriage, for much of the gay rights movement in America, as in Britain, was anathema. I was called a heterosexist, patriarchal, misogynist reactionary, trying to assimilate a wild and hard-fought freedom into bourgeois norms.'[14]

Involuntary Rebels: The Political Triumph of Gay Moderates

Over time, in political terms, the radical queer view that saw homosexuality as inherently subversive and which wanted no part of mainstream society lost out to those who saw the aim of the gay rights movement as ending gay exile from that society. The overwhelming majority of gay people backed the gay-marriage campaign, despite the hostility of many gay activists and the hesitation of some gay rights groups. Writing in 2003, gay radical Peter Tatchell bemoaned the fact that 'Gay politics have been downgraded from radical campaigns to change society to the more modest goal of equal rights within the status quo.' Tatchell was contemptuous of this agenda, describing those who did not endorse his radical views in the following terms: 'Desperate for a queer place at the straight table, they promote a gay version of traditional family values.' Tatchell bemoaned the 'rightward shift', which he said had 'coincided with an influx into the gay movement of conservative-inclined middle-class professionals, who have hijacked it for their own squeaky clean, middle-of-the-road values'.[15]

The dilemma of gay rights activists who make claims in the name of the gay or 'LGBTQ+ community' but who have often been disappointed in the failure of the gay and lesbian 'civilian' population to embrace radicalism is common in revolutionary movements. Karl Marx bemoaned the lack of 'revolutionary ardour' among the British working class and concluded that what was needed was a revolutionary communist elite who would act in the name of the working class.[16] Similarly, the views of ordinary Black and Hispanic voters in the US have proved notably divergent from some of the policies, such as defunding the police or ending deportations that activist groups endorsed in their name. What queer radicals failed to understand was that, like everyone else, most gays and lesbians were not inherent rebels, not consciously strongly political and generally wanted a quiet life. They did not want to be constantly in the role of critic, rebel or campaigner. The idea of always being on the outside critiquing things didn't appeal to most people (though it probably does appeal to those who are attracted to political activism).

One of the things that is most valuable about the advance of gay rights for gay people is the chance it offered to be included within the institutions, such as marriage, which structured and marked the course of the lives of their families, friends and neighbours. After all, for most people, isn't it a happier and more fun way to live to happily join in wedding celebrations, knowing that you now have the right to get married yourself, than to be the party pooping ideologue, sitting on the side of the dance floor casting disapproving looks and struggling to be heard over the music as you bend the ear of a fellow guest about the patriarchal history of the institution of marriage?

With the limited exception of political lesbians (that is women who chose lesbianism as an expression of their feminism), most gay people were not rebels because they were gay. Rather they were gay and had thereby had the role of rebel foisted on them by a society that regarded their sexuality as placing them beyond the pale. Queer radicals might enjoy the sense of being rebels and being distant from the mainstream particularly if, like the 'queer' journalist Terrell Jermaine Starr, criticized by James Kirchick,[17] they are in the growing number of younger people who identify as queer but are opposite-sex attracted and therefore have the option of taking up insider status if they tire of the role of outsider. But, for most gay people, the problem with society's treatment of homosexuality was that it *imposed* the role of rebel and outsider on gay people, whether they wanted that role or not.

What this meant was that more moderate approaches were always likely to provide strong competition to gay radicalism. While many lesbians shared the feminist critique of marriage as a patriarchal institution, lesbian sexual culture was notably monogamous and relationship-focused, meaning that the question of the legal status of long-term unions was always going to come up. Although gay men had, on average, a less relationship-focused sexual culture, the sobering effect of the AIDS crisis probably accelerated a move away from radicalism. Free love no longer promised to be carefree. What is more, having seen lovers exiled from the bedside of their dying partners or kicked out of the homes they had shared with their boyfriends, gay men were acutely aware of the day-to-day impact of the legal discrimination. It is hard to tell a man kicked out of the home he shared with his partner and blocked from inheriting any of his property that his focus on having his relationship recognized is bourgeois conformism and he should focus on overturning the notion of marriage and transforming society.

Having felt the hard edge of exclusion from mainstream institutions and protections, gay men were understandably unwilling to wait for the success of a wider world revolution in social norms to have this exclusion addressed. While the 1970s had seen the flowering of radical gay groups like the Gay Liberation Front, and the decline of the more apologetic groups of the pre-Stonewall riots era, the late 1980s and 1990s saw increased prominence for sober, lobbying-focused organizations like the Human Rights Campaign. Indeed, in the UK Stonewall was founded at the end of the 1980s by activists who were explicit about the fact that they despaired of the factionalism and ineffectiveness of more radical campaigners and wanted a moderate face for the gay rights movement.[18]

The 1980s and early 1990s were a difficult time. The Thatcher and Reagan governments were both notably anti-gay. The Thatcher government even introduced a ban on the 'promotion' of homosexuality by local authorities in 1988. The AIDS crisis also diverted attention and increased hostility among the general public. But, at the same time, incremental progress continued. In France the Socialist government equalized the age of consent in 1981. In the UK entrapment of gay men by so called 'pretty police' was subject to increasing criticism and declined,[19] and in the US, the 1980s saw the end of sodomy bans in Alaska, New York and Wisconsin.

Gay activists made significant progress in making left-wing parties like Labour in the UK and the Democrats in the US more sympathetic to their cause (though both were out of power at the time). A gay speaker addressed the Democratic Convention in 1980 and the British Labour Party had endorsed the principle of legal protection from discrimination by the end of the decade.[20] When the atmosphere improved in the late 1990s, the fact that more extensive progress could be envisaged did not bring about a surge of radicalism. Instead it was very mainstream goals such as employment discrimination legislation, the right to military service and eventually recognition of gay marriage, not the abolition of all traditional structures, that became the focus of gay activism.

The waxing and waning of the influence of non-radical voices in the gay rights movement is not surprising. In the 1970s and 1980s only small numbers of people were willing and able to buck intense societal pressure and be openly gay. Anyone willing to be a member of a gay organization was likely to have a fairly rebellious temperament and therefore to have a tendency towards radical politics. As societal pressure eased in the late 1990s and early 2000s more and more people of a less rebellious bent came out and the membership of gay organizations was likely to become less positively disposed to radical ideas. When, in the mid 2010s, the main objectives of moderates (employment protections, marriage rights etc) were achieved, more moderate and conservative people were likely to disengage from activist groups, meaning that radical influence could once again rise.

Janus-Faced Nature of Gay Male Politics

However, even during the heyday of moderate and conservative gay politics, radicals need not have been totally disappointed in gay men. The political aims of the gay rights movement may have oscillated between approaches that saw few downsides to sweeping changes in sexual and familial norms and more conservative approaches that were more suspicious of radical change. But the sexual culture of gay men has not followed the same pattern. Apart from the period of the AIDS crisis when fear drove reductions in casual sex, gay men have maintained a sexual culture whose norms appear to attribute few downsides to radical departures from traditional approaches to sex. Gay male sexual culture has remained notably libertine in comparison to heterosexuals and lesbians. This led to a Janus-faced approach under which, with the rise of moderate gay politics, there has been something of a contrast between political goals and social reality.

The strength of free-wheeling, anything goes approaches to sex among gay men is readily understandable. Gay people came to the freedom bestowed by the sexual revolution from a fundamentally different starting point from heterosexuals. For straight people, the sexual revolution consisted of a gradual dismantling of a web of norms around what constituted a legitimate and socially acceptable sexual relationship. For example, socially legitimate sex ceased to belong to married couples alone. Social acceptability was steadily extended out from married couples to encompass the relationships of cohabiting couples and then further to cover more casual relationships. The stigma associated with having children out of wedlock also gradually declined.

For gay people, the process was different. Under the old dispensation there hadn't been *any* form of same-sex sexual relationship that was regarded as legitimate. This affected how the sexual freedom they received related to broader social structures and relationships.

It meant that the evolution of norms around same-sex relationships did not amount to a gradual dismantling of a web of norms surrounding such relationships or the expansion of a pre-existing category of legitimate gay relationships. Instead, gays and lesbians started from a blank, or nearly blank, slate. Though the underground world of pre-sexual revolution gay bars and cruising grounds no doubt had its own rules, there was no precedent for open same-sex sexual and romantic relationships in wider society, no agreed norms to pass on to young gay people about how they might best manage their sexual and romantic lives and no established ideas for what the ultimate goals of gay dating should be.

In this context, there were a number of factors that meant that it was highly likely, even inevitable, that the sexual culture gay men would develop on relatively libertine lines. Because men are, on average, more interested in casual sex, sexual variety and paraphilias, without the constraining factor of women in their sexual world, gay men were always going to have more opportunities for no-strings or adventurous sexual encounters than straight men. Lesbian sexual culture, on the other hand, reflected the female relative lack of interest in casual sex and was notably monogamy- and relationship-focused.

In addition, John Maynard Keynes' famous insight that 'Practical men, who believe themselves to be quite exempt from any intellectual influence, are usually the slave of some defunct economist' applies well beyond the arena of economics.[21] We are inevitably influenced by philosophies and ideologies whether or not we are aware that this is happening. It was usually gay sex rather than homosexuality per se that was penalized by the law (though social stigma attached to people who were thought to be gay whether or not they were celibate). The central claim of the sexual revolution was that people should be able to do whatever they wanted with their own bodies. As the gay rights movement picked up momentum in the 1970s the arguments which were gradually winning gays and lesbians freedom in more and more countries across the West were ones that relied heavily on the importance of individual autonomy in sexual matters.

In addition, having had the entirety of their sexual expression, from hookups in public toilets to steady monogamous relationships, judged and deprecated in the recent past, gay men have understandably been reluctant to judge or accept judgement of any consensual sexual behaviour. For gay men, the mixture of this ideological debt to individual autonomy and the greater male desire for casual sex resulted in a sexual culture that 'disenchanted'[22] sex more comprehensively than in among any other groups. Gay male sexual culture became notable for open attitudes to non-monogamous relationships and the development of venues such as saunas or 'dark rooms' in which men could engage in sex with large numbers of partners with no expectation of commitment.

Sex but No Marriage

As importantly, the main institution through which heterosexual male sexuality was channelled towards long-term commitment, namely marriage, was not available to gay people. For heterosexuals the key change brought about by the sexual revolution was that the restriction of legitimate sexual activity to marriage was relaxed and sex before marriage was increasingly accepted. Sex was deregulated but marriage remained. Yes, it was taken up with less frequency, notably by lower socio-economic groups, but while the sexual revolution allowed people to have sex before they were married, it was assumed that they would still, eventually, settle down into a marriage or a stable, marriage-like relationship. As the writer Rob Henderson has pointed out, this pattern is particularly notable for higher socio-economic groups. Although such groups have, he notes, generally embraced the rhetoric of sexual freedom and do engage in pre-marital sex, they have remained remarkably attached to fairly traditional patterns in terms of marriage.[23]

For gay people the sequencing was the opposite. For straight people, marriage pre-dated sexual freedom; for gay people, sexual freedom predated marriage. What I mean by this is that the first step in the gay sexual revolution was decriminalization of gay sex while legalization of gay marriage (and therefore the idea of gay sex within marriage) was the final step. This was the opposite of the heterosexual experience in which legitimate sex within marriage was the starting point and sex outside marriage the innovation. This meant that from the early stages of the gay rights revolution right up until around a decade ago, gay people had been given the right to have sex but not the right to build that sexual relationship towards an eventual marriage.

As we know, when the gay rights revolution was getting going back in the 1960s and 1970s politicians who took the decision to decriminalize homosexuality generally did so out of abstract commitments to privacy and liberty or a desire to show tolerance and mercy towards a group viewed as burdened by a defective or sinful sexuality. Decriminalization did not initially affect the general view that homosexuality was immoral and was not intended as a means through which gay people would be able to establish durable and public relationships. Even after gay sex had been decriminalized in England and Wales in 1967 restrictions on using, for example, personal ads to facilitate gay relationships persisted. In 1972 a British underground paper, *The International Times*, lost an appeal against prosecution for conspiracy to corrupt public morals for its decision to include ads from men seeking to meet men in its classified ads section.[24] Homosexuality was still seen as something to be discouraged and gay relationships were to be tolerated not nurtured. This was not a context favourable to channelling male desire in the direction of stability and monogamy.

The Cult of Authenticity

Though Western culture overall has become more open and confessional in relation to sex, Gay male sexual culture also, unsurprisingly, developed a particularly strong tendency to being open and frank about sexual desires and activities. 'Coming out' is a near-sacred element of the life story of most gay people. Being honest about your sexuality involved breaking with the stifling hypocrisy of a life where you were required to lie, actively or by omission, about what is for everyone an important element of their life. With their insistence on honesty and refusal to refrain from mentioning their sexual orientation, gay people have often been accused of making a big deal about something that should be private.

This charge is usually unfair. It ignores the myriad ways in which sexual orientation is explicitly or implicitly acknowledged and mentioned by society in ways that we don't perceive when heterosexuality is involved. The result is an exhausting and involuntary hyper-politicization of simple acts like holding hands or saying to a waiter 'I am just waiting for my wife'. These kinds of things are said and done unconsciously by straight people all the time but for gays and lesbians it can feel like you are saying 'ANNOUNCEMENT! I AM GAY. YOU BETTER NOT HAVE A PROBLEM WITH THAT!' when all you actually wanted to do was say you were waiting for someone. Gay people have their banal daily lives politicized and are then blamed for being too political about their daily lives.

What has usually been asked of gays and lesbians was not discretion or privacy but denial and self-abnegation, that is the taking of active steps to conceal the fact of their orientation and relationships, steps that were never demanded of straight people. This history makes the emphasis placed by the gay movement on 'being your true self' understandable. Given the oppressive experience of concealment and hypocrisy of the pre-gay rights era, the gay rights movement has understandably been an enthusiastic supporter of what the philosopher Thomas Nagel calls 'cult of authenticity' that is, the notion that people should 'let it all hang out' and should be open about their desires and sexual activities.[25] *

My point is that there is a powerful path dependence at work in relation to gay male sexual culture. Throughout the 1970s, 1980s, 1990s and 2000s, as far as society was concerned, the laws and norms around sex and marriage for gay people were a strange reversal of those for straight people. For straight people sex outside marriage was the rebellious act but, conversely in relation to gay people, opposition to gay marriage was much stronger than to decriminalizing gay sex, meaning that it was the idea of gay sex within a marriage that was regarded as more politically scandalous that casual gay sex. The law permitted gays to have sex but did not permit their coupling to build towards marriage.

Louise Perry's suggestion that, although they were imposed with great cruelty on women, the main function of strict rules of the pre-sexual revolution era was the restraining of the more anarchic sexual behaviour of men[26] does look more plausible in light of the fact that the easing of restrictions on homosexuality saw lesbians drifting spontaneously towards monogamous relationships but saw gay men embrace a very freewheeling sexual culture. When gay men in the West began to get the right to have sex from the late 1960s, homosexuality was still seen as scandalous. This meant social respectability was off the table as an option so there were few social norms or institutions to counteract the combination of the greater openness of men to casual sex, the history of furtive encounters from the pre-decriminalization era and the sex positive ideology of the gay liberation movement. These factors came together to produce the highly sexed gay male culture of the 1970s. This culture has proved persistent. Gay marriage arrived on the scene so late in the day that it has not (yet) brought about a major shift and the political atmosphere has generally been improving, meaning there has been no political pressure to change things.

The result is a Janus-faced approach. From the 1990s until the mid 2010s, the gay rights movement pursued moderate political goals focused on inclusion in established institutions. But at the same time a series of factors, including some beyond their control, made it almost inevitable that gay men would maintain a sexual culture whose libertinism and sexual frankness diverge more radically from established norms. This approach is not necessarily hypocritical. It is perfectly possible to want fair play and the chance of inclusion in mainstream institutions and also to believe in a sex-positive, swinging sexual culture. But there is a degree of tension between the centrality of quite conservative 'we just want what straight people want' demands such as same-sex marriage and, on the other hand, the strength of the libertine element of gay male sexual culture and the sex-positive ideology of the gay rights movement. What is more, although there is no moral issue with people having as much casual sex as they like, the anything goes sexual culture does pose problems that are increasingly difficult to ignore.

7

The Downside of Anything Goes

Just how different is gay male sexual culture? The honest answer is, quite different. Surveys show that, as you would expect, gay men exhibit a full range of sexual behaviour from celibacy and monogamy to very high numbers of partners. It is at population level that important differences emerge. At that population level, gay men (or 'men who have sex with men' abbreviated to 'MSM') have significantly higher numbers of sexual partners than straight people or lesbians. This average does conceal very big differences.[1] For example, a British survey showed about one quarter of gay men being in stable monogamous relationships, a quarter reporting more than thirteen partners in the previous year, with the rest somewhere in between.[2]

This echoes the findings in other surveys that also showed that there is a minority of gay men whose very high number of partners push up the average number of partners reported by gay men as whole and account for some (though not all) of the differences in average numbers of partners between MSM and other groups. The overall picture is fairly clear. Gay male sexual culture has many different elements and spans the full range of behaviour. But, on average, gay men are likely to have a notably higher number of sexual partners, to have higher rates of 'concurrency' (that is, having more than one partner at the same time). There is also a significant minority of gay men who report very high numbers of sexual partners.[3]

The response to this from gay people is often a defensive 'straight men would be as promiscuous as gay men if straight women let them'. This is no doubt true. When I first arrived in London, I lived in a student residence that was close to Russell Square, a park that, at the time, was famous as a place where men met for sex. I remember one evening a straight friend of mine who lived in the same residence saying that he was grateful that there was no straight equivalent because if there had been a nearby park full of women wanting to have sex he would be there the whole time and would get no work done.

But the fact that straight men are as interested in casual sex as gay men is not the killer point that some gay men seem to think. After all, the homophobe's objection to male homosexuality does not depend on denying the straight male appetite for no strings sex. It depends on portraying sexual activity between two (or more) men as inherently wrong or unbalanced. Those with anti-gay beliefs could happily accept that gay men have sexual instincts that are no more promiscuous than straight men without affecting their conclusion that sexual relationships between men in which the moderating influence of typical female approaches to sex are absent are inherently unbalanced and wrong.

I reiterate that, morally, there is nothing inherently wrong with the higher level of casual sex among gay men. However, a sexual culture with such significant 'all you can eat' elements does have certain consequences. Gay men have much higher levels of sexually transmitted disease than the rest of the population. It is true that most of these diseases can currently be effectively treated and that with PrEP (anti-HIV medications taken either consistently or before sexual activity) the likelihood that unprotected sexual acts will result in transmission of HIV can be greatly reduced. But, given the level of casual sex among gay men, these treatments have not succeeded in eliminating the transmission of HIV. In the US, 2.4 per cent of young gay men contract HIV each year and the Center for Disease Control estimated that an 18-year-old gay man has a fifty per cent chance of becoming HIV positive by the age of fifty.[4]

Indeed, the success of medical interventions that either reduce transmission or successfully control the virus post-infection has led many sexually active gay men to dispense with the safe-sex measures that were adopted during the 1980s and 1990s. The problem is that there are diseases other than HIV, and their incidence is rising quickly, particularly now that PrEP has reduced fear of condomless anal sex. Men who have sex with men account for the vast majority of syphilis infections in the United States, with the incidence of the disease rising by fifteen per cent year on year.[5] Drug-resistant gonorrhoea is also an increasing problem.

Perhaps more importantly, who is to know that the new HIV is not around the corner? As recent history has taught us, new pathogens do emerge. It was extraordinarily bad luck that the HIV virus was introduced into the gay male population in the US at the very time that gay men were experiencing their first burst of sexual freedom. But, as Randy

Shilts noted in *And the Band Played On*, his famous history of the early years of the AIDS epidemic in the US, even before gay men started showing up in doctors' offices and hospitals in the early 1980s with a baffling range of symptoms, public health experts were worried that the raucous sexual culture gay men had created in places such as New York and San Francisco had created a climate that risked offering an ideal environment for a new disease to spread. Writing of a meeting of gay doctors in San Francisco as part of the Gay Pride weekend in 1980 Shilts recounted:

> A new disease. It was never a formal topic of discussion, but on that weekend [Gay Pride weekend 1980] when gay doctors from across the country gathered in San Francisco, it was discussed occasionally in hallways and over dinners. What would happen if some new disease insinuated itself into the bodies of just a few men in this community? The thought terrified Dr David Ostrow [a doctor who ran a clinic for gay men in Chicago]. [...] Between the bathhouses and the high levels of sexual activity, there would be no stopping a new disease that got into this population [...] he wondered where all the sexually transmitted diseases would end. It couldn't continue indefinitely.[6]

Interviewed in 1987, Paul O'Malley, a gay man who had spent many years working on sexual health in San Francisco, said 'Looking back on that time, I used to think something was going to happen sooner or later. I was worried about a resistant strain of gonorrhoea or syphilis. I didn't think of some new virus ...'.[7] The reality is that, just as battery farms or 'wet markets' with large numbers of animals kept in tightly packed captivity are inherently risky for the emergence of new diseases, for a group to have very high rates of casual sex with large numbers of partners creates a riskily promising context for new diseases to spread. We are now well protected from HIV and, for as long as antibiotics retain their potency, against a number of other diseases. But with a quarter of gay men in the UK reporting over thirteen sexual partners a year (and similar figures elsewhere), any new sexually transmitted disease is going to have a really good shot and spread far and wide before effective treatments can be developed.

The mpox saga of 2022 showed that there are reasons to wonder whether current patterns in the sexual culture of gay men might be posing physical and indeed emotional risks that are just too high. Mpox, or monkeypox as it was then known, is a disease that had been endemic in areas of Africa for some time. But, in May 2022, cases suddenly began to appear elsewhere. It soon became clear that the overwhelming majority of these new cases were among men who have sex with men ('MSM'). In a parallel of what happened with HIV in the US in the late 1970s, it appeared that mpox may have been circulating at low levels for a number of years before suddenly taking off among MSM.[8]

It was pretty clear what kind of behaviours among MSM caused the outbreak to suddenly spread so much more rapidly. *The New England Journal of Medicine* conducted a survey of 528 cases of mpox diagnosed between the end of April and the end of June 2022. Ninety-eight per cent of cases were MSM, mainly men who have high numbers of sex partners (the median mpox case had five partners in the previous three months, 29 per cent had another sexually transmitted infection, just under a third had attended a 'sex on the premises' venue and twenty per cent had engaged in chemsex). In other words, the reason mpox had suddenly begun to spread much more rapidly outside Africa was because it had gained a foothold among gay men, a significant number of whom were having a very large numbers of sexual contacts.

The reaction of gay rights groups and public health officials was instructive. As had been the case with HIV in the early 1980s, many gay health promotion and gay rights organizations were leery of telling people to lay off multiple partner sex, even for a short time, though they did generally advise people to avoid close contact with those who had symptoms. Among public health professionals, a well-meaning desire to avoid stigmatizing gay men led to the issuing of statements that were somewhat misleading.

In an article headlined 'Monkeypox: expert explains why it isn't a "gay disease" and warns of risk of stigma' the online gay paper *Pink News* quoted an infectious disease specialist with the UK Health Security Agency as saying 'We don't want to ask people to have less sex or to change their relationship around sex because there's a context and a history to that, but we want people to be aware this is happening and to be signposted to the right services.'[9] A range of other experts[10] and bodies[11] stressed that 'anyone' could get the disease and shied away from recommending that gay men temporarily reduce their levels of casual sex. The New York City Health Department even put out a press release which contained tips for 'those who choose to have sex while sick' and included advice to cover mpox sores while having sex to reduce transmission risk.[12]

A number of anti-gay figures were only too delighted to point out that the authorities had been willing to shut down most of society to prevent the spread of Covid-19 but were unwilling to shut down gay sex venues to prevent the spread of mpox. The conservative Christian commentator Rod Dreher stated 'I swear, if you could get monkeypox by going to church, Biden and Fauci would be right now sending in the National Guard to weld the doors of houses of worship shut like the Chinese did with Wuhan apartments in Covid.'[13] But it was not only conservatives who worried about this reticence. Jim Down, a gay historian of infectious diseases, wrote in *The Atlantic* of his worries that 'baggage of the HIV/AIDS crisis – including homophobia' – meant that 'public-health leaders are not doing enough to directly alert men who have sex with men about monkeypox'.[14] While he did not advocate closing saunas and darkrooms, he did argue that health agencies should be clearer about the sexual nature of the spread of the disease.

Others were even more critical. Dr Don Weiss of the Bureau of Communicable Diseases at the New York City Health Department felt that the softly, softly approach, which avoided any hint of telling people to avoid sex, was irresponsible. 'If we had an outbreak associated with bowling, would we not warn people to stop bowling?' he asked colleagues.[15] These arguments echoed the anguished debates within gay circles during the early years of the AIDS crisis. Randy Shilts notes how leaders of the first organization to combat the epidemic, the Gay Men's Health Crisis in New York, had largely cut back on unsafe sex themselves by the end of 1982 but were wary of appearing judgemental and of the civil rights implications of closing gay bathhouses.[16]

The advice around mpox did eventually become more frank and a combination of increased vaccination and a significant number of gay men reducing their sexual contacts meant the outbreak petered out. To be clear, I have no criticism of public health bodies for issuing the kind of statements that they felt would be most effective in countering the spread of the disease. But whether or not the public health authorities got their messaging right, the episode highlights how the kind of sexual culture that gay men have created is one that is inherently risky.

We were lucky with mpox. Those who catch it rapidly became unwell and this limited the ability of the virus to spread. But this is not always the case. HIV has a long latency period. People can be infected for years before becoming unwell, meaning that when the virus began to spread in North America, it could spread far and wide before anyone even knew something was wrong. Scientists running a hepatitis B vaccine trial in San Francisco in the 1970s saved blood samples from large numbers of gay men in the city. When these samples were analysed in the late 1980s, they showed that the virus had arrived in the city around 1976. By 1978 only three per cent of the samples contained HIV antibodies. It was not until 1981 that doctors first began to see significant numbers of gay patients with immune deficiency but by this time 36 per cent of the sample were showing evidence of HIV infection. By the time that, in 1984, the public health system recognized that something very serious was going on, fully 62 per cent of the men in the sample had been infected.[17]

Luckily for the world, mpox was not like HIV. It was non-fatal in most cases, had a short latency period and there was an effective treatment already on hand. This meant that doctors were aware quite quickly that something was wrong and those at risk had a chance to moderate their behaviour. Vaccination could further reduce the risk of transmission and serious illness. But, who is to say that the next virus will be like mpox rather than HIV? If mpox had a similar latency period to HIV, the current model of gay male sexual culture would have permitted it to spread far and wide before we even knew something was amiss.

'Fun' Is Not Just Fun

The mpox saga of 2022 was a useful reminder that there is a physical risk inherent in a group having a significant level of frequent multiple partner encounters. With increasing antibiotic resistance and rising awareness of the risk of new pathogens more generally, the optimistic 1970s attitude that medical science had effectively eliminated the risk of serious consequences from sexually transmitted infections now looks like a very brief holiday from reality. But the mpox saga also highlighted downsides involved in the libertine elements of the sexual culture of gay men that go beyond physical ill-health.

The freewheeling sexual culture that has developed among a significant proportion of gay men is based on the 'disenchantment' of sex. On this view, sex is an activity that adults can engage in without it having any particular emotional significance, something that is just, to use the parlance of apps such as *Grindr*, 'fun'. But the somewhat jumpy and defensive reaction of public-health bodies, gay organizations and gay people during the mpox outbreak seemed to indicate that this kind of sexual culture is about something more than just light-hearted 'fun'.

After all, if sex is just a fun leisure activity, why not knock off those activities for a couple of weeks when it emerges that multiple partner hookups in venues such as saunas and darkrooms are fuelling the spread of a virus? This was not like the 1980s, when a frightening new disease was spreading, about which scientists knew little, and when relying on abstinence would have meant asking people to live without sex for an indefinite period. With mpox, scientists already knew a lot about how it spread and its latency period, which meant that only a short period of abstinence would have sufficed to get on top of the problem.

But, as we have already seen, many gay groups and public health bodies were very reluctant to state this openly. Some of this was motivated by an understandable desire to avoid damaging the reputation of gay people in the eyes of the straight majority. Some of it was also motivated by expert knowledge on the part of public health experts who know best what is and is not likely to be effective as a public health message, so I am happy to accept that the reluctance to call for a reduction in sexual partners may have been the right call. But the very fact that experts were so worried that such a call would have been ineffective is instructive, as it seems to undercut the idea that those engaging in frequent multiple-partner sexual activity are merely engaged in light-hearted 'fun'.

If, to adapt Dr Don Weiss' analogy, sex was simply fun and no more meaningful than bowling, then there would not have been such sensitivity about people being told to cool their sexual jets for a few weeks. The long history of stigmatization of all gay sexuality is an important part of the context but we are not in the relentlessly homophobic world of 1981 any more. In 2022, gay sex and, indeed, gay marriage, were legal and the White House was being lit up in rainbow colours for gay-pride celebrations. The reluctance to give frank advice to gay men to reduce their sexual contacts temporarily to avoid the spread of a virus is about more than historical homophobia.

In reality, it was thought that asking gay men to reduce their sexual contacts would be ineffective, not only because gay sexuality had been stigmatized until so recently, but also because sex is not just 'fun'. On one level gay men having frequent 'no strings fun' may seem to be living out the sexual revolution's dream of disenchanted sex to the maximum degree imaginable. But the reluctance of public health experts to call for temporary reduction in gay sexual contacts shows that this sexual activity is not just light-hearted fun but is something about which people feel very intensely.

In other words, sex has not been disenchanted, even for those most enthusiastically living out the sexual revolution's message of disenchantment. As the (gay) writer Andrew Sullivan writes, 'the meeting of two human beings in a sexual encounter can never be a neutral or casual phenomenon. It has meaning and danger, and promise. It betokens a particular form of responsibility as well as liberation.'[18] Indeed, the idea that public health experts thought that it was pointless even to ask people to reduce sexual contacts for a short period does indicate that there may be an element of addiction and compulsive behaviour at work in the supposedly carefree, freewheeling, fast-lane-version of gay sexuality.

The Emotional Costs of Anything Goes

If sex is, unavoidably, something of a big deal, then this raises the issue of whether sex-positive, anything goes approaches to sex might also have an emotional cost. The idea that having your dreams come true may prove a mixed blessing is not new. There is a possibly apocryphal story about the footballer George Best, whose footballing talent and legendary wild living made him a household name in the 1960s and 1970s. In it, a waiter charged with delivering champagne to Best's hotel room walks in to find thousands of pounds of casino winnings scattered on the floor and Miss World lying in the bed. He turns to Best and says 'Where did it all go wrong?'

Many gay men who lived through the second half of the twentieth century will empathize with this tale of getting what you thought you wanted and yet feeling that what you thought would be paradise actually has its drawbacks. It is almost like a fairy tale. A horny, lonely, frightened gay guy in the 1960s is visited by his fairy godmother, who gives him a wish. He asks her to magic away the laws and norms that were preventing him from acting on his sexual desires. The fairy godmother grants this wish and in the ensuing decades the laws disappear and society tolerates the growth of bars, clubs, discos and, later, apps that offered him unparalleled opportunities to live out those desires. But, as in most fairy tales, it turns out that having your wish granted does not necessarily lead to happily ever after. The bars, clubs and, later, apps, as well as the sexual opportunities they provided were great in their way. But they proved not to be the unalloyed blessing the frustrated and isolated wish-maker had expected and had a more complicated relationship to his ability to live happily ever after than he anticipated.

Gay men's literature reflects this ambivalent relationship between freedom and happiness. In the lonely, frustrated, pre-gay-liberation era gay writing was usually misery-based; tales of doomed relationships like James Baldwin's *Giovanni's Room*, tormented blackmail victims, as in the 1961 film *Victim*, which starred Dirk Bogarde, or self-hating men dreading what they assumed would be lonely middle and old age, as in the 1968 play and 1970 film *The Boys in the Band*. When gay liberation got going things didn't need to be so downbeat. It began to be possible for gay-themed work to involve endings other than murder, suicide and loneliness.

E.M. Forster's *Maurice*, from 1971, was a kind of transitional work. It involved a lot of repression and misery but also ended on a hopeful note, with its eponymous main character set to embark on a loving relationship that might endure. By 1973, Jean Poiret's play *La Cage aux Folles* could feature a gay couple without it being necessary for them to be miserable, alone or doomed. By the end of the 1970s, gay rights appeared to be advancing, people were unaware of HIV and there was still blithe confidence that modern medicine had eliminated the risk of serious illness posed by sexually transmitted infections. With gay freedom being a new development, it was natural, probably even wise for gay people to experiment a bit and push the boundaries to see what kinds of relationships worked best for them. But, after quite a short time, voices began to be raised that expressed doubts about whether the resulting highly sexed sexual culture that gay men were creating in urban enclaves might be diverting gay men from the kinds of relationships that would provide deeper and longer-term happiness.

In 1978, a novelist called Larry Kramer wrote a book that lived up to its provocative title *Faggots*. *Faggots* was a cutting and at times vituperative attack on the promiscuity of gay life in late 1970s New York. Although the book had a strident tone, Kramer's motivations for writing it were much softer, almost mushy. As he told an interviewer: 'I wanted to be in love. Almost everyone I know felt the same way. I think most people, at some level, wanted what I was looking for, whether they pooh-poohed it or said that we can't live like straight people or whatever excuses they gave.'[19] Kramer had participated fully in fast-lane gay sexual culture of the time but became convinced that the relentless pushing of sexual boundaries and high level of casual sex were actually preventing gay men from developing more meaningful and lasting romantic relationships.

His memories of the reactions of many of the gay men he spoke to while researching the book are instructive. He noticed how often his interviewees would ask 'Are you writing a negative book? Are you going to make it positive?' all of which made him think 'My God people must be really conflicted about the lives they are leading.'[20] That kind of defensiveness was very understandable. Gay men at the time were in the first flush of freedom. Having grown up in an era when all gay sexuality had been heavily repressed and operating in a still hostile society, they were unlikely to take well to criticism, however well intentioned. Nevertheless, Kramer, who was a naturally abrasive character, decided to write a novel that told it as he saw it.

Even if his advice was well meant, he certainly didn't sugar coat things. The tone he adopted in *Faggots* was harsh, bitter and almost wilfully insulting. Kramer became a pariah among many of his old friends, not least as some of them appeared in thinly veiled and very unflattering form in the text (it even included a very uncomplimentary portrait of the man Kramer would eventually marry). The book's overall message was clear: 'Why do faggots have to fuck so fucking much?' laments one character. Having had a large amount of casual sex over the years, towards the end of the novel the main character, Fred Lemish (who was loosely modelled on Kramer himself), exclaims 'I'm tired of using my body as a faceless thing to lure another faceless thing. I want to love a Person! [...] no relationship in the world could survive the shit we lay on it.'[21]

Although the book's biting and scolding approach alienated many, some of the intensity of the negative reaction was probably because Kramer couldn't be dismissed a traditional finger-wagging conservative moralist. People who would have rolled their eyes at a novel decrying gay promiscuity if it had been written by a Southern Baptist preacher, felt wounded and angry at Kramer, perhaps because for many of them his book had resonated with nagging doubts they had that they didn't want to acknowledge. Here was criticism from inside the tent from someone who had plenty of first-hand experience of what he was writing about. Kramer couldn't be disregarded as someone who was just out to get at gay people. His concern was not with sin but with unhappiness. He wanted gay men to be happy and to find love and saw a culture that emphasized endless short-term sexual opportunity as an emotional dead-end as well as an impediment to gay happiness in the long term.

Faggots was followed in 1980 by Andrew Holleran's novel *The Dancer from the Dance*. This was a more nuanced book that had less of the openly campaigning quality that *Faggots* had but it reflected the same concerns. As the writer Alan Hollinghurst eloquently wrote, it gave 'a critique of a newly evolved world that was also a hauntingly romantic record of its appeal'. The book is a celebration of the sexual freedom that gay men had achieved in New York in the decade following the Stonewall riots. But, in Hollinghurst's words:

> it has darkening hints that the very life being celebrated is in its way an ordeal, Holleran has a feeling eye for the burden of sex addiction, the 'handsome young man ... with half-moon shadows beneath his eyes and the grim expression of someone living for lust'. How compelling this life is, but how wonderful it would be if one were no longer a prisoner of love.[22]

Holleran reflected this ambivalence in speaking of his own life. He was clear that he loved the raucous gay Mecca that was Fire Island. But he also did not hide the fact that he was horrified by 'these awful human relationships [and] the awful emptiness' that was produced by the partying and promiscuity that characterized gay holidaymaking on the island in the 1970s.

There is something deeply unnerving about reading both *Faggots* and *The Dancer from the Dance*. It is not just that both books portray a world that the authors don't know is suddenly about to end in disaster. That is not so unusual. Any contemporary novel that was written about Europe in the early 1910s or about Jewish Europe in the 1930s would be the same. Yes, the fact that, looking back at accounts of gay life in the 1970s, we know what is about to happen and both the authors and the people they are writing about don't, is unnerving. But what is most eery is the sense that both Kramer and Holleran seem to have an inkling, a sense of foreboding, while at the same time being clueless about just how bad things would shortly become. Kramer in particular appears to fulfil the role of the mythological Cassandra, who was fated to see danger but never to be believed. His book is a satire and an overwritten one at that, yet what was intended as a hyperbolic warning uttered by a character at the end of the book, 'you are fucking yourself to death', turned out not to be hyperbole at all.

With the advent of AIDS, the sexual free-for-all of gay New York and other gay metropolises that Holleran and Kramer chronicled came to a tragic end. But it is important not to let the medical catastrophe that was sprung on gay men in the early 1980s obscure the fact that it was the emotional impact of the sexual culture of 1970s gay New York, not fear of a then unknown virus, that underpins both *Faggots* and *The Dancer from the Dance*. We will never know how the sexual sub-culture of gay men in the West would have developed if AIDS had not emerged. But it is notable that, once the crisis receded with the emergence of effective treatments, some of the behaviours that had worried Kramer, Holleran and others in the late 1970s re-emerged, as did the concerns about the emotional impact of those behaviours on gay men.

There is, I hasten to add, nothing morally wrong with consenting adults engaging in whatever and however many sexual acts they want. I don't claim to have lived a life of perfect restraint myself. But might a sexual culture that places such a heavy emphasis on satisfying one's immediate desires also be a sexual culture that hinders people from getting to where they want to go to in the longer term? For gay people, who are disproportionately likely to spend their teenage years, during which their sex drive is highest, unable to express their sexual desires, the possibility of relieving sexual frustration is, of course, a major driver to come out. The greater openness of men to casual sex and the libertine elements of the ethos of gay male sexual culture can provide a welcome chance to burn off some sexual frustrations of their closeted teenage years. So, on one level, as long as we get lucky and no new virus emerges, there might be no problem here. If the sexual mores that have evolved among gay men mean that casual sex is readily available and if lots of gay men decide that they want to have a lot of casual sex, then everyone is getting what they want, right?

Short-Term Desires and Long-Term Goals

The problem here is with the idea of 'getting what they want'. What humans want in the moment is not a very good guide to what they want in the longer term. Consider internet use. If, on waking in the morning, I was asked how many minutes of the day I would like to spend scrolling through social media I would probably say five or ten. But on an average day, it is very likely that I will clock up over an hour. In each individual minute of that hour, it is true that no one is forcing me to read angry tweets so you could say that I 'want' to spend my time that way, but that is not fully true.

The reality is that, like all humans, I face a struggle between my desires in the moment and my longer-term desires. My desire in the moment, to keep scrolling, hinders me from following my longer-term desire to spend my time doing more productive activities than playing online chess or consuming click bait on the internet. This is one of the fundamental elements of the human condition. Some ability to resist in the moment desires is fundamental to a flourishing human life. That is why, even if we accept that gay men who are having a lot of casual sex are doing what they want to do in the moment, that is not the end of the discussion of whether they are getting what they want.

I have a strong suspicion that for many gay men, consistently following in the moment desires for casual sex gets in the way of realizing our longer-term desires. This isn't surprising. Giving in to all of your desires in the moment is not thought of as a healthy or good approach in almost any other area. The desire to stay in bed rather than get up and go to work requires an acknowledgement that while you have a strong desire in the moment to stay in a warm bed with your eyes closed, this desire is incompatible with your longer-term (and more important) desire to pay your bills and have a successful career. The desire to eat chocolate cake may sometimes have to be resisted in order to realize your longer-term desire to remain healthy.

Indeed, it is notable that many of the men who engage most fully in the unconstrained element of gay male sexual culture live lives in which they regularly resist in the moment desires in the service of longer-term goals. The kind of gay clubs in which men tend to dance with their tops off, take drugs and engage in multiple partner encounters (sometimes on the premises in 'dark rooms', sometimes at 'after parties' elsewhere) are full of men who have no problem in recognizing that their in the moment desire to skip going to the gym or to consume refined carbohydrates is something best resisted in order to serve their longer-term goal of having a great body. Why should in the moment sexual desires be any different?

I remember once hearing legendarily promiscuous singer Rod Stewart on the radio describing how, in his wild heyday, he was in the South of France, dropping one supermodel, who had spent the weekend with him, off at the airport with another supermodel arriving on the incoming flight. As he waited for the second supermodel to emerge from the baggage collection he suddenly thought to himself 'God, this is fucking miserable' and decided he needed to settle down. He had a point. Too much casual sex can, despite its undeniable appeal, get in the way of many people's longer-term goals.

Having high numbers of sexual partners is, unsurprisingly, correlated with high levels of sexually transmitted disease. But gay men, with their high average number of sexual partners, also have higher levels of mental health problems, drug abuse and alcoholism. Of course, there may be many reasons for this, including experiences of prejudice and discrimination. But, if societal homophobia was the main cause of poorer mental health, you would expect that these differences in levels of mental health would be steadily disappearing as societal homophobia declines. The fact that this is not the case[23] suggests that, at least for a significant number of people, engaging in an no-holds-barred sexual culture may not be helping with their long-term happiness or flourishing.

The indiscriminately sex-positive approach that came out of the sexual revolution, and which was embraced most enthusiastically by gay men, can end up stymieing the very thing that the gay revolution sought to render possible: enduring gay love. As the gay writer and scholar Reynolds Price wrote in relation to the portrayal in *Faggots* of the sexually frenzied New York of the 1970s:

> the frenzied sexual activity which the male body so readily proved capable of performing made the stated goal of much of that activity literally impossible – if the goal that is, was love or psychic intimacy between men of good sense and reasonable vigor [...] whatever prodigies the male genitals can perform, the human mind is incapable of emotional focus when it's asked to experience so much emotional intensity with so many different objects.[24]

The gay journalist Matthew Todd, writing of the London of the 2010s, had similar thoughts: 'the way we sexualize our culture so heavily and the way many of us [...] have sex so casually leads to us treating each other as objects [...] that's OK if that's all you want. But most of us say that's not all we want.'[25] Todd is right. There are some people who will be perfectly happy and satisfied by having a large number of casual sexual encounters, who do not hope for anything beyond that and who will not feel empty, lonely or dehumanized by the experience. Good for them. But opinion polls say that for most gay people, that is not the case. Large majorities of gay men express the desire for long-term monogamous or near-monogamous relationships.[26]

As Michael Joseph Gross put it: 'When you came out, you did it because you wanted something. Part of what you wanted was sex, but part of what you hoped for was the possibility of being loved as your true self.' For most people, a bit of casual sex might be fine but, overall, they hope for something more enduring and meaningful. Alan Hollinghurst wrote movingly of those heading out to a gay club 'with clear hopes of finding sex, and hopes, more shyly voiced, of at last encountering real love – with the power to soothe the restless hunting for sex and the recurrent need to go out again'.[27] For some people, a large amount of casual sex with no commitment will be compatible with their longer-term hopes and dreams. For others, enjoying casual flings en route to or between more meaningful relationships will provide pleasure and connection. But for a significant number of gay men, Michael Joseph Gross' description of online gay dating is more apt:

Beyond a certain point, though, perpetually settling for Mr Right Now becomes a failure of hope [...] every fuck, we rationalized, was another chance to find a boyfriend. Yet the more we did this, the fainter grew the hope of finding something more meaningful than a hookup. As our hopes faded, we learned to see one another, and finally even ourselves, as things [...] And when, as often happens while cruising online, we diminish the hopes that drew us out of the closet, we reduce sex to a purely physical act.[28]

Over-Burdening Self-Discipline

In the pre-sexual liberation era, social norms heavily constrained people's ability to choose to have sex. For gay people the constraint was total. Seeking sex meant risking social ostracism and often criminal prosecution. The eventual application of the freedoms of the sexual revolution to gay people meant that the pursuit of sex and love no longer threatened to bring down terrible social and legal consequences. That, it hardly needs to be said, is an unambiguously good thing.

But with power comes responsibility. Before the sexual revolution, even for straight people, much of the decision-making about whether to have sex was effectively taken out of their hands: collective social norms did most of the work. Some people still did what they pleased but, for many, the consequences of breaking the rules were just too severe, particularly for unmarried women, gays and lesbians. With the coming of the sexual revolution much more of the burden of taking these decisions was transferred to individuals. The decision to have or not to have sex was now one that could be taken with less fear of pregnancy, ostracism or criminal penalties.

For gay men, operating in the context of a highly sex-positive sexual sub-culture, the forces pushing against a decision to have sex on any individual occasion were particularly weak and the availability of potential short-term partners was high. As the accounts of gay New York in the 1970s show, this presented gay men with a historically unprecedented range of sexual choices. One could try to go on a date, or go to a disco and hope to chat someone up but one could also go to a darkroom, cruising ground or bath house, where sex with multiple men was readily available.[29] The only constraint on doing so would have to come from your energy levels and your ability to say no.

In the era of dating apps, the constraints are even fewer. Apps have transformed straight dating norms too, with the illusion of endless opportunity and the lack of accountability changing dating patterns in ways that many have found disturbing. For gay men who were already operating in an anything goes sexual culture, apps have supercharged short-termist tendencies. You can connect with an endless range of men without even leaving the comfort of your sofa. What is more, even if you do meet someone who might be a good long-term match, there is always the chance of someone slightly better out there.

The psychologist Barry Schwartz has written of the consequences of almost unlimited choice in his 2007 book *The Paradox of Choice*. His key conclusion is that that 'the fact that *some* choice is good doesn't necessarily mean that *more* choice is better'.[30] Schwartz's work focuses on choice more generally rather than anything specific to sex or homosexuality but his work contains notable echoes of the worries voiced by gay novelists and writers about the sexual culture that has evolved among gay men.

For Schwartz, to have no choice is unbearable but absolutely unrestricted choice risks impeding people in their pursuit of what they most value.[31] He notes how research shows that, beyond a relatively low point, increasing the varieties of a product available tends to decrease the amount of the product people purchase as the increase in options leads to rising expectations and dissatisfaction when those higher expectations are not met. People also tend to be less satisfied with the choice of product if they are given a chance to change their mind and take a different option.

This resonates with Matthew Todd's worries that having a lot of casual sex can lead to requirements for 'higher and higher standards of physical perfection [....] Standards can spiral ever upwards until even stunningly attractive people feel they're not good enough.'[32] Greater choice, it seems, may not always lead to greater satisfaction but to a joyless Rod-Stewart-style 'hedonic treadmill', in which people become desensitized to pleasure and feel paralysed rather than empowered by the choices around them. As Reynolds Price puts it 'when orgasmic sex ceases to constitute emotional intensity for its participants, then what remains in the realm of sensory possibility for the deadened veteran [...]?'[33]

As our fairytales show, humans have long been aware of this risk that the pursuit of ever greater levels of pleasure may make it harder for us to engage with the world as it is by producing a kind of hypersensitivity, where any deviation from an ideal becomes intolerable. In Hans Christian Andersen's *The Princess and the Pea*, for example, the princess had had her tastes catered for to such a degree that she found that the presence of a pea under her mattress generated unbearable discomfort. Similarly, an approach that encourages boundary pushing and the wringing of ever greater excitement from casual sex may risk the development of a degree of erotic inflation that causes ordinary sexual pleasures to lose their potency. This brings the risk that people may find themselves regarding sexual encounters that include the kind of minor deviations from sexual ideals that are inevitable when one is dealing with actual human beings, as disappointing and insufficient. The increased availability of pornography and resultant increased 'pornographication' of sexual life (a feature of both gay and straight sexual culture in the internet era) may worsen these tendencies.

The issues posed by unrestricted choice are a phenomenon that affect secular, wealthy, capitalist societies more broadly. Schwartz describes how, paradoxically, as American society has become more individualistic and has given people more control over how they live their lives, self-reported feelings of helplessness have risen. Perhaps, Schwartz wonders, in a line that could have been written in *Faggots* or *The Dancer from the Dance*, 'there comes a point at which opportunities become so numerous that we feel overwhelmed. Instead of feeling in control, we feel unable to cope. Having the opportunity to choose is no blessing if we feel we do not have the wherewithal to choose wisely.'[34]

The Absent Invisible Hand: Living without Rules or Guardrails

The ability of humans to control their desires without any help from social norms is limited. The approach to sex among gay men shows what happens when a sexual culture relies solely on individuals' regulation of their own desires without any of the norms and structures that humans have relied on for centuries to regulate their inevitably chaotic sexual desires (and particularly male sexual desire, which seems especially chaotic). Some people are no doubt able to manage their desires without any help from social norms. Others may be very happy not constraining their desires at all. But a significant contingent find themselves engaging consistently in behaviours that take them further and further from the kind of life they want to lead. After the long history of oppression of homosexuality by traditional mores, the rejection of traditional structures is understandable. But just because we can understand why gay men might be instinctively hostile to traditional sexual rules does not mean that rejecting them wholesale is not damaging.

Indeed, the damage to the self-esteem of gay men wrought by the discrimination of the past (and the present) probably means that gay men have a greater need than others for some kind of structure to help them to channel their sexual desires in fruitful directions. As Michael Joseph Gross wrote in his 2008 critique of gay online cruising and dating, 'Practically every gay man has his own version of [a] secret, which we learned to keep while growing up in the closet: the secret fear that, if we were truly known, we would never be loved.'[35] Gross was writing about internet dating but his point goes for the anything goes and all you can eat elements of gay male sexual culture more generally; a context that places heavy emphasis on physical attractiveness and casual hook-ups encourages a tendency to seek to attract partners by presenting an artificial, sexy, almost pornographied version of yourself.

This is also a problem faced by straight people on dating apps on which their attractiveness is assessed by potential partners on the basis of photos and some limited text, without all of the more human indicators of personality, manner and charm that in-person encounters bring. Many gay men having grown up in a homophobic society are likely to have particularly intense doubts about whether they are fully loveable. This means that it will be especially hard for them to avoid this phenomenon and to engage in the degree of openness to being fully known that is, as the gay author and psychotherapist Walt Odets suggests, key to lasting relationships. Odets describes how:

> Gay teenagers often cannot talk to others about their lives and feelings, and they are often actively prevented from engaging in the exploration of relation-ships that is a natural and supported element of heterosexual adolescence. Gay boys are left with surreptitious sex that must be assiduously segregated from their social lives, and they too often experience that sex with shame

and guilt. Because sex is the only 'relationship' they have been permitted to know, the shame and guilt are easily transferred later to potentially fuller, adult relationships. Integration of sex and relationships remains difficult, and a deficit of intimacy is one consequence.[36]

Engaging in large amounts of casual sex with partners whom you don't get to know very well is not a promising way out of this dilemma. As Odets puts it:

men seeking others are usually seeking more than the release of young male libido: they are seeking emotional connection to others and, in those connections, discovery of themselves – and possibly, enduring relationships. Purely objectified sex is not a probable path to such objectives.[37]

Gay men may be particularly vulnerable in this regard, but the kind of highly de-regulated sexual market that gay men have created for themselves would present real challenges to anyone. To recall G.K. Chesterton's requirement that someone proposing the removal of a gate should first show that they understand the function the gate is serving, many of the rules that limited sexual autonomy in the pre-sexual revolution era were too restrictive. But that does not mean that they served no function at all. The fact that fairly restrictive laws and social norms were in place for centuries in the West and, indeed, that sexual behaviour has been regulated significantly by every known human society should at least make people question whether humans are well adapted to managing their sexual appetites by dint of their self-discipline alone. Indeed, as Jeffrey Weeks notes, the fact that the removal of autonomy restricting laws and norms was followed by a notable increase in marriage counselling organizations and various kinds of therapists seeking to help people with their relationships 'indicates the difficulties of relying on ourselves alone'.[38]

For gay men in the West, the combination of a large pool of willing sexual partners and very few legal or social constraints on engaging in casual sex can lead to the kind of debilitating overload of choice that the psychologist of choice Barry Schwartz worries about. At a certain point, he argues, we can have so much choice that 'choice no longer liberates but debilitates'.[39] In addition, he notes that choosing takes a degree of mental effort and that, while freedom to choose is essential, some forms of choice 'may contribute little or nothing to the kind of freedom that counts. Indeed [they] may impair freedom by taking time and energy we'd be better off devoting to other matters.'[40]

What consenting adults get up to among themselves is their business and, to my mind, perfectly moral as long as they don't hurt others. Like Larry Kramer, my worry is unhappiness, not immorality (though I hope I am expressing it in less harsh terms than he did). I do not share the faith of libertarian economists that the invisible hand of the market will allow a deregulated economy to achieve the best outcomes. Similarly, I think that the sex-positive belief that if we can just remove as many legal and social constraints on sexual choice as possible some kind of invisible hand will guide us to the sexual behaviours that work best for us is unfounded. As Patrick Deneen has noted, the modern idea of freedom as the freedom to indulge your desires stands in contrast to the classical idea in which mastering one's own desires rather than being enslaved by them was regarded as an important part of becoming free.[41]

Now Deneen, who supports the idea of an authoritarian, socially conservative political system, disregards the other dimension necessary for freedom: the need for private autonomy and for the state to avoid coercing individuals to live as the majority tells them to. But, sex-positive libertarians are guilty of the same lack of balance. A lack of rules is not enough for individual flourishing. The reality is that for a significant section of the gay male population the almost unlimited freedom gay male sexual culture has given them is not helping them to live the kind of lives they want to live. On the contrary it can produce a form of enslavement where, shorn of the (previously unduly restrictive) social, legal and cultural norms that for centuries channelled human sexual impulses, they find themselves unable to stop their in-the-moment desires getting in the way of their longer-term and more important goals.

Furthermore, the abundance of sexual choice and frequent giving in to in-the-moment desires have a compulsive, self-sustaining quality. It is not just that, as Schwartz[42] suggests, having an array of options makes it harder for people to choose any one option. The 'hedonic treadmill',[43] that is, the tendency of humans to get decreasing amounts of pleasure and stimulation from experiences the more we have them, leads, as

Schwartz notes, to the pursuit of ever greater novelty and more intense stimulation. For too many gay men the result is plenty of sex that is desired in the moment but which ends up being, as Michael Joseph Gross termed it, 'a failure of hope' or, as Andrew Holleran put it, sex engaged in in 'the hope of love, and getting farther and farther away from any chance of it'.[44] The undiscerning sex-positivity of gay male sexual culture is a hindrance, not a help, in the construction of the kind of lives that most of us want in the long term.

8

The Truth Will Set You Free? The Challenges of Honesty in a Hostile World

Perhaps you think that the physical and emotional costs I have outlined are overblown or that the freedom and pleasure facilitated by the strength of the anything goes element of gay male sexual culture make those costs worth bearing. But, even if this is the case, there is a further problem. As a tiny minority, the freedom of gay people depends on the tolerance of the straight majority. The strength of the libertine element of gay male sexual culture places that culture at the outer boundaries of the territory conquered by that revolution. With the atmosphere turning against the broader sexual revolution, this represents a significant risk.

Our own actions show that we know this. 'The truth will set you free' is an appealing motto that should be particularly appropriate for a movement that has stressed the need for people to come out and be honest about themselves and their identity. But both the gay rights movement, and gay men more generally, have shown a notable fear that when it comes to our sexual culture, the truth getting out may pose a risk to our freedom. There has been a repeated tendency to seek to downplay, or to avoid straight people knowing too much about, the strength of the libertine element of gay male sexual culture and a related tendency to obfuscation when issues related to that libertinism come to public attention.

Campaigners have always known that anything-goes sexual culture is not a vote-winner. Despite high levels of non-monogamy in gay male couples,[1] ads promoting the legalization of same-sex marriage, for example, generally did not tend to spotlight the happy gay couples in which each partner has no issue with the other going to a bath house for casual sex from time to time, or the contented and caring partnership of two leathermen who like to invite a third person into their bedroom every now and again. Instead, they usually focused on what appeared to be monogamous couples whose relationships appeared as close to the straight norm as possible. This was of course frustrating for more radical gays, who have long complained of a tendency to valorize those gay people who appear closer to straight norms and deprecate those who are more 'queer'.[2] It was no doubt also annoying to conservative opponents of gay marriage, who felt voters were being misled.

Whether or not they were right to be annoyed, the conscious attempt to highlight more conservative and tradition-adjacent forms of gay relationships reflected two fundamental realities. The first is that gays and lesbians are a tiny minority, so winning equal rights required them to convince straight voters to back their cause. The second is that convincing straight voters to back gay marriage meant reassuring them that gay sexual mores were not so wildly different from straight ones that allowing gay weddings would risk big changes being made to the institution of marriage. Political campaigns always involve spinning and not all straight marriages follow traditional norms, so there was nothing wrong in running the campaign this way. But what this does highlight is that campaigners were aware that highlighting how gay male sexual norms are often quite different from straight norms would tend to undermine support among straight people for equal legal and social status for gay relationships.

This evasive tendency goes beyond political campaigning. Ironically, given the constant invocation of 'pride' in the gay rights movement, the tension between the moderate political goals of the gay rights movement and the reality of gay male sexual culture has led to a strange dissonance. Gay people increasingly shared in mainstream social institutions with straight people, while often wanting to hide from those people the distinct nature of much of male gay social behaviour. As Michael Joseph Gross commented in relation to the gay online dating and hook-up site *Manhunt*: 'We don't tell straight people about *Manhunt*. We don't even tell them it exists. And, even when we do, we usually don't tell them what it's really like.'[3] In a similar vein, the Irish–Iraqi activist and YouTuber Riyadh Khalaf did a comedy video in which he got his mother to read out the (graphic) messages he received on *Grindr*, the whole point of which was that it was embarrassing to have a straight outsider, let alone your mother, lifting the lid and peering into this aspect of gay male culture.

The Temptations of Obfuscation and 'Iceberg Opinions'

There has also been a notable degree of obfuscation when some of the problems with gay male sexual culture come to public attention. These attempts at obfuscation can take a number of forms. One is by making statements that are technically true but misleading. The mpox outbreak, as previously discussed, is a case in point. When fears around the outbreak were peaking in the summer of 2022, there were numerous complaints from gay organizations about 'sensationalist media coverage'. This coverage, they argued, wrongly linked what they usually called the 'LGBTQ+ community' to the outbreak. This was accompanied by assertions that 'anyone can pass on this disease'.[4]

The (gay) writer on health issues Benjamin Ryan was actually strongly attacked by a number of LGBTQ activists for reporting honestly on the fact that sex between men was what was driving the outbreak.[5] While it was technically correct that anyone could pass on the disease, no amount of obfuscation could conceal the fact mpox was overwhelmingly (98% of cases) being caught and transmitted by gay men and that its spread was being driven by the notably higher than average tendency of gay men to engage in multiple partner casual sexual encounters. Trying to conceal this reality only damaged the credibility of gay organizations as well as fuelling a sense that gay men had something to hide.

A related kind of obfuscation is a rhetorical form of the game 'charades' where the attention of the listener is redirected away from the truth or falsity of a statement to the issue of whether what was said 'looks like' or 'sounds like' some other statement which is agreed to be bad. Taking again the mpox outbreak, media coverage worried that suggestions that gay men curtail their sexual activity until vaccination took place sounded 'uncomfortably similar to conservative attacks on gay culture'[6] or echoed 'the homophobic trope that gay men are vectors of disease'.[7]

Underlying this idea of a 'trope' is that what the speaker actually says represents what I would call an 'iceberg opinion'. By that I mean that, just as with an iceberg only a small portion is visible above the water, in these cases what the speaker has actually said is presumed to be only the acknowledged part of a hidden, much broader and less acceptable set of opinions. The reasoning goes something like this: you may only have said that you are worried about the challenges posed by the high average numbers of sexual partners reported by gay men, but this is just a cover for your wider hostility to gay people. This line of reasoning allows the redirection of attention away from the merits of issue the speaker has raised towards the assumed (sometimes correctly, but sometimes incorrectly) bad faith of that speaker.

This kind of 'shoot the messenger' obfuscation is not exclusive to gays and lesbians. It is shared by advocates of other minorities who feel vulnerable and who are concerned that open discussion of the unvarnished truth might compromise their wider effort to combat discrimination. Discussions around the changing role of Islam in Europe have shown a related tendency. In this case, many who have sincere and reasonable worries about increases in prejudice against European Muslims or against migrants (a large proportion of immigrants to Europe are Muslim) engage in similar distraction tactics. They argue that concerns about the tensions between gay rights and feminism and the predominant beliefs around gender and sexuality among Muslims represent Islamophobic 'tropes' or merely stand in for broader racist or anti-migrant sentiments.[8]

The problem is that those who discuss illiberal attitudes to sexuality among European Muslims or who point to high levels of sexually transmitted disease among gay men often *are* motivated by more general hostility. But this is not always the case and, in any event, finding out whether the information a messenger brings is true is more important than working out whether the messenger is a bad person who is secretly delighted to be the bearer of bad news. But what is most revealing about the desire to obfuscate and to distract is how it shows a worry deep down about the political weakness of your arguments. By seeking to redirect focus and avoid discussion of the issues raised, you are showing that you are concerned that, if the true facts were known, public opinion on those issues might take a turn for the worse.

For gay men, in the end, this obfuscation comes from the fact that many of us are either a little embarrassed about elements of gay male sexual culture or are concerned that greater public knowledge of the full reality of that sexual culture might fuel homophobia and undermine support for gay rights. The fact that allegations of gay promiscuity are regarded as a bigoted calumny while gay rights orthodoxy is also sex-positive and therefore holds that such promiscuity is no bad thing shows a degree of dissonance.

The position that there is nothing inherently morally wrong with promiscuity is in my view correct. But the fact that high levels of casual sex are not morally wrong does not mean that they are ideal or that this reality is not damaging to the gay rights movement in political terms. This is why there is that unease and embarrassment and why open discussion of a part of the sexual culture of gay men provokes an attitude described as 'Don't say it in front of the straights' by the journalist Owen Jones during the mpox outbreak.[9] On some level, many gay men realize that it might be better that the straight majority, on whose goodwill gays, as a small minority, will always depend, remain ignorant about what gay male sexual culture is actually like.

Perhaps this obfuscation and distraction is aimed as much at ourselves as at that straight majority. It is much more comfortable to avoid thinking about the potential issues posed by gay male sexual culture by focusing instead on the effect of the hostility of others (past and present) as the source of all of gay people's ills. Viewing things this way allows us to focus on the flaws of others and to double down on our approach to date, which insists that the removal of prejudice and enhancement of sexual freedom represent the solution to the problems that gay people face.

This also allows us to avoid some emotionally tricky realities. A world in which we recognize that the freedom for which we have had to fight so hard may have some downsides is one that raises all kinds of difficult questions politically and personally. It suggests that some of the problem is internal and lies in our own behaviour. It also implies that the goals pursued by gay rights activists, such as tackling prejudice and enhancing freedom, may be insufficient to solve some of the problems we face. Acknowledging downsides to freedom can feel risky, given that gay people in much of the world are struggling to get any freedom at all. But, painful though it may be and dangerous though it may feel, facing reality is usually the better option. If you have an urgent desire that others not see the overall nature of the sexual culture of your group, might that not be a hint that you should not rule out the possibility that that sexual culture might benefit from some change?

Honesty and Self-Criticism in a Hostile World

In a purely rational world, gay men would be able to think in a relaxed and dispassionate way about what kind of changes to their sexual culture might be beneficial. But to expect them to be able easily to do so is not realistic. This is not just a matter of the usual problem of confirmation bias (tendency to seek out and give extra weight to arguments that confirm our pre-existing beliefs). It is also because sex is a sensitive point for everyone and, even in the most liberal countries of the West, most gay men will have grown up in a society where equal treatment and respect for gay people was absolutely not the norm.

This experience will inevitably have left psychological scars. If you were bullied because of and felt shame about your sexuality when growing up, it can be hard, even decades later, not to bristle at any hint of criticism or to see any questioning or suggestion that things should change as an attack. The fact that homosexuality was so recently stigmatized in the West means it can be extremely difficult not to adopt a defensive approach that considers any suggestion that gay sexual culture might need to change as either an attack by your enemies or unconscionable cooperation with your enemies by your comrades.

It is a particularly big ask to expect people to be open and self-critical when they know that there are large numbers of people who wish them ill and who are only too keen to jump on any admissions of weakness. Worries about the use enemies might make of admissions of doubts about the current model are not irrational or paranoid. The reality is that gays and lesbians do have enemies, and lots of them. Many sexual conservatives now complain about over-reach in the enforcement of anti-discrimination laws, when a baker is sued for refusing to bake a wedding cake for a gay couple, or a registrar is disciplined for refusing to register a gay marriage. 'Why can't you live and let live?' is always the cry.

I am all in favour of live and let live and have wondered about the wisdom of some of the discrimination cases taken. But, for all of their invocations of freedom and tolerance, many social conservatives show little inclination towards living and letting live when the shoe is on the other foot and it is gays and lesbians who are looking for a little live and let live. The Catholic Church is a very recent convert in this regard. In Ireland the Church complains, sometimes with some reason, about the potentially illiberal nature of the pro-gay consensus in Ireland in 2025 but it opposed decriminalization of sex between men as late as the 1990s.[10] Similarly, in Belize in 2011 the Catholic Church, along with a number of evangelical churches, intervened in litigation to seek to uphold the criminalization of gay sex.[11] Catholic bishops in Africa have often been supportive of laws making gay sex a crime, though it should be noted that in 2023 Pope Francis called for an end to criminalization, describing such laws as 'unjust' and emphasizing that there was a distinction between what is a sin and what ought to be criminal.[12]

The inappropriately named 'Alliance to Defend Freedom' is an American NGO, which describes its mission as advocating 'for the right of people to freely live out their faith'. But it has shown no reciprocal desire to respect the freedom of others, particularly that of gay people. In 2003 when the issue of the criminalization of private, consensual gay sex was before the US Supreme Court the Alliance actively intervened and submitted a brief to the Court, arguing in favour of a state power to punish gay adults for their private sexual conduct.[13] Ten years later the Alliance was lauding the decision of India's Supreme Court to uphold the constitutionality of the criminalization of gay sex. 'Societies that uphold natural law are enduring societies, and protecting laws that best allow a society to prosper is the best protection of human dignity' proclaimed the Alliance's Chief Counsel Benjamin Bull. 'The India [sic] Supreme Court', he continued, 'has ruled in the interest of the health of its society rather than the interests of activist groups.'[14]

Similarly, the Muslim Council of Britain, also claims to support mutual respect and tolerance and to some degree adopts live-and-let-live approaches in the UK. But the Deobandi movement, with which the Council is closely associated,[15] and which runs more mosques in the UK than any other group, enthusiastically supports the criminalization of homosexuality (and persecution of apostates from Islam) in South Asia and elsewhere.[16] Live and let live and mutual tolerance apply, it would seem, only where those of your views are in the minority.

Indeed, it is all too easy to forget that the revolution in gay rights in the West is not a worldwide phenomenon. Persecution of gay people, either through outright criminalization or through heavy societal discrimination, remains the norm in most of Africa, Asia and the Middle East.[17] There is a reason that psychotherapists and counsellors place such an emphasis on providing a supportive and non-judgemental atmosphere for their patients. People are much more likely to ask themselves challenging questions, to be willing to see how their behaviour might sometimes not be ideal and to question cherished but possibly damaging beliefs if they don't feel that they are being judged or attacked.

With gay people being treated as outcasts and criminals in half the world, gay men are not in the kind of a supportive and non-judgemental environment that is conducive to searching self-examination. The temptation to deny that there are any negative aspects to the form of gay liberation achieved in the West in case doing so gives ammunition to those seeking to maintain or revive persecution of gay people elsewhere is only to be expected.

Small Lies, Big Truths and Big Lies

All of these factors may make an approach based on distraction and dissembling very tempting. But giving in to this temptation will ultimately be self-defeating. The great historian of post-war Europe Tony Judt was fascinated by occasions when intelligent people, who usually saw themselves as acting from the best of motives, nevertheless ended up trying to deny reality and making assertions that they knew were not true. For him, occasions like the Dreyfus Affair, when key figures in the French Army and their supporters continued to maintain that Alfred Dreyfus (a Jewish officer convicted in the 1890s of selling military secrets) was guilty long after it was clear that he was innocent, can be explained by the idea of 'higher truths'. Defenders of Dreyfus, like the writer Émile Zola, were telling the truth, that is, highlighting the facts that showed that Dreyfus had not committed the offences of which he had been accused. But those opposed to Dreyfus saw themselves as defending a 'higher truth'; that is, as Judt put it, the higher truth that France must come first and it was not in the national interest for the army to be discredited.

Similarly, when numerous well-meaning left-wing intellectuals in Western Europe denied or deliberately ignored the atrocities of the KGB and the gulag, they were telling what they saw as a small lie about the oppressive nature of the communist regime in the USSR that was excused by a bigger or 'higher truth' that, in the end, the downtrodden of the world would benefit from a communist revolution. The problem is that humans' ability to identify big truths in the abstract is not very good.

Small lies add up. As those who ignored the reality of the Soviet Union found out by 1989, when you tell what you think are little white lies to conceal what you regard as small truths that are inconsistent with the big truth you want to protect, you often end up defending a big lie and discrediting the positive elements of your agenda. What, after all, is a big truth other than the accumulation of many small truths? The best way to 'live in truth', to use the term of the famous Czech dissident Václav Havel, is to be faithful to a series of small truths or, as Tony Judt put it: 'the point is to tell it as it is, rather than to find out what the higher truth is and then adhere to it'.[18]

Ignoring, denying or explaining away inconvenient instances where the gay revolution has had downsides will undermine the defence of the gains of that revolution in the long run. The famous American liberal politician Daniel Patrick Moynihan put it memorably when he discussed why it was that liberal and left-wing politics lost out so badly to Ronald Reagan's Republicans in the 1980s. Moynihan's view was that 'The liberal project began to fail when it began to lie.'[19] By this, Moynihan meant that by denying the existence of downsides of the liberalizing reforms of the 1960s and 1970s, liberals had lost credibility with voters and opened the door to the success of conservatives who had opposed this liberalization project in its entirety.

It is certainly tempting to think that the 'big truth' that gay people deserve to live with dignity and freedom excuses the 'small lie' that denies the existence of any troubling aspects to liberated gay life. But the truth is that such an approach will ultimately be self-defeating. We are unlikely to be able to conceal the nature of gay male sexual culture from the straight majority forever. Not all questioning of elements of gay male sexual culture represents an 'iceberg' opinion that hides a wider hostility to homosexuality and gay people. The gay rights revolution is a work in progress. Admitting to ourselves that it needs refinement need not be discrediting of the whole enterprise. Indeed, it is the only way. It will be difficult to be effective defenders of gay freedom if we remain embarrassed for straight people to know what the sexual culture produced by that freedom is actually like.

Like it or not, gay people, as a small minority, will always be dependent on the goodwill and tolerance of the straight majority. A swing against some elements of the sexual revolution is probably already underway and, even if that is not yet the case, some swing is inevitable at some stage. Such a swing could leave gay people out on a limb. The current model of gay liberation, with its sex positivity and general 'anything goes' attitude to sex, is situated at the outermost edges of that revolution and so will be particularly vulnerable to any restrictive or conservative trends.

Pretending that this is not the case, or attributing homophobic bad faith to anyone who won't pretend not to have noticed troubling features of gay male sexual culture, is not a solution. The idea that the straight majority would not have sufficient interest in what gay men are getting up to to bother curtailing gay freedom is inconsistent with the historical record. For most of the last thousand years gay freedom was inconsistent with the wider moral framework for regulating sexual behaviour in the West and criminalization of male (and less often female) homosexuality was one of the most frequently used ways of dealing with this inconsistency. Indeed, criminalization is currently the preferred method in many areas of the world, most notably a majority of predominantly Muslim countries and a significant number of the largely Christian countries of sub-Saharan Africa.

We need to be realistic about the fact that the libertine nature of gay male sexual culture could become a growing political liability over time, particularly if society overall takes a conservative turn. Will many of our allies come out to fight for our freedom if we insist that doing so requires fighting for *Grindr* and group sex? There are very good reasons to think that the perception that gay rights go hand-in-hand with anything-goes approaches will damage our chances of maintaining political support. Indeed, it is because gay rights are seen as the 'blow that completes the most destructive demolition work of the sexual revolution', as Jonathan Rauch put it, that steps such as gay marriage have triggered such fierce conservative opposition and why LGBT+ issues have been a key force for pushing conservatism in the post-liberal direction it is taking in the US.

This is not to say that *Grindr* or group sex should be banned but that we may well need to find ways of standing over gay freedom that do not involve such a strong commitment to an 'anything goes' ethos. Indeed, the idea that this is not possible, that homosexuality can be tolerated only if a society has virtually no standards at all for sexual behaviour, is one that is homophobic as well as toxic to the long-term political viability of gay freedom. If gay rights are to thrive in a more conservative atmosphere, a version of gay freedom that at least some of those of a more conservative bent can live with may become a necessity.

There will be no more propitious moment than the present for such a movement. Western society is currently about as un-homophobic as it is ever likely to get. The worry that open discussion of the drawbacks of sexual freedom and of the reality of gay male sexual culture may give ammunition to reactionary homophobes is reasonable. But denial and obfuscation won't work in the long term. As things stand, social attitudes towards homosexuality have, at least for the moment, been so transformed that gay people in the West have, for now, room to think and speak honestly about the drawbacks in the current model of gay liberation without having to worry that doing so risks recriminalization. Tolerance of homosexuality has come to be seen as one of the key markers of the progress of Western liberal democracies but this championing of gay rights as a fundamental value of Western societies is often driven by other considerations to a great degree and might not last.[20]

It would be much better to have the honest discussion and to take steps to address the problems of the current model of gay liberation now, when public opinion and political, economic and cultural institutions are on board with a range of gay rights that would have shocked the most optimistic campaigner in the 1980s, than to try to do so at a time when gay rights may be under much more political pressure.

9

A Dose of Modesty

The gay movement is therefore faced with two forms of over-reach, which have their origins in the over-confident belief that sexual freedom is an unqualified good that is destined to progress over time. Both reflect the over-confidence of the wider liberal project that sees liberal freedoms as unalloyed positives that have history on their side. A dose of modesty is in order. A durable form of gay freedom would be both modest in its political goals and in its recognition of the downsides of our movement. In political terms, the gay rights movement needs to abandon the idea that it is part of a wider process in which challenges to ever-wider sets of norms and institutions are regarded as an element of historically inevitable progress. In social terms, gay male sexual culture needs to step away from the idea that the removal of constraints and choice in sexual matters is an unqualified good and that maximization of freedom and choice is always beneficial.

The political solution is in some ways the easier one. The gay rights movement, like liberal movements more broadly, should recognize that, just as its past success was not pre-ordained, its continued success is not guaranteed. Given that the level of freedom and recognition that gay people have won in recent decades in the West is unprecedented, just holding on to what we have achieved would be a very good result. Recognizing that the cause of gay freedom is not being cheered on by history should therefore lead to greater caution than has been the case to date.

This means thinking more carefully about how to maximize our allies and minimize our enemies. The current approach, which links the gay rights movement to an ever-expanding list of other causes, is one which does the opposite. Instead of reassuring moderates that our needs can be accommodated without much else changing, the gay rights movement has been insisting that gay rights are part of a much wider package of LGBTQIA+ rights, which requires ongoing and ever-wider change to all established structures. The symbol '+' is particularly damaging in this regard, as it suggests that the movement aims at changes so open-ended that it requires changes to accommodate concepts and identities that have not yet achieved linguistic categorization.

With the broader atmosphere turning against sexual revolution, which allowed gay rights to advance, this is, to put it mildly, a risky approach. When the challenges to gay freedom come to be fought, gay rights activists need to ensure that the fighting is done on territory that is favourable to their side. If they fall into the trap of allowing support for gay rights to be portrayed as also requiring wider hostility to any traditional norms around sex, gender and the family the chances of success will be diminished. If gay organizations insist that 'LGBTQ+' rights are a package deal and that they will consider you homophobic if you do not support a wide range of other controversial positions, including the participation of biological males in women's sport, support for medical interventions for minors who feel they may be trans, or the active celebration of kinks such as furries (people with a sexual interest in anthropomorphic animals), then many people will decide they are indeed homophobic, and will not rally to the gay cause on other issues.

Social conservatives know this very well, which is why the 2024 Trump campaign consistently highlighted some of these very issues at rallies, as well as in an expensive ad campaign in swing states. These ads contributed significantly to shifting the race in Trump's favour.[1] You may agree or disagree that there are tensions between gay rights and some of the claims made by trans rights campaigners. But, in the light of the deteriorating political climate, the approach adopted by most gay rights organizations until the mid 2010s, namely, that including trans issues within the scope of the gay rights movement was too risky, looks more appropriate than one that insists that the movement can afford to widen its goals. Indeed, doing so would simply mirror the approach sometimes adopted by trans rights campaigners on occasions when linking their claims to gay rights claims would have damaged their cause.[2] Indeed, given cratering levels of support for trans-rights in recent polls, trans rights activists should themselves question whether the tactics they have pursued and the merging of their cause into a wider LGBTQ+ campaign have served their interests.

Rather than thinking of the gay rights movement as part of a wider movement that questions and challenges an ever-widening range of norms around sex, gender and family, it should be seen as a movement that seeks to prevent people from being punished or discriminated against because they are attracted to their own sex, and nothing more. This should be the *only* norm whose acceptance is required to be considered a supporter of gay rights. The gay rights movement should be a movement for the class of people who are same-sex attracted, not a movement for those seeking to dismantle all traditional norms around sex.

This is, of course, controversial. As far back as 1968, the sociologist and gay rights activist Mary McIntosh was critical of approaches that viewed homosexuality in this way because they allowed gay people to be gay 'without rejecting the norms of society'.[3] But it is increasingly clear that those approaches are exactly what the gay rights movement needs. In an era where it is clear that conservative swings in society are, to say the least, a distinct possibility, we need a version of gay rights that can survive in an atmosphere where the norms of society are neither being dismantled nor becoming ever more permissive.

Even if many gay people will inevitably have sympathy with some or all of the arguments made by those campaigning for trans rights, or for radical changes in other areas, this does not mean that those causes are one and the same. The profusion of letters and symbols that has transformed the gay rights movement into the LGBTQIA+ movement must be reversed. The fact that some people may not feel that the terms gay, lesbian or bisexual fully represent their individual identity is just an inevitable side effect of the imperfect nature of language. It does not mean that endless letters should be added to reflect nuances of individual identity. The effect of doing this is to make the movement appear alienatingly narcissistic in its obsession with minor variations in identity. For those whose identity is such that they don't identify with the categories of lesbian, gay or bisexual at all, then questioning whether the gay rights movement is the correct vehicle for them to assert their rights, rather than adding a new letter, is the better approach.

We must also be careful to resist the temptation constantly to push the boundaries and to slide from seeking tolerance to seeking active endorsement. Gay people need the right to live their lives. They do not need to be praised for doing so. The fact that drag, for example, is regarded as a legitimate (usually adult-themed) form of entertainment should be enough. We don't need to then go further and push for it to be in schools or children's libraries. Having the right not to be discriminated against at work for being gay does not mean that employers need to actively celebrate gay identities. Pushing the boundaries and requiring more and more active endorsement not only aggravates those who might otherwise be happy to have a 'live-and-let-live' attitude towards homosexuality, it is also psychologically unhealthy in that it departs from Gloria Gaynor's wise advice to be what you are without looking for praise or for pity.

It may be gratifying for those who grew up in an atmosphere where even the mention of homosexuality was avoided to see workplaces festooned with rainbow flags and pro-gay slogans. Having experienced oppression, it may also be satisfying to see the tables turned and for businesses to shun anti-gay customers or HR departments to investigate those expressing anti-gay views. In the US, the temptation to respond to a loss of power in the political arena by wielding power in areas, such as the corporate arena, where you might still have it will be particularly strong. Giving in to this temptation would be short sighted. That corporate power is unlikely to last. Although there are many people sincerely committed to gay rights working for them, the commitment of corporations, law firms, banks and the like to the gay cause is skin deep. This is not just because corporations exist primarily to make money, though that is the case. It also because, as pro-Trump tech investor Marc Andreessen has said,[4] those at the upper echelons of corporate life are very keen to be thought of as good people by their elite peers. Corporate leaders are rarely renegades, and certainly not renegades in ways that would get in the way of making money.

There is a reason that the law firm whose firing of a young gay lawyer with AIDS in the late 1980s was the inspiration for the film *Philadelphia* was getting top scores on the Stonewall and Human Rights Campaign employer rankings by the 2020s. It was anti-gay when that was both the more prestigious position to take, as well as being the position that avoided ruffling clients' feathers and getting in the way of making money. When changes in public opinion had shifted this calculus, law firms, banks and others all changed too.[5] I am sure that those who drove pro-gay changes in these firms were not being cynical. Their desire to bring about what they saw as positive change was almost certainly sincere. But, because most people go with the flow, their colleagues were only convinced to go along with these changes because of shifts in attitudes to homosexuality, particularly among the elite. We would be kidding ourselves if we were to think that law firms like Baker McKenzie or banks like Goldman Sachs, which were not there for gay people in the bad old days, will stand by us if the social and political atmosphere changes.

Indeed, when the first draft of this book was first being written, back in early 2023, the prediction of a corporate volte-face on gay (and other DEI) issues was just that, a prediction. But things have shifted with astonishing speed. In the autumn of 2024, even before Donald Trump had won back the White House, Toyota announced it would no longer sponsor pride events, while Ford announced it was stepping back from participating in the Human Rights Campaign's LGBTQ+ index.[6] Following Trump's victory, this trickle became a flood, as what the writer Ian Leslie termed 'the Great Vibe Shift' in corporate American took place.

As Leslie notes, this shift has followed the patterns described by Timur Kuran. 'Preference falsification', which had discouraged dissent from pro-DEI (including pro-gay) norms, when those norms appeared to be universally held by the elite, has been replaced by a 'preference cascade', in which previously suppressed opposition to these policies suddenly became public. Companies who had insisted that their commitment to DEI represented their deepest values have dispensed with these deep values with head-spinning speed. Meta, Amazon, McDonalds, Walmart, Target, Harley Davidson and others, all have announced that they are scaling back or abolishing their DEI programmes, with some going so far as donating to Trump's inauguration fund to show their loyalty to the new regime.[7] Google and Meta have also announced that they are stepping back as sponsors of Sydney's Gay and Lesbian Mardi Gras celebrations.[8]

The shamelessness of the speed of the about turn on these issues is quite something. All the protestations that pro-gay and other DEI ventures were about the deepest values of these companies were junked as soon as being pro-LGBTQ+ no longer looked like the path to money and prestige. But, even if corporations were not so fickle, it would still have been a mistake for the gay rights movement to rely on them as a means to achieve its goals. The movement should never have sought to have corporate life marked by pride flags, events that actively celebrate homosexuality, semi-mandatory 'ally' groups and ideologically driven EDI training that defines holding pro-gay beliefs as a matter of professional competence. This always risked turning into an alienating requirement of adherence to an orthodoxy that was likely to be as short lived as it was illiberal. The shoe has only been on the pro-gay foot for a small number of years. The potential backlash may be so much worse than the over-reach that preceded it. If gay people undermine the ideas of free speech and private autonomy we may regret it if and when, as may well already be happening, the shoe goes back to the anti-gay foot on which it spent many centuries and those principles become our only defence.

These changes will be tough to pull off. It is hard to wean yourself off the very flattering and reassuring idea that your movement is part of an 'arc of history that bends towards justice'. It may also be emotionally difficult for those gay rights campaigners who share sympathy with wider causes to step back from the exciting project of changing the whole world and to focus on doing what is necessary to protect gay rights alone. But, difficult as this may be, it will probably be easier than achieving the social change required. Shifting gay male sexual culture away from the belief that more choice and more freedom in sexual matters are always good things cannot draw on many of the resources that a comparable project among straight people could use.

The 'asymmetries' between men and women in relation to interest in casual sex that Louise Perry highlights are absent from the sexual world of gay men. Other possible sources of restraint on the male libido are also more difficult for gay people to access. For straight people, religious norms or reversion to more traditional notions of marriage could perform this function. But, given the persistent hostility of most major religions to homosexuality, religion is unlikely to be able to act as a major resource for a sexual culture that questions short-term desires and nurtures long-term gay relationships. While gay marriage exists, it is so recent that, unlike straight marriage, it has no significant history of playing the role as the sole forum for legitimate sexual activity. A young straight person saving themselves for marriage would be seen as an oddity, though with young straight people becoming notably cooler on casual sex this could change. However, a gay man saving himself for marriage would be regarded as unhinged, something that is unlikely to change any time soon.

It is, to say the least, unrealistic to imagine that many gay men will end up prayerfully walking down the aisle in white tuxedos to symbolize their virgin status. But that doesn't mean that the only other option is a 'whenever and whatever you feel like doing, go ahead!' approach that encourages people not to resist in the moment sexual urges for casual sex and which rejects the notion that a degree of sexual frustration and unmet desire is a necessary element of a balanced sex life. Religion may struggle to act as a direct source of moderation of sexual norms. But, as Tom Holland has pointed out, religious sensibilities and norms can have a vigorous secular after-life in which they guide behaviour and intuitions in ways that are often invisible to non-believers.[9] Christian teachings such as those that see humans as flawed creatures with desires that may lead them astray reflect fundamental instincts about human nature. These norms have been so deeply woven into Western culture that their insights may be of assistance even to those of other faiths or those uninterested in or hostile to organized religion. This could help gay men recognize some of the unhelpful dynamics in their current sexual culture.

Such recognition requires listening to the very longstanding worries that come out in gay literature, surveys of gay men's lives and statistics on sexual and mental health. It also involves acknowledging the gap between the numbers of gay men who express a desire to be in long-term monogamous or near-monogamous relationships and the number who actually are in such relationships. All of these speak to the reality that, while the freedom we have won is wonderful and a net positive overall, it comes with drawbacks that need to be managed. Restrictions on sexual freedom were not all irrational impediments to human flourishing. Every society in the world has needed rules and guardrails to help us manage our chaotic sexual desires. Contemporary gay men are not exceptions to this need. Attempting to remove all, or almost all, constraining norms and relying on self-discipline alone has not worked. There is a tension between short-term desires and long-term plans that an ethic that encourages people to act on their desires does not help.

Some frustrated sexual desire should be seen as a necessary element of a balanced sex life. The desire for sex, like the desire for food, is, after all, a biologically driven and recurring desire. Being a bit indulgent and gorging yourself on a tasty fattening meal from time to time is fine. Gorging yourself several times a week is unlikely to definitively satisfy your desire for food. It is more likely to lead to the creation of ongoing cravings for unhealthy types and amounts of food. Similarly, an approach that encourages people to be led by and not to resist their in-the-moment sexual desires is not likely to lead to 'getting it out of your system' but to a self-sustaining habit that can impede your desire to move beyond casual encounters.

Current norms make it very hard for men to move beyond the Saint Augustine stage of asking God to make him chaste 'but not yet'. In the 1970s, gay 'clones' interviewed by the anthropologist Martin Levine complained that they were tired of casual sex and wanted a boyfriend, yet still found themselves having one-night stands.[10] Half a century later, the gay dating apps of the 2020s are full of profiles whose authors declare themselves sick of hookups and keen to date, who all somehow seem to end up proposing casual encounters to those they contact.

What we desire in the moment may, for gay men as much as for everyone else, take us further from, not closer to, where we want to go in the long term. The sexual ethic predominant among gay men risks depriving them of the mental tools they need to counteract a sexual short-termism ('I am only hooking up tonight, my real plan is a boyfriend') that can undermine more important goals. While a quick casual encounter can bring pleasure and can temporarily ease the sting of loneliness, it can also deprive you of the energy to fully pursue the kind of relationship that would relieve that loneliness more permanently. I know a number of men who say they want a long-term relationship but who also confess that because they find it so easy to meet men online for casual encounters, they can't muster the enthusiasm to go through all of the travel, hassle and awkward conversation of a first date, nor indeed to face the let-down when, as will be the case with most first dates, it doesn't go anywhere.

Recognizing the usefulness of at least some sexual frustration also involves taking a step away from the idea that sex is 'just sex' and accepting that it is a potentially chaotic and powerful force. This approach involves breaking with a key tenet of the sex-positive approach by recognizing that sex cannot be, to return to Aaron Sibarium's term, fully 'disenchanted'.[11] Despite some sex-positive rhetoric, no one really believes that sex is trivial. Even those who are highly sex-positive regard rape as a very serious crime. Yet this understanding requires us to accept that being raped is not like being forced to play tennis with someone. That is only possible if we accept that there is something special that distinguishes sex from other activities.

Similarly, while there are arguments either way as to whether legalizing prostitution would be beneficial or not to those who sell sex, the idea that sex can just be work like other forms of work isn't really believed by anyone either. Take for example, the scandal that erupted in Ireland in 2023 when it was revealed that, amid severe shortage of rental accommodation, some landlords were looking to rent out properties on the understanding that the tenants would have sex with them in return.[12] If sex is just a form of work, then this should not have been a problem. After all, most employees are engaging in work partly so that they can pay their rent. But it was rightly recognized that having to have sex with your landlord to keep your tenancy was absolutely not the same as having to work in an office or a pub to do the same.

Sex is too powerful to be a cost-free or risk-free option. There is a contradiction at the heart of the approach of those who, like many gay men in cities like New York and San Francisco in the 1970s, most enthusiastically adopted free love culture: sex was both an intense source of pleasure and focus in their lives but was also, according to the belief system of the free love movement, 'just sex', that is, an activity with no particular significance that could be engaged in without consequence. This is a mirror image of the improbable claim made by advocates of homeopathy that homeopathic treatments can have powerful curative effects but also, being only water, cannot do you any harm. Something cannot be both trivial and intensely positive at the same time.

The same can be said of the free-love approach that sees open relationships as being a liberation from oppressive rules around monogamy. Such relationships typically require rules that are at least as elaborate as those they replaced. In *Michael Tolliver Lives!*, a 2007 book named for its central character, who was the star of Armistead Maupin's famous *Tales of the City* series, Michael finds himself in a marriage in which he and his husband are both allowed to have sex outside their marriage. But this freedom is subject to a number of provisos, such as that they avoid sleeping with mutual acquaintances, never sleep over and never bring men back to their shared house. Michael also finds his husband's regular visits to gay saunas stressful and upsetting.[13]

This chimes with what sex therapist Dr Ian Kerner, who works with non-monogamous couples, told *Glamour* magazine. Such couples, he says, 'are much more anxious around breaches of trust', noting that they can see 'the slightest variation' as betrayal and are 'vigilant about the terms of their agreement'. Some couples, he notes, end up 'like lawyers with 100-page emails back and forth'.[14] Open relationships may or may not provide a degree of additional sexual pleasure that makes all of the negotiation, rules and jealousy management worth it, but they are not evidence that sex can be 'just sex' or that removing rules results in carefree freedom.

The offer made by the no-rules, anything-goes, sex-positive ideology of the sexual revolution to gay men is one that is too good to be true. It appears to offer cost-free maximization of pleasure in an environment free of the constraints of the relative female lack of interest in casual sex. It suggests that you can avoid the frustration of unsatisfied sexual curiosity by pushing your sexual boundaries as far as you like without ending up on a hedonic treadmill. It implies you can avoid the sting of loneliness by having casual sex without compromising your drive for a long-term relationship and promises that you can have all the stability of a monogamous relationship without the frustration of giving up sex with other people.

You don't need to be religious or a traditionalist to recognize that something that sounds too good to be true probably is too good to be true. Gay male sexual culture can and should recognize that trade-offs are an unavoidable part of life. Complete sexual frustration is not good but seeking to satisfy all of your sexual desires is not good either. Some frustration is necessary for a balanced approach to sex. With a quarter of gay men reporting more than thirteen partners per annum and a mismatch between the number of gay men who say they want to be in a relationship and the number who are in one, we are not getting the balance right. Less can be more.

Limits and Discretion and the Value of (Mild) Hypocrisy

Although adapting 'anything goes' in the direction of 'less can be more' sounds simple, it is unlikely to be that way in practice. Even if gay men can recognize the unhelpful dynamics in their sexual culture and step away from sex positivity this will not change the reality that, without the restraining influence of women, gay men will always be, on average, somewhat more tempted to have casual sex than women. They will also be more likely to be able to find a partner who is similarly interested in a no-strings encounter than straight men. Gay men are therefore likely to continue to have more casual sex than average and gay married men are likely to fail to adhere to monogamy more often than is the case in straight or lesbian marriages. This means that it might well be necessary to rely on a degree of discretion, even moderate hypocrisy, to make this more restrained sexual culture workable.

A sustainably 'less is more' approach among gay men therefore probably also requires a step away from the 'cult of authenticity' described by the philosopher Thomas Nagel: that is, the notion that people should be fully open about their desires and sexual activities. Gay men have a particularly strong tendency to be frank and open about their sex lives. This comes partly from the broader cultural trend, reinforced by social media, in which people make ever more of their personal lives public. Celebrities, for example, are praised for being 'honest' or 'open' when they discuss intimate parts of their lives, while differences between public and private behaviour are seen as dishonest and unhealthy. These cultural trends are strengthened among gay men by the sex-positive ethos of the gay rights movement and the legacy of the closet. In the recent past, both gays and lesbians were forced to be discreet about their sex lives, on pain of being shunned, loss of employment or even criminal punishment. It is understandable, therefore, that their liberation movement stressed the value of openness and authenticity.

However, the fact that ideas of privacy and discretion have often been wielded against gay people does not mean that rejecting them entirely is a good idea. Indeed, full openness can have real disadvantages for the political future of the gay rights movement, for the viability of attempts to shift gay male sexual culture in a 'less is more' direction and, ironically, for sexual freedom. As Nagel argues, being overly open about your sex life involves a failure to see how discretion actually protects true freedom. We all have thoughts and desires that would shock or embarrass others and almost everyone has done or said things, particularly in the heat of a sexually intimate moment, that they would be embarrassed to see on the front page of a newspaper. As he puts it: 'the idea that everything should be out in the open is childish and represents a misunderstanding of the mutually protective function of conventions of restraint'.[15]

If gay men dialled back the degree of frankness they tend to display about their sex lives it wouldn't just weaken the 'anything goes' atmosphere of gay male sexual culture. It would also protect their sex lives and fantasies from what Nagel calls 'the crippling effect of the external gaze', that is the unavoidable self-consciousness and limitation on intimacy that happens when you know that your intimate behaviour may not remain private.[16]

Accepting that casual sex and open relationships might benefit from a little less open acknowledgement, and that our sex life in general ought to be shielded by a bit more voluntary privacy than is currently the case would have significant benefits. It may allow us to get the dual benefit of dampening down the volume of casual sex and lessening the potential political damage to gay rights done by the association of homosexuality with libertinism, while also enhancing true private sexual freedom for everyone.

Is this not pure hypocrisy? The political theorist Judith Shklar, whose childhood as a Jewish girl in Soviet Latvia gave her the appreciation for liberal values and a fear of their fragility, would, I think, disagree. For Shklar, tolerance of moderate hypocrisy is a valuable attribute of a liberal society. As David Runciman writes in his admiring account of Shklar's well-known work *Ordinary Vices*, 'you tolerate things not because you think that they're acceptable, but because even though you think they're unacceptable you have to live with them'.[17] Indeed, as he points out, one of the most valuable elements of liberal modernity is that 'it allowed the space for people [...] to live out something of their lives on the stage and also to hide something away'. In that world with such privacy, there will always be hypocrisy. But discretion and hypocrisy allow us to accept imperfection and to share social space with others in a harmonious way.[18]

The idea is not that gay men should pretend to be monogamous and then fully live out libertine norms in private. They should instead take an approach under which gay male sexual culture sincerely embraces the idea that having a lot of casual sex is not an ideal approach, that some frustrated sexual desire is part of a balanced life and that monogamy (while not ideal for everyone) is in general desirable, while accepting the reality that many of us will occasionally fail to live up to these principles. Although, as a matter of law and morality, we ought to be free to decide to have as much casual sex as we like and to have non-monogamous relationships, that does not mean that there cannot be cultural norms that regard doing so as less than ideal. Having the right to do something does not mean that society must regard that thing as no less ideal than any other option. As David Runciman puts it, there is freedom in an approach under which 'standards are believed in but not always upheld'.[19]

Paying the Price of Admission

Among gay men, current approaches often go beyond the Shklar-style discreet acceptance that monogamy may not always be upheld. Data from the US in the 2010s found that gay male couples in civil unions (gay marriage was yet to be legalized at a federal level) had more encounters outside their relationship than straight or lesbian couples. They also had these encounters much more often with the permission of their partner (only four per cent of married straight men had had sex outside their relationship with their wife's permission; the equivalent figure for gay men was forty per cent).[20] The gay advice columnist Dan Savage has famously advocated a 'monogamish' approach that is, as he put it, 'a more realistic sexual ethic [that] would prize honesty and a little flexibility and, when necessary, forgiveness over absolute monogamy'.[21]

The problem with this openly open approach is two-fold. First, despite high levels of non-monogamy, a number of surveys have shown that polyamory is not what most gay men aspire to. A 2018 survey reported that a large majority (66%) of gay men aspired to having a monogamous relationship, with a further 22 per cent wanting one which was 'mostly monogamous', a figure very close to the ninety per cent desire for monogamy seen in a *Gay Times* survey in the same year.[22] These figures appear to indicate a gap between what gay men aspire to and what they are doing, and therefore that a sexual culture that exerted a greater degree of pressure towards monogamy may be helpful to people in achieving their longer-term goals.

Of course, people may find that the monogamy to which they aspired as singletons is harder in practice than they expected. But, even if openly non-monogamous relationships worked perfectly well for most gay couples, there would still be a problem, at least in relation to those who are married. Gays and lesbians rejected the option of a separate but equal status for their relationships. Given the history of discrimination against homosexuality, separate but equal would inevitably have felt like yet another instance of gay people being assigned a lower social status. But one of the key points of contestation in debates around the legalization of gay marriage was between opponents who argued that the legalization of same-sex marriage would change the meaning of their own (mixed-sex) marriage, and proponents who insisted that legalizing same-sex marriage would only change things for the same-sex couples then excluded from the institution.

I was dismissive of the opponents' arguments at the time but now have to concede that their point was not totally without foundation. Marriage is a social institution and, if gay male couples both insist on their right to participate in the institution of marriage but also flout its traditional requirement of monogamy, then this may indeed affect the degree to which marriage overall is regarded as a monogamous institution.

The tension should not be overstated; after all, not all heterosexual marriages are paragons of fidelity. Indeed, as Jonathan Rauch notes, in the US (as in many countries) even under the old, pre-sexual revolution dispensation, a certain amount of adultery was expected.[23] This has continued into the modern era. A 2001 survey of research in the *Journal of Family Psychology* estimated that between a fifth and a quarter of married people had sex outside their marriage.[24] However, this toleration of a degree of adultery did not undermine the essentially monogamous character of the institution of marriage because any toleration was dependent on a degree of discretion that allowed others not to see what was going on; something that is incompatible with the gay tendency to prizing authenticity and deprecating discretion.

Marriage in the West was monogamous for a very long time before gay couples sought the right to marry. When gay people asked for marriage to be opened up to them, their slogan was that they were looking for 'equal marriage' or, in France, 'mariage pour tous'. Our request was for equal access to an institution we knew to be monogamous. We did not ask for marriage to be changed so that it would include same-sex couples *and* cease to be monogamous (the campaign would likely have failed if we had). Given this, it is not unreasonable to consider that married gay couples who don't want to have or feel incapable of having a monogamous relationship have a duty to maintain, at least publicly, the monogamous nature of marriage by accepting a duty of reasonable discretion so that (perhaps beyond their close friends) their broader social circle of family, colleagues, neighbours and friends (and in some cases, even their spouse) can successfully look the other way. It makes both ethical and political sense to reduce the cost to social conservatives of accommodating gay rights by publicly abiding by the conventions of an institution to which gay men asked to be admitted, even if this means stepping away from the streak in gay male culture that regards norms of discretion about extra-marital liaisons and sex in general as hypocritical and oppressive.

As with most outcomes in liberal societies, monogamy eased by discretion and moderate hypocrisy is a very imperfect outcome. But it is better than the alternatives of possibly unattainable rigid monogamy between men or the damaging insistence that anything that gay men have the right to do must be considered to be the cultural and moral equivalent of the ideal. A duty of discretion would tend to keep a lid on the extent of extra-marital activity. By dampening down the 'anything goes' atmosphere it may also help with the overall goal of moving gay male sexual culture more generally away from the vulnerable outermost boundaries of the freedom won by the sexual revolution, as well as reassuring straight allies that embracing gay equality does not have to mean a broader undermining of established institutions and norms.

Cultural Change Not Coercion

Both the step away from sex positivity and the embrace of discretion (or hypocrisy if that is how you see it) should come about via cultural change, not coercion. Social conservatives like Patrick Deneen are right to highlight how modern notions of freedom underplay the classical idea of freedom as including mastering one's own desires to some degree. But they are wrong to then throw out the equally valuable notion of freedom as the right, ultimately, to choose one's own course in life and not have intimate matters dictated by wider society.

While the state should not seek to legislate for private sexual morality of consenting adults, this does not mean that cultural norms can never distinguish between behaviours that are regarded as conducive to flourishing and those that are not. The aim should be to adapt the kinds of behaviours and attitudes individuals want to cultivate or restrain in themselves and the kinds of things people (individually and collectively) see as desirable or undesirable.

The hope is that individual changes in attitudes among gay men that recognize the limits of the current approach will collectively mould their shared culture and affect what is seen as desirable and prestigious and what is seen as undesirable and low prestige. People would, of course, remain free to dissent from these norms and to live their sex lives in ways that are seen as undesirable or low prestige, but social pressure, maybe even embarrassment, would nudge people towards more restraint and discretion in dealing with their in-the-moment sexual impulses.

This is obviously not a quick fix and is less satisfying than the kind of concrete legal and policy proposals that you can make in other areas. There is no gay parliament that can pass legislation and most of the activist groups that claim to speak for gay people are hopelessly unrepresentative. Although a good liberal would resist coercive measures, there might be some steps that official bodies could take. Materials produced by charities and state bodies to help young people who are coming to terms with their sexuality could be tweaked to be a little less sex positive and to be a little more frank about the health risks of sex with large numbers of people. They might even include advice on the tensions between short-term and long-term goals. But, overall, the main work would have to be done by social norms, through gay men individually stepping back from their historic reluctance to form negative views on any form of consensual sexual activity, their reluctance to say anything that appears to be sex negative, and their reluctance to cultivate in themselves an approach to sex that values restraint and resistance over in-the-moment desires.

Whether such a change in mores would succeed in changing practices is uncertain. Any change would be gradual (or, as with many changes in social mores, slow, then fast once a tipping point has been reached). But, at a certain point, if enough individuals adapt their views, then collective norms will reflect this. Gay social norms would begin to regard sexual over-indulgence in the same way that over-eating or drinking too much alcohol are seen: not necessarily immoral but low-prestige behaviour that is generally regarded as not being good for you.

Proposing changes in social norms rather than technological or policy fixes is, of course, frustratingly vague, and limiting the male libido will always be a big challenge. But vagueness does not mean weakness. After all, it was the millions of individual adaptations in how gay people viewed themselves and in how straight people viewed homosexuality that drove the massive transformation in the fortunes of the gays and lesbians in the West in the past five decades. If society can be persuaded to change its view of gay people in a fundamental way, can gay men not be persuaded to make somewhat less fundamental changes in how they see themselves and their sexual culture?

What this project amounts to is an attempt to enmesh gay male sexuality in the broader web of social norms on which straight people have long relied, to channel their desires in directions that serve their long-term goals. To some extent, this involves changing the story we have told ourselves about gay freedom. That story is a wonderful story of liberation. But the story of a liberation movement should be different from the story of a successful government. Throwing off oppressive rules does not mean that life with no rules will be enjoyable or politically sustainable.

We are all on a constant process of learning and adaptation and we should be open to the idea that the norms that won us our freedom may not be the best ones to live by once that freedom has been achieved. Almost every change involves trades-offs. Our opponents were wrong to oppose the liberation of gay people. But, though it may be hard for us to acknowledge, that does not mean that there were no elements of wisdom in their beliefs. The best victory of all would be to use that wisdom in making our free lives as flourishing and durable as possible.

10

Conclusion: Reform from Revolution

This book arose out of a sense of unease about the sustainability of the unprecedented freedom that gay people have won in most of the West over the past half century or so: the sense that, despite an undoubted run of successes, the gay rights movement is more vulnerable than people think. Rather than representing confidence, the profusion of rainbow flags, lanyards, corporate endorsements and invocations of the 'right side of history' seemed to me to represent a nervy, brittle form of triumphalism that was papering over insecurity.

The most obvious aspect of this insecurity was insecurity about the political future. Despite triumphalist rhetoric of historically inevitable victory, the persecution of gay people has shown no signs of abating in many areas of the world. Worse, even in the heartland of gay rights, the kind of fading of opposition that you would expect if the movement really did have history on its side was not happening.

Across the West, the advance of liberalism that 'end of history' thinking believed permanent had come to a shuddering halt. As part of this wider questioning of the post-1968 worldview, many people, including those widely seen as its beneficiaries, were cooling in their attitudes towards the sexual revolution on which the gay rights revolution depended for its success. At the same time, in the United States the brief apparent reconciliation of much of the right to gay rights was being threatened by the rise of a traditionalist and openly authoritarian wing of the Republican Party. Europe had also seen the rise of anti-gay populism alongside demographic shifts, which placed a question mark over the steady advance of pro-gay sentiments.

The second aspect of the insecurity related to the kind of freedom we had achieved. For all of the invocations of pride and being yourself, there seemed to be a certain desire among gay men to avoid straight people actually seeing what much of the sexual culture of gay men was actually like. There was also a kind of cognitive dissonance in which polling data, mental health statistics and much of the best gay literature all spoke to a sharp difference between what gay men wanted long term and what their sexual culture was encouraging. This seemed to sit uneasily with the continued uncritical embrace of the idea that pushing the boundaries of sexual freedom still further was what gay people needed.

The central argument of this book has been that if gay freedom is to take on a more balanced and sustainable form, it will be necessary for the gay rights movement both to realize how vulnerable its victories are and to break with the libertine, freedom-and-choice-maximizing ethos of the sexual revolution. If gay freedom can be portrayed as being radically inconsistent with moderate conservative approaches to sex, gender and family, its chances of long-term survival will be low.

There is a paradox here. In the bad old days when homosexuality was shocking to most people and gay-specific arguments would have struggled to gain traction, the anything-goes ethos of the sexual revolution provided a shield behind which the gay rights movement could advance. This allowed gay people to live openly for the first time and unleashed a process of desensitization which led to most of the wider public ceasing to regard homosexuality as inherently shocking and immoral. But the sexual revolutionaries' confidence that their cause could continually expand its ambitions and that people can live without any of the guardrails on which humans have relied for centuries to channel their inevitably chaotic sexual desires now looks like over-confidence. This places gay men in a bind. Only anything-goes revolutionary change with what went before could have made us free but sticking with revolutionary change may make our freedom unsustainable.

Some backlash against revolutions is almost inevitable, even when the revolution in question is regarded as largely positive. Just as the fall of communism in Central and Eastern Europe was followed, once the initial burst of freedom had been enjoyed, by a backlash driven by rising awareness of the drawbacks of both capitalism and liberal democracy, the sexual revolution is unlikely to be immune from rising awareness of its costs and nostalgia for elements of the old order.

Mainstream Western gay rights organizations seem oblivious to these dangers and unable to adapt their goals to changing reality. Although they sometimes use apocalyptic language in relation to the threats that gay rights (now repurposed as 'LGBTQ+ rights') face, their actions tell another tale. In contrast to previous cautious approaches, they have shown no recognition that the expansion of their goals may swell the ranks of their enemies, nor any fear that this expansion could cause existing rights to be lost. Similarly, gay men have shown little inclination to adapt their sexual culture, even though it is proving unhelpful both politically and in terms of helping gay men to achieve their longer-term goals.

Things have to change. The costs to gay men both in terms of health, happiness and political vulnerability of the current dispensation are becoming clear. It will be much harder to defend gay freedom success-fully if we cannot come up with a version of that freedom that is acceptable to those who are open to some degree to the need to treat gay people humanely but who retain a belief in monogamous marriage, gender roles and sexual restraint. The current approach also imposes a cost on lesbians. Although lesbian sexual culture does not present the same kind of challenge to traditional norms, given the joint nature of our liberation project, lesbian freedoms will not be spared in an anti-gay backlash.

In this book I have proposed a two-part solution to the bind in which the gay rights movement finds itself. The first part of this solution is to embrace a degree of modesty and to focus on holding on to what we have, not expanding our goals. If the unprecedented freedom gays and lesbians have won is vulnerable, we need to decide what elements of that freedom we will prioritize defending. If the gay rights movement stakes the future of those rights on the success of a much wider set of campaigns such as trans issues and if it links tolerance of homosexuality to the queer commitment to question all established norms and institutions, the chances that the current gay rights settlement will survive this century will be significantly diminished.

Indeed, a step away from this maximalist idea of gay rights would be mirroring the trajectory followed by the gay rights movement in the period of its greatest political success between the late 1990s and mid 2010s, when it walked away from radical politics and won the battles for things like marriage rights and employment protections. Although radical gay activists had hoped that the gay rights movement would be one that was part of a radical change in the whole of society, what actually occurred was more limited: gay rights campaigners achieved what Peter Tatchell dismissively described as the 'modest goal of equal rights within the status quo'.[1]

This inclusion (which was no mean feat) enhanced the freedom of gay people to choose the kind of life they wanted to live. Gays and lesbians could now choose whether to be outsiders and rebels (or 'queer' to use the preferred term of radicals) or be part of the mainstream. When a school friend and I both came out after leaving (an all-boys) secondary school in the mid-1990s, it was reported back to me that when one guy in our class was told we were gay he had exclaimed 'Lads, can you believe we had gays in the class?!' as if we had been like the Special Operations Executive agents the British parachuted into occupied France in the Second World War: enemy spies, walking around with radios concealed in our school bags, tapping out morse-code messages to gay headquarters from quiet corners of the school. He wasn't someone I remember as particularly homophobic; he was only reflecting the idea that gays were inherently other. If you were gay, you couldn't just have been a class member. You must have been some kind of outsider flying under the radar. Yet, when our twenty-year school reunion rolled around, the email inviting us said, with no fanfare and without almost anyone noticing, that 'wives and husbands' were invited to drinks at a pub the night before. Sure, my friend and I (and the two others who had later come out) could still choose to be rebels and outsiders if that was what we wanted, but we no longer had to accept that status if we didn't want to.

The effect of this ending of the involuntary outsider status of gay people has been to break the link between queerness and homosexuality. Those straight people who crave outsider status should be sensitive to the long imposition of outsider status on gay people before asserting that this desire means that they are queer and therefore in some way associated with gays and lesbians. To seek out a queer identity is to revel in the status of outsider. To assert that homosexuality is inherently queer leaves gay people permanently and definitionally excluded from the mainstream. The idea that there is an inherent link between gay people and a man who asserts that he is queer, although exclusively attracted to women, therefore goes directly against a key objective of the gay rights movement, namely, the ending of the involuntary imposition of outsider status on gay people.

If being gay does not, of itself, exclude you from mainstream life, then gay people have no particular claim over the status of queer. This, of course, raises a question mark as to whether LGBTQ (let alone LGBTQIA+) is a meaningful category. I would suggest that it is not. If a straight person can be queer and, following the success of the gay rights revolution, a gay person can be mainstream (if that is what they choose), what necessary connection is there between LGB and Q? The gay rights movement should cease to promote the idea that there is a necessary connection between gayness and the queer ideals of transgression and distance from the mainstream.

The second part of the solution I have proposed is to reverse-engineer a reform outcome in relation to the still-revolutionary sexual culture of gay men; that is, to produce a sexual culture that breaks less decisively with traditional norms by bolting on to gay male sexual culture some of the restraints and channelling mechanisms that humans have relied on for centuries to manage their inevitably chaotic sexual impulses. This would also involve accepting that the enormous boon of inclusion brings with it some obligations, most notably in relation to the monogamous nature of marriage (and even if fulfilling these obligations occasionally involves a degree of moderate hypocrisy shielded by discretion).

Reverse-engineering these changes onto a sexual culture that grew out of a revolution which, at the time, had very good reasons to be sex-positive and hostile to ideas of discretion will be tricky. If you had a time machine and the ability to enact whatever social changes you wanted, you might go back and do gay liberation in a different way. Ideally it would have been possible to achieve gay liberation without needing to hitch the gay freedom wagon to radical change in all sexual mores. This would have involved convincing the straight majority that homosexuality ought to be accepted not because anything goes but because there is nothing wrong with it per se.

Publicly accepted gay relationships would not have entered the social world as a something to be tolerated only because of a wider overturning of all of the established norms around sex. Instead they would have made their debut in a context in which at least some of the web of social norms (including a degree of sexual restraint) that were used to channel straight male sexuality would have been applied to gay male sexuality (lesbians needed no assistance in this regard). Under this approach, gay marriage would have been introduced at the same time as decriminalization of gay sex, thus ensuring that there were structures in place to favour the development of a view of gay sexual encounters as part of wider emotional and potentially enduring relationships rather than only as an end in themselves.

But this is, of course, a counter-factual fantasy. Neither gay marriage nor the idea that homosexuality was morally on a par with heterosexuality had any significant political support in the 1960s and 1970s. It was only by piggybacking on the wider deregulation of sexual life that gay rights could advance. But, now that the sexual revolution has allowed gay people to live openly, our existence cannot be denied. We can now have greater success arguing for gay rights because everyone knows that we are here. When post-liberals propose an authoritarian state that would take away gay freedom, they now have to openly address the issue of what that would mean for gay people in a way that their authoritarian predecessors, operating in an era when almost everyone was in the closet, did not. If we can come up with a version of gay rights that does not involve wider challenges to all conservative norms then a conservative swing in wider society need not be the mortal threat to our rights that it currently represents.

The task of bolting reformist structures on to a gay male sexual culture that was the outcome of revolution not reform will be complicated. A host of factors mean that absolute transformation is not possible. Gay male sexual culture is not the most fertile territory for principles such as sexual restraint. But that does not mean that valuable change is impossible. As Judith Shklar argued, it is possible to sincerely believe in principles, while accepting that at times people will fail to live up to them.

Sincerely believing in the value of a more restrained approach could have a positive impact beyond the political survival of gay freedom. Gay male sexual culture could change. It could encourage people to question whether yielding to in-the-moment desires is always a good thing and whether less could really be more in sexual terms. It could encourage men to try to lead rather than be led by their desires. It could push them to be more honest with themselves about whether their in-the-moment actions really are bringing them closer to where they want to end up long term, thus avoiding emulating Saint Augustine's approach of asking God to make him chaste 'but not yet'. It could encourage a culture in which oversharing about your sexual escapades is viewed as undesirable and where discretion keeps a lid on extra-marital activity, while providing cover for genuine intimacy and true inner freedom.

What both of these solutions amount to is the kind of liberal-reformist approach to homosexuality that appals radicals and will annoy some of those for whom it seems reactionary or too timid in its worries about the views of straight people. But the sad, though irrefutable fact is that gays and lesbians are, in all countries, a small minority whose freedom will always and everywhere depend on the kindness, or at least the acquiescence, of strangers. We need to keep a majority on side and that majority will be more likely if we can appeal to people beyond radical and ultra-liberal circles.

Given the duration and depth of the hostility to homosexuality, the deliverance of gay people from the clutches of rejection and persecution in the past half-century has been miraculous. The fact that gay marriage was unthinkable in 1960 but accepted in 2020 should give us pause for thought. It should bring home to us the reality that the fact that it was unthinkable in 2020 that gay marriage could be repealed does not mean that we will still have it in 2080. If, in a hundred years' time, we have lost gay marriage and discrimination protections but gay sex is still legal, gay people will actually still be doing better than we were for most of Western history.

It is very striking how prominent the issue of gay rights has been in the critique of Western liberalism offered by figures like Putin, Orbán and their supporters.[2] As things stand, gay rights are seen by conservatives as a threat to almost all of their norms around family, sex and gender. By renaming gay rights LGBTQ+ rights, most gay organizations are, if anything, encouraging them in this view. This has only reinforced the tendency among social conservatives towards making the rolling back of gay rights one of their top priorities. Once we accept that history has not loaded the dice in favour of ever advancing sexual freedom, it becomes clear how much of a threat this is. As a 2024 book by Kristina Stoeckl and Philip Ayoub showed, opposition to gay rights is increasingly transnationally networked and has been successfully mimicking the kind of campaigning tactics used to great success by gay rights groups in the past.[3]

A swinging of the societal pendulum in a conservative direction is inevitable at some stage. While many, maybe most, social conservatives will never be reconciled to gay rights we need to ensure that our movement has a place for moderates who are persuadable. For those who are not persuadable, it will be helpful to our cause if they do not see gay rights as their most important target. A form of gay rights that can to appeal to, or at least not appal, those who are unwilling to junk traditional approaches to sex, family and gender is therefore a necessity for the long-term durability of the gay rights movement.

A few years ago, while walking with my brother in Dublin, I bumped into a former secondary-school classmate of mine and his wife. We started chatting. I can't remember exactly what we discussed but do remember him unself-consciously mentioning a friend of his and 'his husband'. The reason this banal interaction stuck with me is because I remembered sitting in the back of a car with the same classmate in the late summer of 1995 when we had just finished school. A mutual friend had access to his parents' car and a group of five of us ended up driving around aimlessly. At one stage we drove past a park which, unbeknownst to me, had a reputation as a place where gay men would meet for sex. As we passed, the same classmate rolled the window down and shouted 'Fucking Faggots' at the top of his voice.

I remember trying to look as though I hadn't noticed, worried that any kind of reaction would blow my cover. But his action barely created a ripple in the car. The conversation continued as if nothing of note had happened. And that was because nothing of note had happened. No one thought that shouting out of the window meant my classmate had a particular bee in his bonnet about gays. The facts that gays were awful, that their activities in the park were illegitimate and would rightly annoy him and that rolling down the window to shout his disapproval was a normal, unremarkable thing to do were all just features of the social water in which we swam back then. Yet, a quarter of a century later, here was the same person chatting amiably and unself-consciously about his male friend's husband. The change was total and had not, to my knowledge, come from anguished thought or lengthy reflection on the wrongness of his former approach. Instead, as an 18-year-old guy in the Ireland of 1995, he had reflected the predominant view of his time and place and in 2021, as a 44-year-old, he was doing the same.

What a miracle that is. To succeed in relieving gay people of the centuries-long status of joke, scandal and hated outsider to the extent that a man being married to another man was an unquestioned, unremarkable background fact in a banal conversation represents a political, legal and social success of an improbable magnitude. But the fact that, in much of the West, most people can no longer imagine how they used to feel about homosexuality does not mean that this revolution is invulnerable.

The central argument of this book is that this wonderous deliverance is more vulnerable than we think. A ball-boy in a tennis tournament in 2025 is in no danger of being publicly mocked for being gay by an international tennis star. Even if he were mocked, there would be an outpouring of support for him and mystified anger at the perpetrator. But, what is even better, that ball-boy will know that, though no one is guaranteed a good life, he has a fair shot at one. When he resigned from Mrs Thatcher's government in the 1990s, Sir Geoffrey Howe told the House of Commons that the Prime Minister's approach to European integration meant that, when negotiating with other European states, it felt like he was going out to play cricket when the team captain had broken the bats before the first ball was bowled.

That is how it was for young gay people for centuries. As they stepped up to play for a flourishing and happy adulthood, they found their bats had been broken by society before they even started. Finally, in most of the West, a young gay or lesbian has their happiness in their own hands to (almost) the same degree as anyone else. They can be confident that, unlike the future that was faced by most of their gay or lesbian predecessors, their friendships, family and career need not be damaged in advance by the mere fact of their homosexuality.

That is a miracle. A miracle that only a tiny percentage of gay people in history have had the fortune to experience and which could easily not last. Changing the stories we have told ourselves about gay freedom will be hard. Thinking that freedom was an unalloyed good gave us a comforting clarity of purpose, allowed us to see our problems as always coming from the outside and never challenged us to consider whether there was any tiny kernel of insight to be found in our opponents' positions. Regarding the advance of gay rights as being on the right side of history not only reassured us that the future was secure but also allowed us to see our opponents as not just wrong but as outdated and passé. Uncomfortable as it may be, asking ourselves a few hard questions seems a very small price to pay to maximize the chances of keeping that miracle going.

Notes

1 *Deliverance?*

1 *The Rough Guide to Ireland 1990* (Rough Guides, 1990).
2 *General Social Survey: Key Trends: Sex and Sexual Orientation.* https://gssdataexplorer.norc.org/trends (United States); National Centre for Social Research, *British Social Attitudes.* https://natcen.ac.uk/british-social-attitudes (United Kingdom).
3 Richard Jago, 'Something, You Know, Just Clicked', *Guardian*, 10 July 2001.
4 Charles Taylor, *Modern Social Imaginaries* (Duke University Press, 2004).
5 Anita Kurimay *Queer Budapest 1873–1961* (University of Chicago Press, 2020), p. 40 and ch. 6.
6 Ibid., p. 4.
7 Aaron Sibarium, 'Three Theses about Cuties', *American Compass*, 23 September 2020. https://americancompass.org/three-theses-about-cuties/
8 *See Gay and Bisexual Men's Health*, Centre for Disease Control, 29 February 2016. https://www.cdc.gov/msmhealth/mental-health.htm
9 Michael Joseph Gross, 'Has Manhunt Destroyed Gay Culture?' *Out.com*, 4 August 2008. https://www.out.com/entertainment/2008/08/04/has-manhunt -destroyed-gay-culture
10 Archie Bland, 'Monday Briefing: Gay and Bisexual Men Are Most at Risk of Monkeypox. Why Aren't We Saying So Clearly?' *Guardian*, 25 July 2022. https://www.theguardian.com/world/2022/jul/25/monday-briefing -monkeypox-gay-bisexual-men-public-health-who

2 *An Incidental Revolution*

1 *Sex and the City*, season 2, episode 6.
2 Kiffer G. Card et al., 'Using Google Trends to Inform the Population Size Estimation and Spatial Distribution of Gay, Bisexual and Other Men Who Have Sex with Men: Proof of Concept Study', *JMIR Public Health and Surveillance*, 7 (11), 2007.
3 *See* General Social Survey identity polling available at: https://sda.berkeley.edu /sdaweb/analysis/?dataset=gss16
4 Louise Perry, *The Case against the Sexual Revolution* (Polity, 2022), p. 6.

5 Stefan Zweig, *The World of Yesterday: Memoires of a European*, trans. Anthea Bell (Pushkin Press, 2011).

6 Louise Perry, *The Case against the Sexual Revolution*, p. 163.

7 Philip Larkin, *Annus Mirabilis*.

8 Douglas Murray, *The Madness of Crowds* (Bloomsbury 2019), p. 50.

9 Betty Friedan, *Life So Far: A Memoir* (Simon and Schuster, 2001), p. 221.

10 General Social Survey 'Key Trends'. https://gssdataexplorer.norc.org/trends

11 National Centre for Social Research, *British Social Attitudes*. https://natcen.ac.uk/british-social-attitudes

12 'Opinion publique sur l'homosexualité', *Statistica*. https://fr.statista.com/statistiques/1022931/jugement-homosexualite-france/

13 *See* Jeremy Bentham, 'Offences Against One's Self: Paederasty Part 1', published in Louis Crompton, *Journal of Homosexuality*, 3 (4), Summer 1978.

14 Jeffrey Weeks, *Making Sexual History* (Polity, 2000), p. 7.

15 Judit Takacs, 'The Double Life of Kertbeny' in G. Hemka (ed.) *Past and Present of Radical Sexual Politics* (UvA, Mosse Foundation) pp. 26–40.

16 David Halperin, 'How to Do the History of Male Homosexuality', *GLQ A Journal of Lesbian and Gay Studies*, 6 (1), 2000: 87–124.

17 Mary McIntosh, 'The Homosexual Role' in Kenneth Plummer (ed.) *The Making of the Modern Homosexual* (Barnes & Noble, 1981) p. 37.

18 Tom Holland, *Dominion: The Making of the Western Mind* (Basic Books, 2019) pp. 274–5.

19 Clayton J. Whisnant, *Queer Identities and Politics in Germany: A History, 1880–1945* (Columbia University Press 2016).

20 Anita Kurimay, *Queer Budapest 1873–1961* (University of Chicago Press, 2020), pp. 49, 86 and 87.

21 Stephen Jeffery-Poulter, *Peers, Queers and Commons* (Routledge, 1990), ch. 2.

22 Ibid., p. 39.

23 Scott Gunther, 'Building a More Stately Closet: French Gay Movements since the Early 1980s', *Journal of the History of Sexuality*, 13 (3), July 2004: 32.

24 *The Report of the Committee on Homosexual Offences and Prostitution* CMND 247, 23 October 1957.

25 Lesbian sex had not been criminalized because it was approved of but because female sexuality was largely overlooked.

26 See the statement that decriminalization took California 'one step farther from 1984', quoted in Randy Shilts, *The Mayor of Castro Street* (Atlantic Books, 1982), p. 125.

27 Quoted in *The Times*, 4 July 1967.

28 Stephen Jeffery-Poulter, *Peers, Queers and Commons*, p. 82.

29 Quoted in *The Times*, 28 July 1967.

30 *Dudgeon v. United Kingdom* Case 7525/76, Judgment of 22 October 1981.

31 *Bowers v. Hardwick* 478 US 186 (1986).

32 *Lawrence v. Texas* 539 US 558 (2003).

33 Stephen Jeffery-Poulter, *Peers, Queers and Commons*, p. 98.

34 Dennis Altman, *Homosexual Oppression and Liberation* (New York University Press 1971).

35 Jeffrey Weeks, *Making Sexual History*, pp. 190–1; 81.

36 Kevin Mumford, 'The Miscegenation Analogy Revisited: Same Sex Marriage as a Civil Rights Story', *American Quarterly*, 57(2), June 2005: 523.

37 Evan Wolfson, *Why Marriage Matters: America, Equality and Gay People's Right to Marry* (Simon and Schuster, 2004).

38 *See* Christopher Caldwell, *The Age of Entitlement: America Since the Sixties* (Simon & Schuster, 2021).

39 Steven Epstein, 'Gay Politics, Ethnic Identity' in Edward Stein (ed.) *Forms of Desire: Sexual Orientation and the Social Constructivist Controversy* (Garland, 1990), quoted in Jeffrey Weeks, *Making Sexual* History, p. 69.

40 Council Directive 2000/78/EC of 27 November 2000 establishing a general framework for equal treatment in employment and occupation OJ L303 2.12.2000 pp.16–22 (EU). *Egan v. Canada* [1995] 2 SCR 513, *Ley Federal para Prevenir y Eliminar la Discriminación* (Mexico), the Sex Discrimination Amendment (Sexual Orientation, Gender Identity and Intersex Status) Act 2013 (Australia), *Bostock v. Clayton County* 590 US (2020) (US).

41 Ronan McCrea, 'Regulating the Role of Religion in Society in an Era of Change and Secularist Self-doubt: Why European Courts Have Been Right to Adopt a Hands-Off Approach', *Current Legal Problems*, 2022: 111–35.

42 Jonathan Rauch, 'Red Families, Blue Families, Gay Families and the Search for a New Normal', *Journal of Law and Inequality*, 28(2), Summer 2010: 333.

43 Eli Finkel, 'How Self-Expression Replaced Love as the Most Important Part of a Marriage', *The Cut*, 19 September 2017.

44 Jonathan Rauch, 'Red Families, Blue Families, Gay Families and the Search for a New Normal': 333.

45 *Ghaidan v. Mendoza* [2002] EWCA Civ 1533, Judgment of Buxton LJ paragraph 35.

3 Sexual Freedom and the End of History: The Post-Liberal Moment

1 Francis Fukuyama, *The End of History and the Last Man* (Free Press, 1992).

2 Anita Kurimay, *Queer Budapest 1873–1961* (University of Chicago Press, 2020), p. 18.

3 Lukasz Szulc 'How LGBT Rights Became a Key Battleground in Poland's Election', *LSE Europe Blog* 26 September 2019; '"Climate" and "LGBT"

chosen as Polish Words of the Year for 2019', *Notes from Poland*. https://notesfrompoland.com/2020/01/06/climate-and-lgbt-chosen-as-polish-words-of-the-year-for-2019/

4 'Il Comune di Milano Interrompe le Registrazioni dei Figli di Coppie *Omogenitoriali' Sky ItaliaI*, 13 March 2023. https://tg24.sky.it/cronaca/2023/03/13/milano-interrompe-registrazioni-figli-coppie-omogenitoriali; Barbie Latza Nadeau and Jack Guy, 'Italy Starts Removing Lesbian Mothers' Names from Birth Certificates', *CNN* 21 July 2023. https://edition.cnn.com/2023/07/21/europe/italy-lesbian-couples-birth-certificates-scli-intl/index.html; Davide Ghilglione, 'Italy Leaves Children of Gay Parents in Limbo', *BBC News*, 18 March 2023. https://www.bbc.co.uk/news/world-europe-64967517; 'Hungarian Government Proposes Same-Sex Adoption Ban', *BBC News*, 11 November 2020. https://www.bbc.co.uk/news/world-europe-54902048

5 Tony Luckhurst, 'Hungary Bans LGBTQ+ Pride Marches', *BBC News* 19 March 2025. https://www.bbc.co.uk/news/articles/c5y0zrg9kpno; Leonie Kijewski, 'Hungarian President Vetoes anti-LGBTQ Law', *Politico*, 22 April 2023. https://www.politico.eu/article/hungary-president-katalin-novak-vetoes-viktor-orban-anti-lgbtq-law/

6 E.g. Owen Jones, 'Anti-Zealots, Know This: History Will Judge You', *Guardian*, 15 December 2017.

7 Quoted in Tony Judt, *When the Facts Change* (Vintage, 2015), p. 331.

8 Louise Perry, *The Case against the Sexual Revolution* (Polity, 2022), p. 6.

9 Philip Hensher, 'City Slicker Loses His Way', *Guardian*, 10 June 2007.

10 Julia Yost, 'New York's Hottest Club Is the Catholic Church', *New York Times*, 9 August 2022.

11 Molly Olmstead, 'Uh, Can the NYT Please Not Treat Catholic Reactionaries as a Fun, Sexy, Trend Story?' *Slate*, 11 August 2022. https://slate.com/news-and-politics/2022/08/nyt-dimes-square-trad-catholic-op-ed.html

12 James Pogue, 'Inside the New Right, Where Peter Thiel Is Placing His Biggest Bets', *Vanity Fair*, 20 April 2022.

13 Louise Perry, *The Case against the Sexual Revolution*, p. 186.

14 Vicente Valentim, *The Normalization of the Radical Right: A Norms Theory of Political Supply and Demand* (Oxford University Press, 2024).

15 Matthew Rose, *A World After Liberalism* (Yale University Press, 2021), p. 2.

16 Christopher Caldwell, *The Age of Entitlement* (Simon and Schuster, 2020), pp. 100–1.

17 Patrick Deneen, *Why Liberalism Failed* (Yale University Press, 2018), p. 53.

18 Quoted in Christopher Caldwell, *The Age of Entitlement*, p. 93.

19 Ibid., p. 93.

20 Ken Bredemeier, 'Trump Endorses Hungary's Orbán for Re-election', *Voice of*

American News, 3 January 2022. https://www.voanews.com/a/trump-endorses
-hungary-s-orban-for-reelection-/6380295.html; 'Trump and Musk Express
Support for Spanish Far-Right Vox', *GBC News,* 23 February 2025. https://
www.gbc.gi/news/musk-and-trump-express-support-spanish-far-right-vox

21 John Burn-Murdoch, 'Why the MAGA Mindset Is Different', *Financial Times,*
7 March 2025.

22 Patrick Deneen, *Regime Change* (Forum, 2023), p. 146.

23 *See* Ian Ward, 'The New Right's Man in the Ivory Tower', *Politico,* 6 August
2023 as well as Patrick Deneen, *Why Liberalism Failed* (Yale University Press,
2018); Patrick Deneen, *Regime Change.*

24 Patrick Deneen, *Regime Change,* p. 94.

25 Patrick Deneen, *Why Liberalism Failed,* p. 113.

26 Ibid.

27 Ibid., p. 5.

28 Ian Ward, 'The New Right's Man in the Ivory Tower', *Politico,* 6 August 2023.

29 Patrick Deneen, *Regime Change,* p. 94.

30 Ibid., p. 181.

31 Ian Ward, 'The New Right's Man in the Ivory Tower'.

32 Patrick Deneen, *Regime Change,* p. 158.

33 Theo Burman, 'Support for Same Sex Marriage Is Declining', *Newsweek,* 25
June 2024. 'Republican Support for Same-Sex Marriage Is Lowest in a Decade,
Gallup Poll Finds', NBC News 29 May 2025. https://www.nbcnews.com/nbc
-out/out-politics-and-policy/republican-support-sex-marriage-lowest-decade
-gallup-poll-finds-rcna209762

34 Matthew Rose, *A World After Liberalism* (Yale University Press, 2021), p. 4.

35 Ian Ward, 'The New Right's Man in the Ivory Tower', *Politico,* 6 August 2023.

36 John Riley, 'Trump Taps Anti-LGBT Matt Gaetz for Attorney General', *Metro
Weekly,* 13 November 2024. https://www.metroweekly.com/2024/11/trump
-taps-anti-lgbtq-matt-gaetz-for-attorney-general/

37 Adrian Vermeule, *Common Good Constitutionalism: Recovering the Classical
Legal Tradition* (Polity, 2022).

38 'Republicans Put Abortion Disagreements Aside at "Unity" Convention', *BBC
News* 19 July 2024. https://www.bbc.co.uk/news/articles/c9r3nz67v9lo

4 The Illusion of the Universal Appeal of the Sexual Revolution

1 A proportion of this chapter appeared originally in Ronan McCrea, 'Regulating
the Role of Religion in Society in an Era of Change and Secularist Self-doubt:
Why European Courts Have Been Right to Adopt a Hands-Off Approach',
Current Legal Problems, 75 (1), 2022: 111–35. Reproduced with kind permission
of *Current Legal Problems.*

2 David Coleman, 'Immigration and Ethnic Change in Low-Fertility Countries: A Third Demographic Transition', *Population Development Review*, 32(3), 2006: 401–4.

3 Pew Research Center, 'The Global Divide on Homosexuality Persists', 25 June 2020. https://www.pewresearch.org/global/2020/06/25/global-divide-on -homosexuality-persists/

4 Dirk-Jan Janssen and Peer Scheepers, 'How Religiosity Shapes Rejection of Homosexuality Across the Globe', *Journal of Homosexuality*, 66 (14), 2019: 1974–2001.

5 Pew Research Center, '10 Key Findings about Religion in Western Europe', 29 May 2018. https://www.pewresearch.org/short-reads/2018/05/29/10-key -findings-about-religion-in-western-europe/

6 Pew Research Center, 'Where Is the Most Religious Place in the World?', 9 August 2024. https://www.pewresearch.org/short-reads/2024/08/09/where-is -the-most-religious-place-in-the-world/

7 Pew Research Center, 'The Religious Composition of the World's Migrants; Spotlight on Europe', 19 August 2024. https://www.pewresearch.org/2024/08 /19/geographic-spotlights-a-closer-look-at-4-migration-stories/

8 Sarah Carol, 'Like Will to Like?: Partner Choice among Muslim Migrants and Natives in Western Europe', European Association for Population Studies. https://epc2014.eaps.nl/papers/140065

9 Sarah Carol, 'Intermarriage Attitudes Among Minority and Majority Groups in Western Europe: The Role of Attachment to the Religious In-Group', *International Migration*, 51 (3), 2013: 67–83.

10 Sarah Carol, 'Measure for Social Integration: Mixed Marriages between Muslims and Non-Muslims Are Accepted but Rare', WZB/The Berlin Social Science Center, 29 November 2019. https://bibliothek.wzb.eu/articles/2014/f-18970.pdf

11 Pew Research Centre, 'Europe's Growing Muslim Population', November 2017. https://www.pewresearch.org/religion/2017/11/29/europes-growing-muslim -population/

12 A.C. Alexander and C. Welzer, 'Islam and Patriarchy: How Robust Is Muslim Support for Patriarchal Values?', *International Review of Sociology*, 21 (2), 2011: 247–76.

13 *See* R. Inglehart and P. Norris, 'The True Clash of Civilizations', *Foreign Policy*, 82 (2), March/April 2003: 62–70.

14 Sarfraz Manzoor, *They: What Muslims and Non-Muslims Get Wrong about Each Other* (Headline, 2021).

15 Frances Perraudin, 'Half of British Muslims Think Homosexuality Should Be Illegal Poll Finds', *Guardian*, 11 April 2016.

16 *See* 'The Gallup Coexist Index 2009: A Global Study of Interfaith Relations'.

https://ec.europa.eu/migrant-integration/sites/default/files/2009-05/docl
_8511_392761152.pdf

17 Shadi Hamid, 'France's False Choice: Can Liberal Societies Come to Terms with Religious Illiberalism?' *Atlantic*, 28 January 2015 and 'Selon l'Ifop, 65% des lycéens musulmans placent l'islam au-dessus des lois de la République', *Marianne*, 9 December 2021. https://www.marianne.net/societe/education/selon-lifop-65 -des-lyceens-musulmans-placent-lislam-au-dessus-des-lois-de-la-republique.

18 Ibid.

19 *The Pew Forum*, 'Muslims in Europe: Economic Worries Top Concerns about Religious and Cultural Identity', 6 July 2006. https://www.pewresearch.org /global/2006/07/06/muslims-in-europe-economic-worries-top-concerns-about -religious-and-cultural-identity/

20 'US Muslims Concerned about Their Place in Society but Continue to Believe in the American Dream', *Pew Research Center*, 26 July 2017. https://www .pewresearch.org/religion/2017/07/26/findings-from-pew-research-centers -2017-survey-of-us-muslims/

21 Donna Ferguson, 'We Can't Give in: The Birmingham School on the Frontline of Anti-LGBT Protests', *Guardian*, 26 May 2019. Jean-Pierre Stroobants 'En Belgique, plusieurs écoles incendiées après une campagne d'extrémistes religieux contre l'éducation sexuelle', *Le Monde*, 18 September 2023.

22 Jaweed Kaleem, 'As Muslims' Status as Political Punching Bag Fades, Some Are Fighting Against LGBTQ+ Acceptance', *LA Times*, 25 September 2023.

23 Shadi Hamid, 'Muslims v. Democrats: A Story of Betrayal: Disputes over Sexual Ideology Put to a Test the Left's Commitment to Cultural Diversity', *Wall Street Journal*, 27 July 2023.

24 Paul Bickley and Nathan Mladin, 'Religious London: Faith in a Global City', *Theos*, 2020. https://www.theosthinktank.co.uk/cmsfiles/Religious-London -FINAL-REPORT-24.06.2020.pdf

25 'Opinion publique sur l'homosexualité', *Statistica*. https://fr.statista.com /statistiques/1022931/jugement-homosexualite-france/

26 Helen Corbett, 'George Galloway Criticised for "Blatant Homophobia"', *Independent*, 4 May 2024. https://www.independent.co.uk/news/uk/george -galloway-rochdale-chris-bryant-britain-momentum-b2538454.html

27 Mark Lilla, *The Stillborn God* (Knopf, 2007); Charles Taylor, *A Secular Age* (Harvard University Press, 2007).

28 Shadi Hamid, *Islamic Exceptionalism* (Saint Martin's Griffin, 2017).

29 Olivier Roy, *Secularism Confronts Islam* (Columbia University Press, 2007).

30 Lyman Stone, 'The Conservative Fertility Advantage', Institute for Family Studies, 18 November 2020. https://ifstudies.org/blog/the-conservative-fertility -advantage

31 Patrick Weil, 'Why the French Laicite is Liberal', *Cardozo Law Review*, 30, 2009: 2699.

32 *See* Office of the UN High Commissioner for Human Rights, 'UN Human Rights Experts Urge Denmark to Halt Sale of "Ghetto" Buildings', 23 October 2020. https://www.ohchr.org/en/press-releases/2020/10/un-human-rights-experts-urge-denmark-halt-contentious-sale-ghetto-buildings?LangID=E&NewsID=26414

33 Ronan McCrea, 'Regulating the Role of Religion in Society in an Era of Change and Secularist Self-Doubt: Why European Courts Have Been Right to Adopt a Hands-Off Approach', *Current Legal* Problems, 75 (1), 2022: 111–35.

34 Ivan Krastev, 'Liberal Europe Must Learn Some History Lessons to Survive', *Financial Times*, 22 December 2024.

35 Tony Judt, *Postwar: A History of Europe since 1945* (Penguin, 2005).

36 Christopher Caldwell, *The Age of Entitlement* (Simon and Schuster, 2020), pp. 45, 46, 49.

37 Robin Morgan, 'Goodbye to All That', *Rat Magazine*, February 1970.

38 Catherine A. MacKinnon, *Towards a Feminist Theory of the State* (Harvard University Press, 1989) and Andrew Dworkin, *Pornography: Men Possessing Women* (Putnam, 1981).

39 Louise Perry, *The Case against the Sexual Revolution* (Polity, 2022); Mary Harrington, *Feminism against Progress* (Swift Press, 2023).

40 Judith Green, 'Powerful Critique, Dismal Prescription: A Review of the Case against the Sexual Revolution', *Radical Notion*, 7. https://theradicalnotion.org/tag/issue-7/

41 Ross Douthat, *The Decadent Society* (Simon and Schuster 2021), p. 53.

42 John Burn-Murdoch, 'The Relationship Recession is Going Global', *Financial Times,* 11 January 2025.

43 *Ladele v. London Borough of Islington* [2009] EWCA Civ 1357 CA and *Eweida and Others v. United Kingdom* [2013] ECHR 37. I should state that I acted for the National Secular Society in its in intervention in this case before the European Court of Human Rights.

44 'Trump and Musk Express Support for Spanish Far-Right Vox', *GBC News*, 23 February 2025. https://www.gbc.gi/news/musk-and-trump-express-support-spanish-far-right-vox

45 Gideon Rachman, 'Vance's Real Warning to Europe', *Financial Times*, 17 February 2024.

46 'LGBTQ+ Rights: Gallup Historical Trends'. https://news.gallup.com/poll/1651/gay-lesbian-rights.aspx

47 Louise Perry, *The Case Against the Sexual Revolution*, p. 186.

5 Hubris: The Gay Movement Over-Reaches

1 Andrew Sullivan, 'Gay Rights and the Limits of Liberalism', *Substack*, 23 June 2024. https://andrewsullivan.substack.com/p/gay rights-and-the-limits-of -liberalism-be4

2 Stonewall, 'What is the Workplace Equality and How is it Scored?' https://www .stonewall.org.uk/build-workplace-works-lgbtq-people/uk-workplace-equality -index

3 Stonewall Workplace Equality Index: https://www.stonewall.org.uk/top-100 -employers/what-workplace-equality-index-and-how-it-scored.

4 Human Rights Campaign, Corporate Equality Index: Executive Summary. https://reports.hrc.org/corporate-equality-index-2023#executive-summary. I owe the tithe analogy to an anonymous reviewer of the manuscript.

5 Andrew Sullivan, 'John Derbyshire's Poisonous Paranoia about Gays', *Salon* 26, June 2003. https://www.salon.com/2003/06/26/derbyshire_2/

6 *R (on the application of Ngole) v. University of Sheffield and Health and Care Professions Council* [2017] EWHC 2669.

7 *Smith v. Trafford Housing Trust* [2012] EWHC 3221.

8 John Rawls, *Theory of Justice* (Belknap Press, 1971).

9 'What Is LGBTQIA+?' The Center. https://gaycenter.org/community/lgbtq/

10 James Kirchick, 'From Gay to Queer', *Liberties*, 3(3). https://libertiesjournal .com/articles/from-queer-to-gay-to-queer/

11 The Pew Forum 'The Experiences of LGBTQ Americans Today' 29 May 2025. https://www.pewresearch.org/social-trends/2025/05/29/the-experiences -of-lgbtq-americans-today/. 'Transgender Law: An Overview, The National Center for Lesbian Rights. http://www.nclrights.org/our-work/transgender-law /transgender-law/; Sean Bugg, 'Trans Mission', *Metro Weekly*, 18 August 2004. https://www.metroweekly.com/2004/08/trans-mission/

12 *Goodwin v. United Kingdom*. Application 28957/95, Judgment of 11 July 2002 (Grand Chamber).

13 Jerome Hunt, 'A History of the Employment Non-Discrimination Act', *American Progress*, 19 July 2011. https://www.americanprogress.org/article /a-history-of-the-employment-non-discrimination-act/

14 Sean Bugg, 'Trans Mission', *Metro Weekly*, 18 August 2004. https://www .metroweekly.com/2004/08/trans-mission/

15 Chuck Colbert, 'HRC Apologises to Trans Community, Pledges Push for Broad LGBT Bill', *The Bay Area Reporter*, 10 September 2014.

16 Natacha Kennedy, 'Stonewall Holding Back on Transgender Equality', *Guardian*, 20 October 2010.

17 Reubs Walsh, 'Why Stonewall's Decision to Lobby on Trans Issues was the Right

One', *Pinknews*, 17 February 2015. https://www.thepinknews.com/2015/02/17/comment-why-stonewalls-decision-to-lobby-on-trans-issues-was-the-right-one/

18 Jamie Grierson, 'Stonewall Calls for Gender-Neutral X Option for UK Passports', *Guardian*, 5 April 2017.

19 'Transgender Group to Protest outside HRC Headquarters', *Advocate*, 30 April 2004. https://www.advocate.com/news/2004/04/30/transgender-group-protest-outside-hrc-headquarters-12260

20 Mark Lilla, *The Once and Future Liberal: After Identity Politics* (Hurst, 2017), p. 59.

21 Ibid., p. 35.

22 Yascha Mounk, *The Identity Trap: A Story of Ideas and Power in Our Time* (Penguin, 2023), p. 268.

23 Julie Bindel, 'No, United Nations. "Trans-Lesbians" Are not Lesbians: When Did the LGBTQQIA2S+++ "Community" Become an Unbreakable Wifi Code?', *Daily Telegraph*, 13 October 2023.

24 Mark Lilla, *The Once and Future Liberal: After Identity Politics* (Hurst, 2017), p. 24.

25 *Accelerating Acceptance 2023*, Gay and Lesbian Alliance Against Defamation. https://assets.glaad.org/m/23036571f611c54/original/Accelerating-Acceptance-2023.pdf

26 Raymond Aron, *Thinking Politically: A Liberal in an Age of Ideology* (Routledge, 1997).

27 Human Rights Campaign, Press release, 'For the First Time Ever, Human Rights Campaign Officially Declares "State of Emergency" for LGBTQ+ Americans; Issues National Warning and Guidebook to Ensure Safety for LGBTQ+ Residents and Travelers', 6 June 2023. https://www.hrc.org/press-releases/for-the-first-time-ever-human-rights-campaign-officially-declares-state-of-emergency-for-lgbtq-americans-issues-national-warning-and-guidebook-to-ensure-safety-for-lgbtq-residents-and-travelers

28 Andrew Sullivan, 'Is There a Way to Acknowledge America's Progress?', *New York Magazine*, 17 January 2020.

29 'Annual GLAAD Study Shows Further Decline in LGBTQ Acceptance among Younger Americans', Gay and Lesbian Alliance Against Defamation, 24 June 2019. https://glaad.org/releases/annual-glaad-study-shows-further-decline-lgbtq-acceptance-among-younger-americans/

30 'Opinion publique sur l'homosexualité', *Statistica*. https://fr.statista.com/statistiques/1022931/jugement-homosexualite-france/

31 Theo Burman, 'Support for Same Sex Marriage is Declining', *Newsweek*, 25 June 2024.

32 'Gallup Historical Trends: LGBTQ+ Rights'. https://news.gallup.com/poll/1651/gay-lesbian-rights.aspx

33 Ibid.

34 Matthew Smith, 'Where Does the British Public Stand on Transgender Rights In 2022? There Has Been an Erosion of Support for Trans Rights since 2018' YouGov, 20 July 2022. https://yougov.co.uk/society/articles /43194-where-does-british-public-stand-transgender-rights-1?redirect_from= %2Ftopics%2Fsociety%2Farticles-reports%2F2022%2F07%2F20%2Fwhere -does-british-public-stand-transgender-rights

35 National Centre for Social Research, *British Social Attitudes 2023*. https:// natcen.ac.uk/events/british-social-attitudes-2023

36 Andrew Sullivan, 'Gay Rights and the Limits of Liberalism'.

37 Ibid.

6 *The King Is Dead! Now What? Radical and Moderate Versions of Gay Freedom*

1 Gilbert Keith Chesterton, *The Thing: Why I Am a Catholic* (Dodo Press, 1929).

2 Ross Douthat, *The Decadent Society* (Simon and Schuster, 2021), p. 109.

3 Ibid., p. 110.

4 Louise Perry, *The Case against the Sexual Revolution* (Polity, 2022), p. 178.

5 Jonathan Rauch, 'Red Families, Blue Families, Gay Families and the Search for a New Normal', *Journal of Law and Inequality*, 28 (2), Summer 2010: 333.

6 Louise Perry, *The Case against the Sexual Revolution*, p. 15.

7 Mary Wollstonecraft, *A Vindication of the Rights of Woman* (1792), ch. 12.

8 Patrick Deneen, *Why Liberalism Failed* (Yale University Press, 2018).

9 Gay Liberation Front Manifesto 1971 (as revised in 1978).

10 Kim I. Mills, 'Gay Groups Try to Put Distance between Themselves and Paedophile Group', AP, 13 February 1994. https://web.archive.org/web /20201027000651/https://apnews.com/article/c64e816cac5b0fa1194dd40f57 6813b2

11 *Baker v. Nelson* 409 US 810 (1972).

12 Andrew Sullivan, 'Here Comes the Groom: A (Conservative) Case for Gay Marriage', *New Republic*, 28 August 1989.

13 Andrew Sullivan, *Virtually Normal: An Argument about Homosexuality* (Picador, 1995).

14 Andrew Sullivan, 'I Cried as Obama Finally Came Out', *The Times*, 13 May 2012.

15 Peter Tatchell, 'I'm Right Wing, Respectable and Gay: You're Just Gay', *Guardian*, 30 November 2003.

16 Quoted in Patrick Deneen, *Regime Change* (Forum, 2023), p. 89.

17 James Kirchick, 'From Gay to Queer', *Liberties* 3 (3). https://libertiesjournal .com/articles/from-queer-to-gay-to-queer/

18 Stephen Jeffery-Poulter, *Peers, Queers and Commons* (Routledge, 1990), pp. 245–49.

19 Ibid., pp. 167–73.

20 Ibid., ch. 12; Randy Shilts, *And the Band Played On* (Saint Martin's Press, 1987), ch. 1.

21 John Maynard Keynes, *The General Theory of Employment, Interest and Money* (Palgrave Macmillan, 1936).

22 Aaron Sibarium, 'Three Theses about Cuties', *American Compass*, 23 September 2020. https://americancompass.org/three-theses-about-cuties/.

23 Rob Henderson, '"Luxury Beliefs" Are the Latest Status Symbol for Rich Americans', *The New York Post*, 17 August 2019. https://nypost.com/2019/08/17/luxury-beliefs-are-the-latest-status-symbol-for-rich-americans/

24 Harry Cocks, 'Conspiracy to Corrupt Public Morals and the "Unlawful" Status of Homosexuality in Britain After 1967', *Social History*, 41 (3): 267–84.

25 Thomas Nagel, 'Concealment and Exposure', *Philosophy and Public Affairs*, 27 (1), Winter 1998: 3–30.

26 Louise Perry, *The Case against the Sexual Revolution*.

7 The Downside of Anything Goes

1 Paula England and Eliza Brown, 'An Unequal Distribution of Partners: Gays versus Straights', 1 July 2016. https://contexts.org/blog/an-unequal-distribution-of-partners-gays-versus-straights/; Sarah E. Jackson et al., 'Sociodemographic Behavioural Correlates of Lifetime Number of Sexual Partners: Findings from the English Longitudinal Study of Ageing British', *Medical Journal Sexual and Reproductive Health*, 45(2); Sarah Nelson Glick et al., 'A Comparison of Sexual Behavior Patterns Among Men Who Have Sex With Men and Heterosexual Men and Women', *Journal of Acquired Immune Deficiency*, 60 (1), 2012: 83–90.

2 Partnership Patterns and HIV Prevention among Men Who Have Sex with Men (MSM), National AIDS Trust (July 2010). https://www.nat.org.uk/sites/default/files/publications/July-2010-Parternship-Patterns-and-HIV-Prevention.pdf

3 Ibid.

4 Puja Seth, Tanja Walker and Argelia Figueroa, 'CDC-funded HIV Testing, HIV Positivity, and Linkage to HIV Medical Care in Non-Health Care Settings among Young Men Who Have Sex With Men (YMSM) in the United States', *AIDS Care*, 29 (7), 2017: 823–7; *see also* 'CDC Warns Gay Men of "Epidemic" HIV Rates', *Lifesite.com*, 8 July 2013. https://www.lifesitenews.com/news/epidemic-1-2-of-gay-men-will-have-hiv-by-age-50-if-current-rates-continue-w/

5 Oliver Neil Refugio and Jeffrey D. Klausner, 'Syphilis Incidence in Men Who Have Sex with Men with Human Immunodeficiency Virus Comorbidity and the Importance of Integrating Sexually Transmitted Infection Prevention into HIV Care', *Expert Rev Anti Ther*, (4), 16 April 2018: 321–31.

6 Randy Shilts, *And the Band Played On* (Saint Martin's Press, 1987), pp. 18–20.

7 Christine Russell, 'Map of AIDS' Deadly March Evolves from Hepatitis Study', *Washington Post,* 1 February 1987.

8 Ian Sample, 'Monkeypox May Have Been Circulating in the UK for Years Scientists Say', *Guardian,* 25 May 2022.

9 Patrick Kelleher, 'Monkeypox: Expert Explains Why it isn't a "Gay Disease" and Warns of Risk of Stigma', *Pink News,* 24 May 2022. https://www.thepinknews.com/2022/05/24/monkeypox-gay-sex-disease-bisexual-virus/

10 Victoria A. Brownworth, 'Media Must Separate Monkeypox Risk From Stigma', *Philadelphia Gay News,* 25 May 2022. https://epgn.com/2022/05/25/analysis-media-must-separate-monkeypox-risk-from-stigma/

11 Press Statement: 'UNAIDS Warns That Stigmatizing Language on Monkeypox Jeopardizes Public Health', *UNAIDS,* 22 May 2022.

12 'Debate over Monkeypox Messaging Divides NYC Health Department', *New York Times,* 18 July 2022.

13 Rod Dreher, 'The Price of Pride: Woke Public Health Authorities Still Lack Courage and Credibility when it Comes to Monkeypox', *American Conservative,* 30 July 2022.

14 Jim Downs, 'Gay Men Need a Specific Warning About Monkeypox: Tiptoeing Around the Issue Carries its Own Risks', *Atlantic,* 28 May 2022; and Jim Downs, 'Asking Gay Men to be Careful Isn't Homophobia', *Atlantic,* 13 August 2022.

15 'Debate over Monkeypox Messaging Divides NYC Health Department'.

16 Randy Shilts, *And the Band Played On* (Saint Martin's Press, 1987), p. 210.

17 R.H. Byers Jr et al., 'Estimating AIDS Infection Rates in the San Francisco Cohort', *AIDS,* 2(3), June 1988: 207–10. https://pubmed.ncbi.nlm.nih.gov/3134915/; Bruce Lambert, '10 Years Later Hepatitis Study still Yields Critical Data on AIDS', *New York Times,* 17 July 1990.

18 Andrew Sullivan, *Love Undetectable: Reflections on Friendship, Sex and Survival* (Knopf, 1998), p. 39.

19 Quoted in Eric Marcus, *Making Gay History* (Harper Collins, 2002), p. 196.

20 Quoted in Ibid.

21 Larry Kramer, *Faggots* (Random House, 1978).

22 Andrew Holleran, *The Dancer from the Dance* (with an introduction by Alan Hollinghurst) (Vintage, 1999).

23 *See Gay and Bisexual Men's Health* (Centre for Disease Control, 29 February 2016). https://www.cdc.gov/msmhealth/mental-health.htm; *see also* the extensive discussion of the higher levels of poor mental health among gay men in Matthew Todd's *Straight Jacket: How to Be Gay and Happy* (Bantham Press, 2010) and Walt Odets' *Out of the Shadows* (Penguin, 2020).

24 Reynolds Price, 'The Way of All Flesh', *LA Times,* 4 June 2000. https://www.latimes.com/archives/la-xpm-2000-jun-04-bk-37074-story.html.

25 Matthew Todd, *Straight Jacket*, p. 311.
26 Lewis Corner, '90% of Gay Men Say They Want a Monogamous Relationship According to New Study', *Gay Times*, 26 March 2018. https://www.gaytimes.co .uk/life/90-of-gay-men-say-they-want-a-monogamous-relationship-according -to-new-study/; *see also* the clear majority preference among gay men for monogamous (66%) or mostly monogamous (22%) relationships, seen in the Buzzfeed and Whitman Insight Strategies LGBTQ in America Survey June 2018. https://www.buzzfeednews.com/article/dominicholden/lgbtq-in-the-us -poll
27 Andrew Holleran, *The Dancer from the Dance* (with an introduction by Alan Hollinghurst) (Vintage, 1999), p. xi.
28 Michael Joseph Gross, 'Has Manhunt Destroyed Gay Culture?' *Out.com*, 4 August 2008. https://www.out.com/entertainment/2008/08/04/has-manhunt -destroyed-gay-culture
29 *See* Martin Levine, *Gay Macho: The Life and Death of the Homosexual Clone* (New York University Press, 1998).
30 Barry Schwartz, *The Paradox of Choice: Why More Is Less* (Harper Perennial, 2004), p. 3.
31 Ibid., pp. 20–4.
32 Ibid., p. 152.
33 Reynolds Price, 'The Way of All Flesh', *LA Times*, 4 June 2000. https://www .latimes.com/archives/la-xpm-2000-jun-04-bk-37074-story.html
34 Barry Schwartz, *The Paradox of Choice*, p. 103.
35 Michael Joseph Gross, 'Has Manhunt Destroyed Gay Culture?'
36 Walt Odets, *Out of the Shadows* (Penguin, 2020), pp. 139–40.
37 Ibid., p. 164.
38 Jeffrey Weeks, *Making Sexual History* (Polity, 2000), p. 169.
39 Barry Schwartz, *The Paradox of Choice: Why More Is Less* (Harper Perennial, 2004), p. 2.
40 Ibid., p. 4.
41 Patrick Deneen, *Why Liberalism Failed* (Yale University Press, 2018), pp. 23, 37.
42 Barry Schwartz, *The Paradox of Choice*, p. 96.
43 The term was coined by psychologists Philip Brickman and Donald Campbell, *see* 'Hedonic Relativism and Planning the Good Society' in M.H. Appley (ed.), *Adaptation Level Theory: A Symposium* (Academic Press, 1971), pp. 287–302.
44 Andrew Holleran, *The Dancer from the Dance* (with an introduction by Alan Hollinghurst) (Vintage, 1999), p. 226.

8 The Truth Will Set You Free? The Challenges of Honesty in a Hostile World

1 Liza Mundy, 'The Gay Guide to Wedded Bliss', *Atlantic*, June 2013.

2 Carl F. Stychin, 'To Take Him "at His Word": Theorizing Law, Sexuality and the US Military Exclusion Policy', *Social and Legal Studies*, 5, 1996: 179.

3 Michael Joseph Gross, 'Has Manhunt Destroyed Gay Culture?' *Out.com*, 4 August 2008. https://www.out.com/entertainment/2008/08/04/has-manhunt -destroyed-gay-culture

4 Samuel Lovett, 'Monkeypox: Charities Warn Against Stigmatisation of Gay and Bisexual Groups Amid Outbreak', *Independent*, 25 May 2022. https:// www.independent.co.uk/news/health/monkeypox-cases-gay-bisexual-men-uk -b2087216.html

5 https://x.com/benryanwriter/status/1814748936629805452

6 Wilfred Chan, 'Rightwing Media Embraces AIDS-Era Homophobia in Monkeypox Coverage', *Guardian*, 10 August 2022.

7 Skylar Baker-Jordan, 'Is Your Monkeypox Panic Homophobic? It Might Just Be', *Yahoo! News*, 2 June 2022. https://sg.news.yahoo.com/voices-monkeypox-panic-homophobic-just-145854691.html?guce_referrer=aHR0cHM6Ly93d3cuZ2 9vZ2xlLmNvbS88&guce_referrer_sig=AQAAAF1R-g8L4EpL_9xpGrhgnq7-4sM0bLjxLiVRGJlk-3e5q6WAGBvjez6eIrLQL2AH6SMLu0mK0s0tmZYIG3 ZdlxNEHnNlHAwwSuQyc046ROQ7yUXMoMo0oBHOs9yUxcopILDc6R8 aEyp58dQHkMIfjkw9q_gfy3YCyq00YkYUgvhk

8 *See*, for example Alexander Dhoest, 'LGBTs In, Muslims Out: Homonationalist Discourses and Counterdiscourses in the Flemish Press', *International Journal of Communication*, 14, 2020: 155–75.

9 Archie Bland, 'Monday Briefing: Gay and Bisexual Men Are Most at Risk of Monkeypox. Why Aren't We Saying So Clearly?' *Guardian*, 25 July 2022. https://www.theguardian.com/world/2022/jul/25/monday-briefing -monkeypox-gay-bisexual-men-public-health-who

10 *See* Patrick James McDonagh, *Homosexuals Are Revolting: A History of Gay and Lesbian Activism in the Republic of Ireland, 1973–1993*, Ph.D. Thesis awarded by the Department of History and Civilization, European University Institute, Florence, 2019.

11 Owen Bowcott, 'Global Campaign to Decriminalise Homosexuality to Kick off in Belize Court', *Guardian*, 16 November 2011. https://www.theguardian .com/world/2011/nov/16/global-campaign-decriminalise-homosexuality-belize -court?INTCMP=SRCH

12 'Pope Francis Calls for End to Anti-Gay Laws and LGBTQ+ Welcome from Church', *Guardian*, 25 January 2023. https://www.theguardian.com/world /2023/jan/25/pope-francis-calls-for-end-to-anti-gay-laws-and-lgbtq-welcome

13 'This Right-Wing Powerhouse Wants to Make Gay Sex Illegal', *Huffington Post*, 19 November 2014. https://www.huffpost.com/entry/this-right-wing-legal-pow_b_6185878

14 'India Supreme Court Refuses to Engage in Judicial Activism in Landmark Decision', The Alliance Defending Freedom, 13 December 2013.

15 'British Muslims Reject Trial by Media of the Deobandi Movement', *Muslim Council of Britain*, 7 September 2007. https://mcb.org.uk/british-muslims-reject-trial-by-media-of-the-deobandi-movement/

16 'Darul Uloom Deoband Slams Supreme Court 377 Verdict, Says Islam Forbids Homosexuality', *India.com*, 6 September 2018, https://www.india.com/news/india/darul-uloom-deoband-slams-supreme-court-377-verdict-says-islam-forbids-homosexuality-3277424/#:~:text=The%20top%20court%20delivering%20separate,social%20morality%20which%20will%20prevail.&text=New%20Delhi%3A%20One%20of%20the,Court%27s%20decision%20to%20decriminalise%20homosexuality

17 'Map of Countries That Criminalise LGBT People', *The Human Dignity Trust*, https://www.humandignitytrust.org/lgbt-the-law/map-of-criminalisation/. There are also a number of countries where same-sex sexual activity is not criminalized but where anti-gay discrimination is intense.

18 Tony Judt and Timothy Snyder, *Thinking the Twentieth Century* (Penguin, 2012), pp. xvi, 287; *see also* Tony Judt, *Postwar: A History of Europe Since 1945* (Penguin, 2005).

19 Steven F. Hayward, 'Standing Pat', *Claremont Review of Books*, 11 (1&2), Winter/Spring 2010/11.

20 Christopher Caldwell, *Reflections on the Revolution in Europe* (Penguin, 2009), ch. 8.

9 A Dose of Modesty

1 Peter Singer, 'What Progressives Must Learn from Trump's Campaign', *Project Syndicate*, 14 November 2024. https://www.project-syndicate.org/commentary/what-progressives-must-learn-from-trump-campaign-by-peter-singer-2024-11

2 E.g. in the campaign to allow marriages between transwomen and men and transmen and women: *Goodwin v. United Kingdom* Application 28957/95, Judgment of 11 July 2002 (Grand Chamber).

3 Mary McIntosh, 'The Homosexual Role' in Kenneth Plummer (ed.) *The Making of the Modern Homosexual* (Barnes & Noble, 1981), p. 33 (this was a 1981 reprint of an argument she first made in 1968).

4 'How Democrats Drove Silicon Valley into Trump's Arms', *New York Times*, 17 January 2025. https://www.nytimes.com/2025/01/17/opinion/marc-andreessen-trump-silicon-valley.html

5 'Baker McKenzie Earns Top Score on Corporate Equality Index for 13th Consecutive Year', 30 November 2023. https://www.bakermckenzie.com/en /newsroom/2023/11/corporate-equality-index-for-the-13th-consecutive-year. 'Philadelphia Screenplay Suit to Reach Court', *New York Times*, 11 March 1996. https://www.nytimes.com/1996/03/11/business/philadelphia-screenplay -suit-to-reach-court.html

6 Iker Del Rio, 'Toyota and Ford Scale Back LGBTQ and DEI Initiatives amid Political Pressures', *Ket Mag Brussels*, 7 October 2024. https://ket.brussels/2024 /10/07/toyota-and-ford-scale-back-lgbtq-and-dei-initiatives-amid-political -pressures/. Taylor Nicole Rogers and Gregory Meyer, 'Walmart to Curb Diversity Efforts in Face of Pressure Campaign', *Financial Times*, 26 November 2024.

7 Ian Leslie, 'Notes on the Great Vibe Shift', 18 January 2025. https://www .ian-leslie.com/p/notes-on-the-great-vibe-shift?utm_source=substack&utm _medium=email; Anjli Raval, Emma Jacobs and Taylor Nicole Rogers, 'The DEI Backlash: Employers "Reframing not Retreating"', *Financial Times*, 3 February 2025.

8 Josh Taylor, 'Meta and Google Opt Out of Sydney Mardi Gras and Move away from DEI in US', *Guardian*, 20 February 2025. https://www.theguardian.com /australia-news/2025/feb/20/meta-and-google-opt-out-of-sydney-mardi-gras -2025-sponsorship-dei-us

9 Tom Holland, *Dominion: The Making of the Western Mind* (Basic Books, 2019), ch. 21.

10 *See* Martin Levine, *Gay Macho: The Life and Death of the Homosexual Clone* (New York University Press, 1998).

11 Aaron Sibarium, 'Three Theses about Cuties', *American Compass*, 23 September 2020. https://americancompass.org/three-theses-about-cuties/

12 Barbara Soares, 'What I Heard as an Undercover Renter: "Cash … Or Some Other Way"', *RTE Investigates*, 27 July 2023. https://www.rte.ie/news/investigations -unit/2023/0727/1396683-what-i-heard-as-an-undercover-renter-cash-or -some-other-way/

13 Armistead Maupin, *Michael Tolliver Lives!* (Harper Collins, 2007).

14 Andrea Syrtash, 'What It Really Means to Be Monogamish', *Glamour Magazine*, 9 May 2016. https://www.glamour.com/story/what-is-monogamish

15 Thomas Nagel, 'Concealment and Exposure', *Philosophy and Public Affairs* 27 (1), Winter 1998: 3–30.

16 Ibid.

17 David Runciman, *The History of Ideas* (Profile Books, 2024), p. 243.

18 Ibid., p. 245.

19 Ibid., p. 247.

20 Liza Mundy, 'The Gay Guide to Wedded Bliss', *Atlantic,* June 2013.

21 Mark Oppenheimer, 'Infidelity Will Keep Us Together', *New York Times*, 3 July 2011.

22 Lewis Corner, '90% of Gay Men Say They Want A Monogamous Relationship According to New Study', *Gay Times*, 26 March 2018. https://www.gaytimes.co .uk/life/90-of-gay-men-say-they-want-a-monogamous-relationship-according -to-new-study/; *see also* the clear majority preference among gay men for monogamous (66%) or mostly monogamous (22%) relationships seen in the Buzzfeed and Whitman Insight Strategies LGBTQ in America Survey June 2018. https://www.buzzfeednews.com/article/dominicholden/lgbtq-in-the-us -poll

23 Jonathan Rauch, 'Red Families, Blue Families, Gay Families and the Search for a New Normal', *Journal of Law and Inequality*, 28 (2), Summer 2010: 333.

24 Quoted in Mark Oppenheimer, 'Infidelity Will Keep Us Together', *New York Times*, 3 July 2011.

10 Conclusion: Reform from Revolution

1 Peter Tatchell, 'I'm Right Wing, Respectable and Gay: You're Just Gay', *Guardian*, 30 November 2003.

2 For a particularly notable example *see* Kristina Stoeckl and Philip Ayoub, *The Global Fight Against LGBTI Rights* (New York University Press, 2024), pp. 257–8.

3 Ibid.

Index